RELATIONSHIPS&
COMMUNICATION
in East Asian Cultures:
China, Japan and South Korea

Guowei Jian • George Ray

Kendall Hunt
publishing company

Cover image © 2016, Shuttestock.com

Kendall Hunt
publishing company

www.kendallhunt.com
Send all inquiries to:
4050 Westmark Drive
Dubuque, IA 52004-1840

Printed in the United States of America

CONTENTS

ACKNOWLEDGMENTS

GUOWEI JIAN AND GEORGE RAY

This book is about human relationships and cultural communication. The very process of producing this book is an exercise in building, renewing, and maintaining various relationships in our personal and professional circles. Although the book project is now complete, the relationships we cultivated in this process will last for a very long time. This book project deepens our appreciation for the contributions of many people in our relational networks. We'd like to take this opportunity to express our gratitude and acknowledge their contributions.

First and foremost, we would like to thank the students who have taken our course *Communication and Human Relationships in East Asian Societies* at Cleveland State University. Your intellectual curiosity and open-mindedness are the engine and fuel for this book. It is through the stimulating conversations with our students that the idea of this book first emerged. It is also our students' insatiable thirst for knowledge that has propelled us to develop our idea into its current form.

Second, we would like to extend our gratitude to each contributing author in this book. Without your dedicated effort, this project simply would not have succeeded. We deeply appreciate your cooperation in meeting the various deadlines throughout the project. Most importantly, we value the intellectual rigor you have exercised in authoring each chapter and the rich content you have provided for our readers as a result.

We also owe a great debt of gratitude to people at Kendall Hunt. Especially, we are thankful for the great support we received from our acquisition manager Sean Skinner, senior project coordinator Michelle Bahr, and copy editor Raguraman Gurusamy. Sean was instrumental in recognizing the potential of this project and supporting us in the entire process.

Finally, we acknowledge Cleveland State University where we work. Especially, we thank our colleagues in the School of Communication for their support and encouragement.

NOTES ON CONTRIBUTORS

Yanrong (Yvonne) Chang, Ph.D. is Associate Professor of Communication at the University of Texas-Rio Grande Valley, USA. She was the recipient of the 2003 Dissertation Award of the Language & Social Interaction Division of the National Communication Association (NCA). Her research interests are culture and communication, language and social interaction, cultural identities, persuasion, and ethnography of communication. Her works have appeared in *Communication Teacher, Chinese Journal of Communication, China Media Research, the International Journal of Intercultural Relations, Journal of Intercultural Communication, Narrative Inquiry,* and *Discourse & Society,* among others.

Chin-Chung Chao, Ph.D. is Associate Professor of Communication at University of Nebraska at Omaha, USA. Her primary research interests span conflict management, leadership, intercultural communication, organizational communication, and media communication. She served as the President of Association for Chinese Communication Studies (ACCS) in 2011–2012 and the Chair of Asian/Pacific American Communication Studies Division (APACS) in 2012–2013. In addition, she has served on the editorial boards of the *Journal of Intercultural Communication Research* (2011–2016) and *Journal of International and Intercultural Communication* (2015–2017).

Jensen Chung, Ph.D. is Professor of Communication at San Francisco State University, USA. His research interests include organizational communication, leadership communication, and intercultural communication. His current primary research interest is in the *chi (qi)* theory of communication. His research appears in *Computer Information System, Mass Communication Research, Communication Quarterly, Communication & Society, The Howard Journal of Communications, Intercultural Communication Studies, Intercultural & International Communication Annual,* and *China*

Media Research, among others. He has served on various editorial boards of communication journals.

Eun-Jeong Han, Ph.D. is adjunct faculty in the Tim Russert Department of Communication and Theatre Arts at John Carroll University, USA. Her research interests include (1) intercultural/interracial/interethnic relationships and stereotypes of minorities, (2) social identities constructions and negotiations, (3) global migration and immigrants, and (4) second-language learning/teaching. Dr. Han's research has been published in various scholarly journals including *Journal of Intercultural Communication Research, Asian Journal of Communication,* and *Journal of Broadcasting and Electronic Media.* In addition, she presented numerous papers in the annual conventions of ICA (International Communication Association) and NCA (National Communication Association).

Juyoung Jang, Ph.D. is a visiting scholar in the Chao Center for Asian Studies at Rice University, USA, where she was a postdoctoral fellow. She is interested in identifying the determinants and role of social capital in familial and sociocultural contexts, including intercultural families and transnational families. Her current research focuses on how parents develop social capital using information and communication technology. Her works have been published in family science and psychology journals such as the *Journal of Family and Economic Issues, Computers in Human Behavior,* and *Cyberpsychology, Behavior, and Social Networking.*

Guowei Jian, Ph.D. is Associate Professor of Communication at Cleveland State University, USA. His research interests include organizational communication, leadership, and intercultural communication. He also studies work participation and civic engagement. His research appears in *Communication Research, Communication Monographs, Organization, Management Communication Quarterly, International Journal of Business Communication, Discourse & Communication,* and *The Handbook of Business Discourse,* among others. He currently serves on the editorial board of *Management Communication Quarterly* and *Journal of Applied Communication Research.*

Jaerim Lee, Ph.D. is Assistant Professor in the Department of Child Development and Family Studies at Seoul National University, South Korea. She received a doctoral degree in family social science with a minor in family policy from the University of Minnesota, USA. Her research interests include parent–child relationships in emerging adulthood, family dynamics in the context of intergenerational transfer (e.g., child care by grandmothers and inheritance), family and work of employed mothers, and family diversity (e.g., childless couples). Her works have been published in journals such as the *Journal of Marriage and Family*, *Family Relations*, and the *Journal of Family Issues*.

Jaesub Lee, Ph.D. is Associate Professor of Communication at Valenti School of Communication, University of Houston, USA. His research interests include leadership and relationship communication in organizations, social justice, risk and crisis communication, public relations, and health literacy. He, with co-author Dr. Robert L. Heath, recently published an article in Risk Analysis (Online First, 2015): Chemical manufacturing and refining industry legitimacy: Reflective management, trust, precrisis communication to achieve community efficacy (DOI: 10.1111/risa.12504).

Soyoung Lee, Ph.D. is Associate Professor in the Department of Family and Child Studies at Montclair State University, USA. Her research interests include family diversity and mutual relationships between communities and families, including immigrant and global families and family life education program development and evaluation. She has served as a board member of the National Council on Family Relations and is the current Chair of the Inclusion and Diversity Board Committee. She is a Certified Family Life Educator.

Susan Orpett Long, Ph.D. is Professor of Anthropology at John Carroll University, USA, and founding director of its East Asian Studies program. She has conducted research in Japan and the United States on families, gender, medical systems, elder care, and end-of-life decisions, authoring *Final Days: Japanese Culture and Choice at the End of Life* (University of Hawaii Press, 2005) and editing *Caring for the Elderly in Japan and the US: Practices and Policies* (Routledge, 2000), *Lives in Motion: Composing Circles of Self and Community in Japan* (Cornell East Asia Series, 1999), and co-editing *Capturing Contemporary Japan: Differentiation and Uncertainty* (University of Hawaii Press, 2014).

Reiko Nebashi-Nakahara, Ph.D. is Professor of Intercultural Communication at School of Information and Communication, Meiji University, Japan. She received her Ph.D. from Michigan State University. Her main research interest is personal development in intercultural settings focusing on various cultural groups such as migrated families in Japan, Japanese families overseas, foreign students, and employees in multinational corporations. She has been serving several journals and associations as an editor and a board member and is currently an editor for *Journal of Intercultural Communication*.

George B. Ray, Ph.D. is Professor of Communication at Cleveland State University, USA. Professor Ray's principal area of research is language and social interaction. He has conducted ethnographic research in Appalachian communities, studied micro-level interactional processes during initial encounters and in physician–patient communication, and has also investigated language attitudes toward Standard American English and New Zealand English. In 2009, he published *Language and Interracial Communication in the United States: Speaking in Black and White*. His research has appeared in prominent journals such at *Communication Monographs, Social Psychology Quarterly*, and the *Journal of Language and Social Psychology*.

Linda G. Seward, Ph.D. is Professor of Communication Studies at Middle Tennessee State University, Murfreesboro, USA. Her primary interests are in cultural diversity, whether within the United States or in cultures around the world. She has taught in four study abroad programs and contributed to study abroad orientations. She was selected as a participant in the ASIANetwork Japan Seminar as well as for a Malone Fellowship to study the Middle East. She has served on the Executive Board for the Study of Communication, Language and Gender (OSCLG) and is on the editorial board of *Women and Language*.

Sachiyo M. Shearman, Ph.D. is Associate Professor in the School of Communication at East Carolina University, USA. She teaches courses such as Cross-Cultural Communication, Conflict and Communication, Social Influence, and Research Methods at the undergraduate and graduate levels. Her research has been published in journals such as *Communication Quarterly, Communication Research Reports, Human Communication Research, Journal of Intercultural Communication Research, Journal of Family Communication, The International Journal of Human Resources Management*, and *Asian Journal of Social Psychology*.

Miai Sung, Ph.D. is Professor in the Department of Home Economics at Korea National Open University, South Korea. She has researched the change or continuity of traditional Korean family values and norms, especially family concepts, filial piety, family lineage, etc. She also studied post-divorce adaptation, family lives of women-headed families, poverty, and retiree's life satisfaction. She is currently studying sibling relationships, unmarried single women's lives, childless couple's lives, and Korean American's life ritual and identity. She is chief editor of the *Journal of Family Relations* in South Korea.

Dexin Tian, Ph.D. is Professor of Media and Communication Studies at Yangzhou University, China. His teaching and research interests lie in public speaking, intercultural communication, and intellectual property rights from the cultural perspective. He is on the editorial boards of the *Journal of Intercultural Communication Research* and *Journal of International and Intercultural Communication*.

Ming Xie is a research assistant at Institute of Journalism and Communication, Chinese Academy of Social Sciences, Beijing, China. She was a visiting scholar of School of Communication, University of Nebraska at Omaha in 2015. Her research interests are intercultural communication, public policy and communication, religion and communication.

Youqi Ye is a doctoral student in the Graduate School of Information and Communication at Meiji University, Japan. She is also a part-time lecturer in School of Cross-Cultural Studies and School of Modern Management, Sugiyama Jogakuen University, Japan. Her major field of study is intercultural communication. Her research focuses on adjustment of Japanese expatriates and their families and the career development of foreign students in Japan. Her research interests include gender roles, family relations, social networks, and ethnic community.

CHAPTER I
RELATIONSHIPS AND COMMUNICATION IN EAST ASIAN CULTURES: AN INTRODUCTION

GUOWEI JIAN

In September 2013, a local newspaper in Cleveland, Ohio, reported that the top hometown for the freshman class in Case Western Reserve University, an elite private university in the city, was no longer Cleveland or its neighboring city Cincinnati or Pittsburg, but a city nearly 7,000 miles or 12-hour time zones away, Beijing, China (Smith, 2013). On this top-10 hometown list were two other non-U.S. cities: Shanghai, China (No. 3) and Seoul, South Korea (No. 9).

In June 2015, the Fortune Magazine featured a story about "the most American vehicles you can buy" (Callaway, 2015). To qualify as the most American, a car must have at least 75% of its parts made in the United States. Was it a Ford or Chrysler? It turned out that topping the list were two Toyota models, Camry and Sienna. Yes, a Toyota Camry was more American than a Chevy or Buick, and none of the models from Ford or Chrysler even made the list. Also interesting to the story was that when Car.com first compiled the American Made Index ten years ago, 29 vehicles qualified. However, by 2015, this list had shortened to nine.

The two stories above not only reveal an accelerating trend of globalization but also draw attention to the rising impact of East Asian societies, in particular, China, Japan, and South Korea. In the last five decades, each of these societies has found its own path of transformation into a global economic powerhouse: Japan in the 1970s and 1980s followed by South Korea in the 1990s and China in the 2000s. According to the World Bank (2016), the three countries now rank among the top 15 nations in gross domestic product (GDP). The latest trade data show that China, Japan, and South Korea are among the top trading partners with the United States, including both import and export (The U.S. Census Bureau, 2016). Such economic growth in this region has spurred unprecedented levels of exchange and contact with the rest of the world not only in commerce, travel, and politics but also in civic activities, education, and private relationships, such as interracial and/or interethnic marriages and international adoptions. To facilitate the unparalleled increase in intercultural contact with East Asian countries, we are in need of not only the right economic policies and political environment but also the cultural knowledge and sensitivity regarding interpersonal relationship building and maintenance.

Catering to this growing relational need, the overall aim of this book is to introduce to readers cultural and communication concepts, rules, and norms that help build and maintain relationships in the cultures of China, Japan, and South Korea. The book is organized around these three cultures. Within each culture there are three chapters, which focus on (1) family relationships and communication (Chapters 2, 5, and 8), (2) close peer-based relationships, such as friendship and romantic relationships, and communication (Chapters 3, 6, and 9), and (3) professional relationships and organizational communication (Chapters 4, 7, and 10).

Our choice to focus on relationships is not just motivated by a practical demand due to globalization, as suggested above. Equally important to our choice is the realization that a relational-oriented approach to understanding both the physical world and human affairs characterizes East Asian civilizations in both ancient and modern times. Many scholars have convincingly argued that collectivism may not be an accurate descriptor of East Asian cultures (e.g., Nishida, 1996; Yum, 1988). Rather, it is the relationalism or the strong relational orientation that characterizes the cultural milieu of East Asian societies. Social scientific studies have clearly born out this distinctive pattern. In his influential book *The Geography of Thought*, social psychologist Richard Nisbett (2003) made a compelling case that when perceiving the external world Westerners have a tendency to categorize objects whereas members of East Asian cultures have a penchant for discerning relationships among objects; in the social realm, unlike the Western concept of self defined by autonomy, rights, and unique attributes, the Eastern sense of self is largely defined by social relationships and their duties and obligations. It can be argued that to understand the Eastern self one has to understand the multitude of relationships that constitute it. Thus, it is our hope that the relationship focus of this book provides readers with an illuminating view of the East Asian cultures.

Another important feature of this book is that it positions the three East Asian cultures side by side so as to allow readers to appreciate cultural similarities among the three societies while recognizing important, but often, subtle differences. By incorporating the three cultures in one volume the book intends to offer a rich learning experience that resembles a dialogue among the three cultures and the reader's own cultural experience. To facilitate this intercultural dialogue, each chapter draws comparisons with relational and communicative behaviors in the West and discusses the implications for intercultural encounters.

Moreover, the book is designed to blend a social science-based academic rigor with a strong practical orientation so that readers will find the content not only useful as an important scholarly source but also relevant to their everyday communicative and relational practices in business and private lives. All the contributors to this book are social scientists in their respective fields as well as cultural insiders who either grew up or have spent extensive periods of time conducting research and teaching in East Asian societies. Moreover, the book puts an emphasis on introducing to readers native cultural concepts that are often difficult to translate but crucial to know and understand. Thus, each chapter not only presents the cutting-edge social scientific findings on its respective topic but also offers up a distinct sense of cultural authenticity.

Finally, each chapter of this book situates its analysis in a historical context and tries to capture the dynamic cultural transformations over time in its respective relational domain. For example, in Chapter 8, Jang, Lee, Sung, and Lee carefully survey the changing trends in family ideologies in South Korea as the country transitioned from a traditional to modern society. In Chapter 4, Chung effectively traces modern organizational communication practices in China to their ancient philosophical roots. As a result, readers gain a strong historical perspective, which helps deepen the appreciation for the contemporary cultural practices.

The book is intended for three groups of readers. First, scholars could use this book as an important scholarly source regarding communication and relationships in the three East Asian cultures. Second, instructors in intercultural communication and Asian studies could use this book as a main text or supplemental text. Third, the book is useful for a general audience who either seek an understanding of East Asian cultures in general or prepare themselves for traveling, working, or living in the East Asian region.

To help orient readers toward each individual chapter that follows, I would like to address two questions in the rest of this introduction. First, what are the philosophical sources that historically formed the common background connecting these three East Asian cultures? To address this question, I will provide a brief historical account on the intellectual heritage shared by the three societies. Given the limited space and complex nature of this topic, I will briefly discuss two schools of thought, *Confucianism* and *Buddhism*, and how they traveled and gained roots in each of these societies over the span of millenniums. Readers will find that many of the following chapters draw on Confucian and Buddhist thoughts to explain East Asian relational and communicative patterns.

Second, what are the theoretical tools that can help us systematically understand and talk about cross-cultural differences? As evidenced in each chapter of this book, such tools are necessary for a productive intercultural dialogue. Thus, I will introduce several cultural theories upon which many chapters in this book draw to carry out their analysis. Each of these theories serves as a useful conceptual instrument that allows researchers and readers alike to systematically compare cultures and grasp the patterns of similarities and differences. In the following, I will begin with a brief historical sketch of Confucianism and Buddhism as shared cultural heritage of the three societies.

■ Shared Cultural Heritage

For millenniums, the three East Asian societies have witnessed times of peaceful coexistence as well as brutal wars waged against one another. Although the political debate on national boundaries in the present as well as the past continues to this day, few deny the close ties that culture renders across national borders and never stops nourishing the development of each. Scholars agree that Confucianism and Buddhism are among the most profound sources that have contributed to the rich cultural confluence in this part of the world (Holcombe, 2011). To comprehend their deep impact on almost every facet of the cultural life in these societies, it is necessary for us to take a brief historical tour. So let me start with Confucianism.

Confucianism

As a school of thought, Confucianism originated in China over 2,500 years ago. It is a term that represents a large body of teachings, ranging from learning, self-cultivation, and social relationships to ethics and governance. The most famous thinker of Confucianism known to the West is Confucius (551–479 B.C.) along with *The Analects of Confucius* (论语; lunyu), a collection of short passages attributed to the words of Confucius and his students. Confucius is, in fact, a Latinized name given by Jesuit Missionaries in the seventeenth century (Nadeau, 2014). His real name is Kong Qiu with Kong being his family name. People referred to him as *Kong Fuzi* (孔 夫子 ; the Great Teacher Kong). In spite of his consequential role in the development of Confucianism, Confucius was not its founder and there was not a single creator of Confucianism. Confucian ideas existed long before the time of Confucius and continued to evolve after Confucius' death. Confucius' contribution was his transmission and, in particular, his interpretation of the ancient teachings. Over the millenniums, many important Confucian scholars emerged, such as Mengzi (circa 371–289 B.C.), Dong Zhongshu (circa 179–104 B.C.), and Zhu Xi (1130–1200), who transformed and adapted Confucianism to their unique historical times (Fung, 1948).

Confucianism first became an official state orthodoxy in China in the Han dynasty (206 B.C.–220) and served as the ideological basis for the initial formation of the national examination system and a state civil service bureaucracy. It was not until the Tang Dynasty (610–906), however, that the national examination system and state bureaucracy were fully developed when Confucian classics became the official teachings of the state. Although it had experienced various revisions, Confucianism held its dominant intellectual position until the beginning of the twentieth century when modern Western style education system was introduced to China. In the modern era, the Chinese government under Mao Zedong ruled that Confucianism was a reactionary force against Communist revolution and tried to banish it. After Mao's rule, Confucianism has been witnessing a gradual revival with some of its teachings reintroduced into classrooms, media, and broader social discourse.

In Korea, Confucian influence started as early as the second century B.C. (Richey, 2013). During the Three Kingdoms Era of Korea (57 B.C.–668), the ruling class established Confucian schools to train prospective government officials with Confucian classics. Confucian ethics and governance were adopted in setting up administrative bureaucracy (Han, 1971). Later in the unified Koryo Period of Korea (935–1393) Confucian influence continued to grow. For instance, King Ch'ungyol (1274–1308) established a national Confucian academy. In the Yi dynasty (1392–1910), Confucianism was granted the status of official state ideology. King Sejong (1397–1450) was a fervent believer of Confucian teachings and helped expand the Confucian influence to an unprecedented level in the Korean society (Han, 1971). In South Korea today, although Confucianism no longer possesses its official ideological reign as it once did in the feudal era, Confucian values and virtues in regard to learning, self-cultivation, and social relationships continue to exert influence (Richey, 2013). As Koh (1996) observed, Confucianism in the modern Korean society is "hardly visible on the surface and rarely manifests itself in any organization or institution. It survives only at the most basic level of the popular consciousness and in the routines of daily life" (p. 194).

Confucianism entered Japan during China's Han Dynasty (206 B.C.–220). During the Nara period of Japan (710–784), the imperial rulers appropriated Confucian discourse in compiling history and governing the state (Holcombe, 2011). However, it wasn't until the Tokugawa period (1603–1868) in Japan that Confucianism ascended to being the official state ideology in education and governance. Confucian academies mushroomed in local communities. As a result, unlike in previous eras, Confucian teachings began to influence both social elites and commoners alike. During the Meiji period (1868–1912), in spite of the introduction of Western style public education system, the imperial government made Confucian teaching foundational to its moral education. After World War II, although losing its state ideological role, like in modern China and South Korea, the Confucian influence has continued to this day through family traditions and routine conduct of life (Richey, 2013).

Confucian teachings underscore moral conduct in social relationships. According to Confucius, there are five basic human relationships, known as *wulun* (五伦; five relationships), including those between father and son, husband and wife, older brother and younger brother, friend and friend, and ruler and subject. Associated with each relationship are duties and responsibilities, such as filial piety to parents, respect to elders, truthfulness to friends, and loyalty to superior. An example of such teachings can be illustrated in the following passage from *The Analects of Confucius*:

> *The Master said, A young man's duty is to behave well to his parents at home and to his elders outside, to be cautious in giving promises and punctual in keeping them, to have kindly feelings towards everyone, but seek the intimacy of the Good. If, when all that is done, he has any energy to spare, then let him study the refinements of culture"* (Analects 1:6).[1]

---

[1]The translations of passages from *The Analects of Confucius* were by Arthur Waley, trans., *The Analects of Confucius* (New York: Vintage Books, 1938).

Underlying the right relational conduct are Confucian virtues that help define and cultivate a morally superior person (君子; junzi), such as *ren* (仁 ; human-heartedness), *li* (礼; propriety), *yi* (义 ; righteousness), *zhong* (忠 ; loyalty), xiao (孝; filial piety), and *xin* (信 ; sincerity and truthfulness). For Confucius, *ren* represents the "perfect virtual" or "all the virtues combined" (Fung, 1948, pp. 42–43). Passages that embody these virtues, such as, "Do not do to others what you would not like yourself" (Analects 12:2), have served as guidance for relational conduct for generations in East Asian cultures. Zengzi, one of Confucius' students said,

> *Every day I examine myself on these three points: In acting on behalf of others, have I always been loyal to their interests? In interacting with my friends, have I always been true to my word? Have I failed to repeat the precepts that have been handed down to me?" (Analects 1:4).*

Zengzi's words capture a process of Confucian self-cultivation through constant learning, practice, and reflection on everyday relational behaviors.

It is through moral conduct and relational ritual propriety that a Confucian social–political ideal of *harmony* is realized. *Harmony* represents *the Confucian Way* or the ideal order of the world and the condition for human flourishing (Li, 2006; Tu, 2006). Harmony does not mean sameness, uniformity, or agreement. Nor does it suggest avoiding conflict at all costs or blind subordination. On the contrary, harmony is the result of "creative tension" or harmonization of different forces and "the requirement of harmony places a constraint on each party in interaction, and, in the meantime, provides a context for each party to have optimal space to flourish" (Li, 2006, p. 589).

Specifically in regard to relational and communicative conduct, Yum (1988) argued that the Confucian impact could be found in several aspects. Most salient is the fact that how people communicate highly depends on the specific social, relational context. Such factors as age, rank, in-group/out-group simultaneously shape the rules of an interactional process. Yum (1988) also argued that Confucian teachings contributed to the patterns of indirect communication and other-orientedness, which are important features of East Asian cultures. Based on a close analysis of *The Analects of Confucius*, Chang (1997) called to the attention Confucius' emphasis on the connection between communication and morality, such as the relationship between words and virtue and the relationship between words and action.

In many chapters of this book readers will have the opportunity to witness in concrete terms the way in which Confucianism exerts its profound influence on everyday communicative and relational behaviors in contemporary East Asian societies. For example, in Chapters 4 and 10, respectively, Chung and Lee illustrate how employees follow social norms shaped by Confucian values in contemporary Chinese and South Korean organizations.

In addition, to understand Confucianism and its influence, one cannot disassociate it from the ever-changing social, historical contexts. We have to confront those aspects of Confucianism that contradict the moral values of the modern society today. Most notable is its patriarchal ideology that places women in a subservient social position to men. In Chapter 2 on Chinese family relationships and communication, Chang draws a sharp contrast between traditional and contemporary families in regard to Confucian influence and gender role shifts. Her analysis also reveals the intriguing role that the one-child policy played in transforming women's position in the Chinese society.

Buddhism

Like Confucianism, Buddhism as both a religion and a school of thought encompasses a vast array of traditions, teachings, and practices and has a history of over 2,500 years. Since its origination in India, Buddhism has spread first to various parts of Asia in ancient times and then globally in the modern era. As it migrates, three broad traditions have formed: the Theravada tradition, known as southern Buddhism, in the areas of Sri Lanka and Southeast Asia; the East Asian tradition in China, Korea, Japan, and Vietnam; and the northern Tibetan tradition in Himalayan India, Nepal, Tibet, and Mongolia (Gethin, 1998). The East Asian tradition started in China around the first century of the Common Era and grew steadily in the next six centuries. During the Tang Dynasty (618–907), when China was experiencing a remarkable period of economic and cultural prosperity, Buddhism flourished into a major philosophical and religious force. Its teachings were widely studied, accepted, and practiced not only among the intellectuals and bureaucrats but also among the peasants and laborers (Fung, 1948; Poceski, 2014). The deep impact of Buddhism was evident in the works of literature and fine arts during that period, many of which have been well preserved to this day. By the end of the first millennium, the roots of Buddhism were already deeply established in China. Even with the ascension and dominance of Confucianism during and after the Song Dynasty (960–1279), Buddhism never ceased its influence over the mind of Chinese people. In various ways, many teachings of Buddhism and Confucianism have been gradually integrated into people's everyday practices since the ancient times, even when Buddhism as a religion was assailed by modern reformers during the first half of the twentieth century and then by the state during the Chinese Cultural Revolution (1966–1976) under Mao Zedong. Like Confucianism, China's economic prosperity and political stability in recent decades have left room for a gradual revival of Buddhism as both a religion and a school of thought.

Buddhism entered Korea around the fourth and fifth century through diplomatic missions with China. For nearly eight centuries throughout unified Silla (668–935) and Koryo (918–1392) periods, according to Vermeersch (2014), Buddhism became so widely spread and accepted that the Korean societies at the time "deserve to be called Buddhist civilizations" (p. 63). However, during the reign of the Yi dynasty (1392–1910), Confucianism eclipsed the influence of Buddhism and gained the status of official state ideology. As a result, Buddhism went through a long period of decline. In spite of the suppression during the Yi dynasty followed by Japanese colonization (1910–1945) Buddhism was able to rely on the deep influence achieved in previous centuries and survive. In the democratic society of South Korea today Buddhism remains vibrant as a philosophy and religion.

Via Korea, Buddhism was spread to Japan in the sixth century and experienced its golden age in terms of institutional development during the Nara period (710–784) (Blair, 2014). The government sponsored temple constructions and Buddhist practices were integrated into royal rituals. During the Tokugawa period (1603–1868), Buddhism reached every walk of life around the country. In postwar and contemporary Japan, the deep-rooted influence of Buddhism pervades people's private lives and worldview (Blair, 2014).

According to Buddhism, birth and death are not the beginning and end of a being (Gethin, 1998). Rather, one goes through many lifetimes through rebirth or reincarnation and death, or *saṃsāra* (the cycle of death and rebirth). It is believed that one's intentional actions of body, speech, and mind, known as *karma*, in the present life all have consequences upon the suffering and happiness in one's own and others' current and future realms of existence (Gethin, 1998). This pattern of causality is known as *dependent arising*. From a Buddhist view, suffering, or *dukkha*, is a fundamental understanding of reality; we experience suffering because we tend to crave for and attach to objects, feelings, ideas, and ambitions, which are inherently impermanent. Resulting from our attachment and craving is a sense of unsatisfaction, which co-arises with the feelings of greed, aversion, and delusion, and aggravates our sense of suffering. This arising of suffering is also conditioned and caused by our previous deeds—unwholesome intentional actions or bad karma. Leading toward the cessation of suffering Buddhist teachings present an eightfold path, including the right view, right intention, right speech, right action, right livelihood, right effort, right mindfulness, and right concentration. Directly pertaining to communication is the right speech, which asks people to refrain from false, divisive, and hurtful speech and gossip. Relationally, the eightfold path asks people to have right intentions and strive to be desireless, friendly, and compassionate.

Like Confucianism, Buddhist teachings have profound influence on many cultural values and norms in East Asian cultures. In particular, Chuang and Chen (2003) argue that Buddhist impact on East Asian communication behavior includes, but not limited to, the emphasis on intuition, silence, emotional control, empathy, and avoidance of aggressive behaviors. For instance, Buddhist influence on communication can be easily found in East Asian Languages. Take for example the idiom *yi xin chuan xin* (以心传心) in Chinese, *ishin-denshin* (以心伝心) in Japanese (see also Chapter 6), or *ee-sim-jun-sim* (이심전심) (see also Chapters 8 and 9) in Korean, meaning communication from mind (or heart) to mind (or heart), although this meaning may change slightly depending on the relationship context in which it is used. The idiom has its origin in a Chan (or Zen) Buddhist legend in which Huike, a famous Chan Master, received ideas and instructions from his teacher Bodhidharma, the founder of Chan Buddhism, through mind transmission, instead of relying on the exchange of words (Nadeau, 2014). This legend suggests an important thought in Chan Buddhism, which is to learn, understand, and, ultimately, be awakened, not through words or verbal instructions, but intuitive understanding, direct experience, and practice. Moreover, the influence of Buddhism on relationship development is also evident in East Asian cultures. For example, in Chapter 3, Chao, Tian, and Xie expound the impact of the Buddhist concept *yuan* (缘; predestined affinity) on friendship and romantic relationships in China. Their analysis reveals how the idea of rebirth and reincarnation has deeply shaped the Chinese psyche vis-à-vis relational development.

In summary, Confucianism and Buddhism as two schools of thought together have made significant contributions to the rich cultural heritage shared by the three East Asian societies. However, to fully grasp the cultural differences in relational and communicative conduct between East Asian cultures and the West, we also seek help in a set of conceptual tools developed in intercultural communication research. The following introduces these tools that later chapters will employ to cast light on intercultural encounters and cross-cultural comparisons.

■ Theoretical Tools for Intercultural Dialogue

In our everyday life we do not need to be a handy person to know that tools are important to help us fix things, be it a hammer, wrench, or drill. For scholars, tools are also indispensable. A theory is one of those tools scholars use to deal with conceptual tasks. In social sciences, a useful theory is like an effective lens, drawing our attention to patterns of similarities and differences and offering plausible explanations to social phenomena (Deetz, 1992). Another powerful use of theories is that they afford us with a set of vocabularies to give shape to our sensory experiences and allow us to make sense of the seemingly chaotic world we live in. So what are the useful theoretical tools that scholars often apply in understanding cross-cultural differences and intercultural encounters? Although many good theories exist, three, in particular, have been very instrumental and are applied in many chapters of this book. These three theories are Hofstede's (2001; Hofstede, Hofstede, & Minkov, 2010) framework of cultural dimensions, Hall's (1976) high- versus low-context culture, and Ting-Toomey's (2005) theory of face negotiation. In the following, I offer a brief introduction to each of these theories.

Hofstede's Dimensions of Culture

When we systematically compare national cultures by using modern social scientific methods, such as surveys and statistical analyses, what large patterns of differences and similarities can we find? This is the ambitious question that a Dutch scholar Geert Hofstede has attempted to solve since the 1970s. The persistent research efforts by him and his colleagues over the years gradually led to a theoretical framework, which suggests five dimensions by which cultures can be systematically compared (Hofstede, 2001).

These five dimensions are known as power distance, uncertainty avoidance, individualism versus collectivism, masculinity versus femininity, and long-term versus short-term orientation. It needs to be mentioned that although new dimensions, such as indulgence versus restraint, have been proposed in recent years (Hofstede et al., 2010), the five dimensions mentioned above have been most influential and received extensive support from empirical research. Among these five dimensions, three in particular, have been frequently drawn upon in analyzing the differences between East Asian cultures and the West, which are power distance, individualism versus collectivism, and long- versus short-term orientation.

Power distance is about the extent to which less powerful members in a culture accept inequality or unequal power distribution (Hofstede, 2012). Although existing in every society, inequality is viewed differently. In cultures of high power distance, such as East Asian cultures, common people are more receptive of social hierarchy than those in lower power distance cultures, such as the United States. The dimension *individualism versus collectivism* describes the extent to which individuals are related to groups or collectives. In more collectivistic cultures, Hofstede (2001) argues that an individual self tends to be defined by group identities and relational roles while individualistic cultures tend to see self as autonomous and independent. East Asian cultures are found to have a stronger collectivistic tendency than cultures in the West, such as the United States and the United Kingdom. However, as mentioned earlier, the use of the term collectivism is not without controversy. For example, Yum (1988) argues that for East Asian cultures, the emphasis is more on social relationships than "a general collective body" (p. 375). Thus, relationalism is argued to be a more appropriate term than collectivism. Finally, East Asian cultures and the West diverge on the dimension *long- versus short-term orientation*. Long-term oriented cultures, such as China, Japan, and Korea, are found to be associated with stronger future-oriented values such as perseverance and thrift than short-term oriented cultures.

In spite of the debate over some of the dimensions, Hofstede's framework has been widely applied in understanding communication and relational differences. For example, in Chapter 7, Nebashi-Nakahara and Ye effectively demonstrate how the Japanese employment system reinforces collectivistic values through teamwork and decision making in the workplace. In Chapter 10, Lee illustrates how collectivistic values affect the way employees communicate and maintain supervisor–subordinate relationships in South Korean organizations.

Hall's High- Versus Low-Context Cultures

Although narrower in scope than the framework of cultural dimensions introduced above, Hall's theory of cultural variation directly reflects patterns of difference in communication across cultures. In particular, Hall (1976) argues that cultures vary in the extent to which people rely on contextual cues versus verbal expressions during the communication process. East Asian communication is characterized as high context because of its strong emphasis on nonverbal and contextual information to discern, transmit, and construct meaning, whereas people in low-context cultures, such as the United States, depend more on explicit messages. For instance, in Chapter 6, Seward and Long elucidate vividly the pattern of high-context communication in Japan in the form of interactional norms and linguistic practices. Han in Chapter 9 offers examples of how high-context communication characterizes close friendships in South Korea.

Many scholars (e.g., Gudykunst & Ting-Toomey, 1988; Hofstede, 2001) agree that high- versus low-context is in line with Hofstede's cultural dimension *individualism versus collectivism*. This is because the emphasis on shared experience and group integration in collectivistic cultures facilitates mutual understanding and, thus, allows shared social meaning to remain implicit. By contrast, in individualistic cultures, the value on independence and autonomy prioritizes individual voice and demands the use of explicit messages as an essential form of communication and a necessary tool for individual identity construction.

Ting-Toomey's Face Negotiation Theory

The concept of *face* represents a universal human concern about identity and self-worth (Ting-Toomey, 2005). If we recall many of the conflicts we had with others in our daily life, oftentimes, we became upset because our face, that is, our identity and social self-worth (e.g., social image and reputation) were not respected, questioned, or under attack. Face concern is universal because it matters to people regardless of their cultural membership or geographic location. However, what is not universal is in (1) how people orient face when interacting with others, (2) what and how people do with face or *facework*, and (3) what are specific types of face needs (Ting-Toomey, 2005).

First, according to Ting-Toomey (2005), face orientation means the extent to which people direct their attention to one's own face, the other's face, or the mutual face. It is argued that collectivistic cultures tend to be other-face oriented, meaning that one is more concerned with the social image or reputation of the other party with whom one interacts, whereas individualistic cultures are self-face oriented. Does this mean that people in individualist cultures are more selfish or egocentric while those in collectivist cultures more altruistic? The answer is no. The other-face orientation could be the result of the collectivistic assumption that one's own fortune is so tied up with that of others that honoring others' face is deemed a better way to advance one's own interests. So in both types of cultures, people's action could be self-motivated but the face orientation people take varies and is culturally conditioned.

Second, *facework* refers to the actions people take to maintain or manage either self or other's face (Ting-Toomey, 2005). It is well known that cultures vary in the way people conduct facework in various relational contexts. For example, in Chapter 6, Seward and Long describe in detail how Japanese and Americans apply different facework strategies in order to deal with conflict among friends.

Finally, face concerns involve many specific domains, such as autonomy face (e.g., privacy and autonomy), competence face (e.g., intelligence and expertise), and moral face (e.g., integrity and honor) (Ting-Toomey, 2005). It is important for us to recognize that face may refer to or emphasize different domains of meaning for people from distinct cultures in different situations. A good example can be found in Chapter 10 in which Lee introduces the Korean concept of face and highlights how Koreans conduct facework in organizational settings.

In summary, the theories introduced above are useful tools that readers can adopt to systematically conceptualize and examine differences across cultures. However, it is necessary to understand that the broad cultural differences suggested by these theories should not be taken to stereotype individuals with whom we interact because individual level differences can vary a great deal. For example, at the individual level a Chinese can be more individualistic than an American even though at a national cultural level Hofstede's (2001) theory suggests that the United States exhibits a stronger individualistic pattern than does China. Thus, the cultural theories discussed above should not function as bases or assumptions for judgments of another individual. Rather, they should be used to understand general patterns of a culture and sensitize us to potential cultural differences. As a set of cultural vocabularies they should help open up and facilitate a conversation about cultural differences instead of closing down a conversation with ready-made cultural assumptions or stereotypes.

■ Discovering Ourselves through Intercultural Dialogue

American novelist David Forster Wallace began his commencement address at Kenyon College in 2005 with the following parable:

> *There are these two young fish swimming along and they happen to meet an older fish swimming the other way, who nods at them and says 'Morning, boys. How's the water?' And the two young fish swim on for a bit, and then eventually one of them looks over at the other and goes 'What the hell is water?'*

Like water, culture seems banal on its appearance, or even transparent for most people living and breathing in it, but proves to be the hardest to see or talk about (Wallace, 2005). Studying a different culture is simultaneously a process of discovering ourselves because it is in the contrast we see ourselves with clarity and realize the taken-for-granted and socially constructed features of our own culture. Like water enabling life, culture enables social relationships and community and gives shape and meaning to our lives. At the same time, culture constrains our sight and even distorts our sense of reality. Learning from a different culture (Miike, 2012) helps us replace an arrogant sense of certainty with one of open-mindedness and critical sensitivity in how we see the world and ourselves.

Four decades ago Edward Hall (1976) began his influential book *Beyond Culture* with the following observation:

> *There are two related crises in the world of contemporary man. The first and most visible is the population/environment crisis. The second, more subtle but equally lethal, is man himself . . . as well as between the many groups that inhabit the globe; in a word, his relationship to his culture. (p. 1)*

His description of the world at the time reads eerily familiar today. The environmental crisis has reached a breaking point and regional conflicts continue to ravage nations and communities across the globe. To resolve the crises of cultural coexistence and human–environment coexistence, the need for productive intercultural dialogue and negotiation becomes more critical than ever before. It is my hope that the intellectual effort of this book, no matter how humble and diminutive it may seem in front of these colossal crises, will contribute to the collective endeavor toward a peaceful and sustainable world.

References

Blair, H. (2014). Buddhism in Japanese history. In M. Poceski (Ed.), *The Wiley Blackwell companion to East and Inner Asian Buddhism* (pp. 84–103). Malden, MA: John Wiley & Sons, Ltd.

Callaway, S. (2015, June 29). Cars made in America? Chrysler, Ford no longer qualify. *Fortune*. Retrieved from http://fortune.com/2015/06/29/cars-made-in-america/

Chang, H-C. (1997). Language and words: Communication in the Analects of Confucius. *Journal of Language and Social Psychology, 16*, 107–131.

Chuang, R., & Chen, G-M. (2003). Buddhism perspectives and human communication. *Intercultural Communication Studies, 12*(4), 65–87.

Deetz, S. (1992). *Democracy in an age of corporate colonization: Developments in communication and the politics of everyday life*. Albany: State University of New York Press.

Fung, Y-L. (1948). *A short history of Chinese philosophy: A systematic account of Chinese thought from its origins to the present day*. D. Bodde (Ed.). NY: The Free Press.

Gethin, R. (1998). *The foundations of Buddhism*. Oxford, UK: Oxford University Press.

Gudykunst, W. B., & Ting-Toomey, S. (1988). *Culture and interpersonal communication*. Newbury Park, CA: Sage.

Hall, E. (1976). *Beyond culture*. Garden City, NY: Anchor Press/Doubleday.

Han, W-K. (1971). The history of Korea (K-s. Lee, trans. and edited by G. K. Mintz). Honolulu, HI: The University Press of Hawaii.

Hofstede, G. (2001). *Culture's consequences: Comparing values, behaviors, institutions, and organizations across nations* (2nd ed.). Thousand Oaks, CA: Sage.

Hofstede, G., Hofstede, G. J., & Minkov, M. (2010). *Cultures and organizations: Software of the mind: Intercultural cooperation and its importance for survival* (3rd ed.). New York: McGraw Hill.

Hofstede, G. (2012). Dimensionalizing cultures: The Hofstede model in context. In L. A. Samovar, R. E. Porter, & E. R. McDaniel (Eds.), *Intercultural communication: A reader* (13th ed., pp. 19–33). Belmont, CA: Cengage Learning.

Holcombe, C. (2011). *A history of East Asia from the origins of civilization to the twenty-first century*. Cambridge, UK: Cambridge University Press.

Koh, B-I. (1996). Confucianism in contemporary Korea. In W-M. Tu (Ed.), *Confucian traditions in East Asian modernity: Moral education and economic culture in Japan and the four mini-dragons* (pp. 191–201). Cambridge, MA: Harvard University Press.

Li, C. (2006). The Confucian ideal of harmony. *Philosophy East & West, 56*(4), 583–603.

Miike, Y. (2012). Harmony without uniformity: An Asiacentric worldview and its communicative implications. In L. A. Samovar, R. E. Porter, & E. R. McDaniel (Eds.), *Intercultural communication: A reader* (13th ed., pp. 65–80). Belmont, CA: Cengage Learning.

Nadeau, R. L. (2014). *Asian religions: A cultural perspective*. Malden, MA: Wiley.

Nisbett, R. E. (2003). *The geography of thought: How Asians and Westerners think differently . . . and why*. New York: Free Press.

Nishida, T. (1996). Communication in personal relationships in Japan. In W. B. Gudykunst, S. Ting-Toomey, & T. Nishida (Eds.), *Communication in personal relationships across cultures* (pp. 102–121). Thousand Oaks, CA: Sage.

Poceski, M. (2014). Buddhism in Chinese history. In M. Poceski (Ed.), *The Wiley Blackwell companion to East and Inner Asian Buddhism* (pp. 40–62). Malden, MA: John Wiley & Sons, Ltd.

Richey, J. L. (2013). *Confucius in East Asia: Confucianism's history in China, Korea, Japan, and Việt Nam*. Ann Arbor, MI: Association for Asian Studies, Inc.

Smith, R. L. (2013, September 6). Cleveland's economy may get a boost as international students flock to CWRU. *The Plain Dealer*. Retrieved from http://www.cleveland.com/plaindealer

Ting-Toomey, S. (2005). The matrix of face: An updated face-negotiation theory. In W. B. Gudykunst (Ed.), *Theorizing about intercultural communication* (pp. 71–92). Thousand Oaks, CA: Sage.

Tu, W. (2006) The Confucian ethic and the spirit of East Asian modernity. In UNESCO (Ed.), *Cultural diversity and transversal values: East-West dialogue on spiritual and secular dynamics* (pp. 7–13). Paris: UNESCO.

U.S. Census Bureau, (2016). Top trading partners-March 2016. Retrieved from http://www.census.gov/foreigntrade/statistics/highlights/top/top1603cm.html

Vermeersch, S. (2014). Buddhism in Korean history. In M. Poceski (Ed.), *The Wiley Blackwell companion to East and Inner Asian Buddhism* (pp. 63–83). Malden, MA: John Wiley & Sons.

Wallace, D. F. (2005). This is water. Retrieved from http://bulletin.kenyon.edu/x4280.html

World Bank (2016). Gross Domestic Product 2014. Retrieved from http://databank.worldbank.org/data/download/GDP.pdf

Yum, J. O. (1988). The impact of Confucianism on interpersonal relationships and communication patterns in East Asia. *Communication Monographs, 55,* 374–388.

CHAPTER 2
FAMILY RELATIONSHIPS AND COMMUNICATION IN CHINA

YANRONG CHANG

According to Samovar, Porter, and McDaniel (2007), family is one deep structure institution that "unifies a culture, makes each culture unique, and explains the how and why behind a culture's collective actions" (p. 35). Family has been considered and remains the base or cornerstone of Chinese society. Chinese people still value close family relationships and prefer living together with or near their families. Out of the five cardinal social relationships identified by Confucius, which showed the patriarchal nature of Confucianism, three, namely, *fu zi* (父子; father-son), *fu qi* (夫妻; husband-wife), and *xiong di* (兄弟; elder and younger brother), are family relationships. The other two, *jun chen* (君臣; ruler-subject) and *peng you* (朋友; friends), "though not family relationships, can be conceived of in terms of the family" (e.g., ruler–subject relationship can be understood in terms of father–son relationship and that between friends in terms of the relationship between elder and younger brother) (Feng & Derk, 1967, p. 21). Confucianism values family relationships so much that it claims that those who are able to manage their family are able to manage a country or the world. As a matter of fact, in Chinese language, *guo* (国; country) is referred to as *guo jia* (国家; country–family), which virtually equates a country to a family. Family relationships, thus, are foundational for the Chinese society. It would be difficult, if not impossible, to understand Chinese culture and Chinese society without understanding Chinese family relationships.

As Chinese society went through various changes economically, politically, and socially since the founding of New China in 1949,[1] Chinese family relationships have undergone many changes. Some traditional cultural values have been discarded, for example, Confucian beliefs that show contempt for or prejudice against the female sex. Gender roles have undergone dramatic changes since the founding of New China. Many economic, political, and social factors have contributed to the development of new gender roles in contemporary China. In particular, the One-Child Policy, which was implemented between 1979 and 1982 and lasted till 2015, has significantly helped elevate women's status in China (Settles, Sheng, Zang, & Zhao, 2013). The gender role revolution has affected family relationships in that wives are no longer inferior to husbands and daughters are no longer viewed as having less value than sons. Though some traditional Confucian values were cast off, some remain predominant in Chinese society today.

In this chapter, I am going to show that contemporary Chinese family relationships are shaped by the changing gender roles and an interpersonal ideology that is founded on three core Confucian values—filial piety, harmony, and respect for age. I will first delineate the theoretical framework that guides my analysis. Then I will describe new gender roles in contemporary Chinese society and how they redefine family relationships. Following that, I will unpack the interpersonal ideology by describing each of its founding values and how they are enacted or manifested through family communication practices. Arguing that the Chinese interpersonal ideology is based on a collectivistic view of personhood, I will contrast it with the Western interpersonal ideology that assumes an individualistic personhood and highlight major differences in values and family social interaction patterns. Finally, I will conclude with a discussion of changing trends in Chinese family relationships and an outlook on future Chinese family relationships.

---

[1] The People's Republic of China was founded in 1949. After New China was created, various revolutions were carried out to eliminate imperialism, feudalism, and colonialism. One major reform revolved around marriage system. In 1950, New China put into operation the Marriage Law of the PRC that enacted freedom of marriage, monogamy, equality between men and women, and protection of the lawful rights and interests of women and offspring. As a result, it completely abolished the feudal marriage system of arranged and coerced marriages, men's superiority to women, and neglect of the interests of offspring.

■ Culture, Communication, and Family Relationships: Theoretical Perspective

My investigation of Chinese family relationships and communication is grounded in a cultural perspective based on two assumptions. For one, the cultural perspective assumes an inherent interconnection between culture, communication, and relating. Culture is a historically transmitted system of meanings and symbols that members use to help them understand the world, regulate behaviors, and evaluate actions (Geertz, 1994; Hall, 2005; Schneider, 1968/1980). One subset of the cultural meaning system deals with premises about personhood and communication as they are related most specifically to interpersonal relationships. This is known as the interpersonal ideology (Fitch, 2012; Poutiainen, 2015) and it answers questions such as "Who am I?" "How am I related to others?" "What are my duties/responsibilities/obligations in relation to others?" "What are proper or acceptable ways to communicate with others?". Hence, an interpersonal ideology allows people, as group members, to systematically organize various beliefs about what is good or bad, right or wrong, and to act accordingly (Van Dijk, 1998). Within families, the interpersonal ideology guides members to formulate lines of action in relation to others and to judge or evaluate others' actions.

Interpersonal ideology and social interaction are inseparably interconnected. On the one hand, the interpersonal ideology helps make sense of the collective actions of a speech community, namely, why and how people communicate in certain ways in interpersonal relationships. On the other hand, interpersonal ideology is enacted or manifested through communication practices such as patterns of language use and rituals (Fitch, 2012).

A second assumption of the cultural perspective is that communication always happens in specific contexts—social, political, historical, and so on. As a result, communication needs to be examined in light of the contexts in which it occurs.

Guided by the cultural perspective, my examination will highlight the mutual influence of social, political, and historical contexts as well as the interpersonal ideology in shaping Chinese family relationships and communication. Specifically, I will describe the changing gender roles in contemporary Chinese society and their impact on family relationships. In addition, I will unpack an interpersonal ideology that is founded on three core Confucian values— *xiao xin* (孝心; filial piety), *he* (和; harmony), and *zun zhong zhang bei* (尊重长辈; respect for age)—and describe patterns of family communication practices that enact that ideology.

■ New Gender Roles and Contemporary Chinese Families

In the ancient feudal system (211 B.C.–1911) that dominated China for over 2000 years, women had few rights. For example, Confucianism prescribed strict rules of conduct for women, among which were the notorious *san cong si de* (三从四德; three obediences and four virtues). The three obediences for a woman were to *wei jia cong fu* (未嫁从父; obey her father as a daughter), *ji jia cong fu* (既嫁从夫; obey her husband as a wife), and *fu si cong zi* (夫死从子; obey her sons in widowhood). Four feminine virtues were, first, *fu de* (妇德; women's virtue) meaning a woman must know her place and comply in every way with the old ethical code; second, *fu yan* (妇言; women's speech) meaning a woman must not talk too much; third, *fu rong* (妇容; women's appearance) meaning a woman must adorn herself to please the opposite sex; and fourth, *fu gong* (妇功; women's chore) meaning a woman must willingly do all the household chores. Wen (1974) pointed out that these codes of conduct virtually placed a woman "under the control of the male sex from the cradle to the grave" (p. 17). Furthermore, under the feudal system, sons were valued over daughters and only sons inherited from parents while daughters were considered outsiders once they were married.

Ever since the founding of New China in 1949, women started to be liberated from social oppression and began to enjoy equal opportunities of education and employment. The famous slogan that signaled the rise of women in the society is *funu neng ding banbiantian* (妇女能顶半边天; women can sustain half of the sky), coined in 1968 by Chairman Mao Zedong who was credited with raising women's status in China. Later, women are jokingly referred to as "*banbiantian*" (半边天; half of the sky) in Chinese language.

China's economic reform and globalization have also affected changes in domestic gender roles in China. In the 1990s, the Chinese government, in response to the United Nations International Conference on Population and Development in Cairo in 1994 and the fourth World Conference on Women held in Beijing in 1995, made a consistent effort to promote the rights and interests of women and their equality with men. Ever since 1995 the government launched *zhongguo funü fazhan gangyao* (中国妇女发展纲要; programs for

Chinese women's development). Achieving women's social and economic equality with men has also been an important component in China's development of a *hexie shehui* (和谐社会建设; developing a harmonious society) since the 2000s, which aims to protect women by providing them access to health, education, social security coverage, employment, and so on (Attane, 2012). All these efforts helped raise women's status in families and the society, though according to Attane (2012), women's equality with men was unstable and there was still the tendency for women to depend on men.

The biggest contributor to women's dramatic status change may be the so-called One-Child Policy, also known as the policy of *Jihua shengyu zhengce* (计划生育政策; family planning policy) that took effect between 1979 and 1982 as a response to the extreme population growth (Chen, 2003; Dicker, 2014). With the One-Child Policy being implemented, the predominant form of family in China becomes "4–2–1," namely, four grandparents, two parents, one child. By the late 1990s, 95% of preschool-aged children in urban areas were reported to be only children (Settles, et al., 2013, p. 5).

Since only one child was allowed, families that had only a daughter had no choice but to give all attention to the single daughter and invested all resources to help the daughter grow and become successful. Consequently, the One-Child Policy has brought about a breakthrough in gender differences in personal achievements (Feng, Poston, & Wang, 2014; Fong, 2002). Daughters are expected to fulfill duties and responsibilities just as sons do in relation to their parents. This enables daughters to be raised with values similar to those for sons. "Girls born after China's One-Child Policy. . . have more power to challenge detrimental gender norms than ever before, thanks to the decline of patriliny and the absence of brothers for their parents to favor." (Fong, 2002, p. 1098, cited in Settles et al., 2013, p. 14). As a matter of fact, several studies indicate that nowadays Chinese people generally do not have a gender preference for offspring and among those who have a preference most favor a daughter (Deutsch, 2006; Ding & Hesketh, 2006; Settles, et al., 2013).

The One-Child Policy has shifted family relationships. The single child has become the center of a family. All decisions are made with the purpose of bringing up the child so that he or she can become a useful person. As a result, the single child has become the object of intense attention of the entire family, shattering the Confucian father-centered family structure.

Today, more and more females assume leadership roles and become prominent figures in various fields. The surging power of women in China is captured by new linguistic terms such as *nu qiang ren* (女强人; super-woman) and *nu zhu ren* (女主人; female master). As women gain more power and status academically, socially, and financially, wives strive for equality with their husbands at home, though the traditional patriarchal model is still preferred (Feng, et al., 2014). They are no longer under the control of males. Quite ironically, women often overpower their husbands at home by exercising authority and control over them. Such dramatic gender role revolution is attested by new and popular linguistic terms in recent decades in China. For example, men are called *qi guan yan* (妻管严; wife controls tight), *jia ting fu nan* (家庭妇男; house husband), etc. Interactively, among younger Chinese couples, a husband addresses his wife by *lao po da ren* (老婆大人; wife Monsignor) and *tai hou* (太后; queen mother), while a wife addresses her husband by *lao gong* (老公; old eunuch). Studies found that due to the One-Child Policy, husbands were far more likely to help with household chores than the older generation of men who might not do any housework, and in families where the wife made more money, husbands did more housework than the wife (Fong, 2002).

In rural areas, women were found to have gained more power in agriculture due to the fact that there are a large number of single daughters despite the somewhat relaxed One-Child Policy that allows farming families that had only a daughter to have a second child. More and more women run farms largely without help from men. Additionally, when there are no sons available, daughters inherit the family's land and become more important economic stakeholders (Dicker, 2014).

In sum, gender roles have changed dramatically in contemporary Chinese families. The traditional preference of sons or the subjugation of women under the power of men is replaced with more gender equality between husbands and wives and with daughters being valued as much as sons.

■ Chinese Interpersonal Ideology and Family Relationships

Despite the changed gender roles in families, some core traditional cultural values are still upheld strongly and play a key part in shaping Chinese family relationships (Jia, 2006; Yum, 1988). This is, to a great extent, due to the effort on the part of the Chinese government to propagate and educate the traditional values to the public through the use of media and school curricula (Reed, 1995; Wang & Mao, 1996; Zhan & Ning, 2004). In addition, TV commercials also sell such values to the public. Such values permeate school curricula. Mass media are used by the government to revive and reinforce traditional cultural values to combat the incoming and surging western values. For instance, since the 1980s, CCTV (China Central Television) has been featuring an annual Spring Festival Gala—generally a 4–5-hour-long TV program that features singing, dancing, martial arts, traditional folk arts, dramatic skits, comic dialogues, interviews, and so on—on Chinese New Year's Eve when entire families sit and watch the TV shows. Among the programs are those that propagate core traditional family values such as family centeredness, filial piety, harmony, and warm feelings. As observed by Zhu and Berry (2009), Chinese people enjoy the Spring Festival Gala because they identify with the traditional concept of the family.

In addition to efforts on the part of the government, nongovernmental movements have been launched in recent years that aim at a renaissance of traditional cultural values. As a result, contemporary Chinese society witnesses a resurgence of Confucianism. According to the Center for Religion and Civic Culture of the University of Southern California (September 22, 2009), *dujing jiaoyu yundong* (读经教育运动 CREM; the Classic-Reading Education Movement), the nongovernment based movement, focuses on promoting reading and recitation of Chinese classics. In particular, attention is called to the Confucian canonic texts, and there is an emphasis on Confucian moral education and character development of children under 13 years of age.

All these efforts lead to the perpetuation and reinforcement of some core Confucian values. These values influence significantly Chinese people's thoughts, attitudes, and behaviors. Within families, an interpersonal ideology that is composed of three key Confucian values underlies people's actions in relation to others and their judgment of others' actions. Next, I am going to describe each of the three values, *xiao xin* (孝心; filial piety), *he* (和; harmony), and *zun zhong zhang bei* (尊重长辈; respect for age), and show how they are manifested through family interaction patterns.

Xiao Xin (孝心; filial piety)

Filial piety is an important concept in Confucianism. It encompasses sets of social expectations related to younger generations in a family in terms of their duties and obligations in relation to senior family members.

To be filial, children need to *zun lao* (尊老; respect parents), *jing lao* (敬老; honor parents), *yang lao* (养老; provide for parents' physical, financial, and material needs), and *song lao* (送老; handle parents' funeral affairs). *Lao you suo yang, shao you suo yi* (老有所养, 少有所依; caring for the old and nurturing the young) remain fundamental Chinese family virtues (Zhang, 2015).

Contemporary filial piety does not mean exactly the same as when it was first introduced by Confucius. In the feudal system, filial piety applied only to sons; the male children in a family were expected to show reverence to their parents when they were alive and after they died. In contemporary Chinese society, however, daughters are equally expected to fulfill filial responsibilities to their parents (Settles, et al., 2013). Under the influence of the One-Child Policy, filial piety has become even more significant. As one study in 2006 of senior undergraduates shows, the young people in the study felt strongly a concern for their parents' welfare and they considered their parents' wishes when planning for their lives (Deutsch, 2006). According to Deutsch (2006), single child families seemed to produce closer emotional ties between child and parents, and children had a stronger sense of responsibility for their parents' emotional wellbeing. Since they did not have any siblings they also expressed a more intense obligation to take care of their parents.

Filial piety is accomplished through patterns of interaction between children and parents. One way adult children perform filial piety is through regular visitation of parents. Adult children who have jobs or who have established their own families should always find time to visit their parents no matter how busy they are or how far away they live from their parents. Traditional Chinese holidays such as *zhong qiu jie* (中秋节; Mid-Autumn Festival) and *chun jie* (春节; Chinese New Year or Spring Festival) provide opportunities for a family reunion. The Mid-Autumn Festival has always been framed as a family holiday and every Chinese person is taught to visit parents or express his/her longing for home and family during this holiday. Many poems, songs, and proverbs are used to express Chinese people's homesick sentiments through the image of the round moon. One such popular saying is *mingyue qianli ji xiangsi* (明月千里寄相思; the bright moon sends my reminiscences over thousands of miles). Chinese people are expected to enjoy a family meal that features moon cakes and gaze at the moon together. The Spring Festival is the most important holiday in China and lasts generally 15 days. It is the time of family reunions when children are expected to return to their parents' home and enjoy time spent with their parents. *Nian ye fan* (年夜饭; the Chinese New Year's Eve meal) may be the most meaningful meal for Chinese people. At this meal all family members sit around the dinner table with a variety of delicious foods, and the mood is expected to be one of happiness and enjoyment. Those who cannot join their parents (e.g., study abroad, work overseas) should phone or video call parents to wish them good health. Many commercials and TV programs (e.g., Spring Festival Gala) dramatize the warm feelings when children rejoin their parents in family reunion during such traditional holidays.

By the same token, children who refuse to visit their parents are considered *wu qing* (无情; lacking in human feelings) or *bu shi ren* (不是人; nonpersons). The sanctioning power of this expected ritual is so strong that many Western businesspeople shockingly observed that, quite often, many Chinese employees, who are not used to leaving home and doing well on their own in the big cities, would take a long and sometimes hard journey back to their hometowns during Chinese New Year and decide to take off weeks or months at a time or simply resign. They also observed that some Chinese employees seemed to feel an extreme amount of pressure because they have to visit their parents (Upton-McLaughlin, 2013).

Another way people enact filial piety is through providing monetary or material support for one's parents. Married children, including single daughters and sons, are expected to give monthly pensions to parents in addition to buying clothes, foods, or other material things from time to time. Buying parents nutritious food items and health supplements such as vitamins, fish oil, and calcium is considered quite virtuous on the part of children because these products are considered helping keep parents healthy and strong, and prolonging their lives.

A third way to fulfill filial piety is to take care of one's parents when they are no longer able to look after themselves. It is considered utterly unloving for a son or daughter to leave his or her aged parent in the care of a nursing home. A loving child must personally take care of his or her parents' needs. This expectation becomes a huge burden on single children who find themselves torn between personal job or family obligations and those of taking care of their aging parents.

A final way to show filial piety is through burning incense or paying homage to dead parents regularly on the day they passed. It is still a deeply held belief that children who fail to burn incense for their dead parents or who refuse to *kou tou* (叩头; kneel down before parents' graves) are *bu xiao* (不孝; not filial).

He (和; harmony)

Harmony constitutes another key component of the Chinese interpersonal ideology. The earliest meaning of *he* was when Confucius used it to refer to the way various sounds (e.g., animal, people, music) "respond to one another in a mutually promoting, mutually complementing, and mutually stabilizing way" (Li, 2006). Confucianism greatly stresses interpersonal harmony, especially within a family, such as the harmony between parent and child, between husband and wife, and between siblings. A harmonious relationship requires coordination, cooperation, and mutual support between the parties. Harmony is believed to be the highest ideal for Confucianism as a whole (Li, 2006). Even today, harmony is greatly valued in family relationships, as some popular sayings show, for example, *jia he wan shi xing* (家和万事兴; a harmonious family prospers in every way possible) and *he wei gui* (和为贵; harmony is precious). This value of harmony is manifested through some ritual communication practices in Chinese families: (a) dining together, (b) indirect communication, and (c) avoiding conflicts.

Dining together as a family

Communication ritual refers to the repeated sequence of actions, the successful performance of which pays homage to a sacred object (Hall, 2005). In other words, communication rituals enact cultural values. The traditional Chinese cultural value of harmony is communicatively enacted through the ritual of dining together as a family. When meals are ready, each and every family member is called to the table before anyone can start eating. It is considered uncouth if a young child starts eating on his or her own without first calling elder family members to the table. Members are expected to act in unison; that is, when it is time for a meal, everyone should leave behind whatever he/she might be busy with and join the group and eat together. The table is preferably round in shape, symbolizing reunion or perfection. Many Chinese food items also symbolize harmony, for example, *yue bing* (月饼; moon cake or cake in the shape of the round moon), *bao zi* (包子; round steamed dough with stuffing), *man tou* (馒头; round steamed dough without stuffing), *yuan xiao* (元宵; glutinous rice balls), and *xian bing* (馅饼; stuffed pies).

Han xu (含蓄; indirect communication)

The need for creating and maintaining harmonious relationships override all other needs in Chinese families including the need to express one's feelings or opinions. Chinese people are taught not to openly express their true emotions, especially those negative ones (Gao & Ting-Toomey, 1998) since emotions are viewed as dangerous and disruptive to the social harmony (Soto, Levenson, & Ebling, 2005). Therefore, Chinese people are expected to consider others or the group when they decide on what to say or how to say it. It is considered wrong to voice one's opinion or express one's emotions that end up hurting the harmony of the relationship. For example, children are to be severely reprimanded if they keep crying despite parents' repeated orders to stop. For the sake of the group, Chinese people are taught to conceal their true feelings or emotions. Consequently, direct communication is discouraged as it easily leads to friction and discordance (Gao, 1998; Yum, 1988).

Scholars have observed that Chinese people have a strong sense of the distinction between in-group vs. out-group members (Chang & Holt, 1991; Gao, 1998). Family members are considered *zi ji ren* (自己人; one's in-group members) in contrast with strangers who are viewed as *wai ren* (外人; out-group members). Family members constitute a particularistic (Triandis, 2000) social network within which in-group members show respect or reverence to others' face needs or *mian zi* (面子; face). In a particularistic culture, people are treated on the basis of who they are, which is different from a universalist culture that treats people on the basis of universal criteria. Chinese people follow quite different patterns of interaction with their in-groups vs. out-groups. They tend to be considerate, polite, and friendly with in-group members while they can be harsh, blunt, and rude toward out-group members (Gao, 1998).

To create a harmonious atmosphere, Chinese people might choose to joke about a situation that poses potential risks of embarrassment. For example, when family members reunite after long time separation, they tend to tease each other about their hair or appearance in a positive way to break the ice (Chang, 2005).

Face concern is another reason that Chinese people shun from direct communication among family members (Hu, 1944). In Chinese language, face is represented by two characters, *lian* 脸 and *mian* 面, with the former referring to one's moral image and the latter one's social image. Quite often the two characters are combined into *lianmian* 脸面, indicating the inseparability of the two aspects of one's image. It is each family member's responsibility to protect others' face in social interaction. A harmonious family interaction in China is characterized with much laughter and joking. They avoid talking about things that might jeopardize the relationship or each other's face. Engaging in blunt, direct talk (e.g., Scott, 2004) is not preferred among Chinese family members as these conversations can create tension, face loss, or discordance.

According to Gao (1998), *han xu* (含蓄; implicity) as a manifestation of indirect communication is the preferred style of communication in China. It is considered a social rule for Chinese people to communicate, both verbally and nonverbally, in a reserved, implicit, and indirect manner. To be *han xu*, one does not spell out everything and this is believed to help maintain existing relationships and avoid damaging group harmony.

Popular conversational topics for Chinese families are food, health, gossip, children, comments on politics, and so on. Through sharing information or opinions on such innocuous topics, family members establish a sense of togetherness and connection.

Avoiding conflict

Conflict avoidance or prevention is one of the main goals of family relationships. "To the Chinese, conflicts are not treated as problems of communication but rather as detractors from harmony . . . To sincerely display a whole-hearted concern for the other is therefore a gateway to reach a harmonious relationship" (Chen, 2002; Chen & Starosta, 1997–8, p. 5). One way to create conflict-free relationships is through following rules of proper behaviors. In order to handle conflict situations harmoniously, Chinese people take into consideration two factors, *guanxi* (关系; connection/relationship) and *mianzi* (面子; face). It is considered a huge disgrace for family members to fight with one another openly in public. They tend to refrain from expressing disagreements face to face; rather, they maintain a façade of peace and harmony by pretending that nothing is wrong. They may choose to use an intermediary to help them resolve their unavoidable conflict to save face (Chen & Starosta, 1997–8). Through the use of informal intermediaries, Chinese people can avoid directly confronting others, which is considered detrimental to harmony.

Zun zhong zhang bei (尊重长辈; respect for age)

A third core traditional value that constitutes the Chinese interpersonal ideology is the respect for age. Respect for age was one important manifestation of the Confucian concept of *li* 礼 or propriety. Li refers to rules of proper action that help create *zun bei you xu* (尊卑有序; harmonious and orderly human relationships). According to Confucianism, human relationships need to maintain propriety. Age remains the deciding factor along which family relationships are defined and ordered. In contemporary China, age is still a source of interpersonal power; older people command respect from the younger ones.

One way respect for age is manifested is the strict and proper use of kinship address terms. Chinese language contains a meticulous and sophisticated system of kinship terms, the correct use of which enables Chinese people to connect with one another properly (Huang & Jia, 2000). These kinship terms help enact and sustain orderly and hierarchical relationships. One important factor in formulating the kinship address terms is age. The younger in age must not address the older ones by their names; rather, they must be properly addressed with the correct kinship terms. However, it is appropriate and expected that parents or elder siblings address their children or younger counterparts by first names or nicknames. For instance, children in a family must not address their parents or grandparents by names. The same is true with uncles and aunts. In Chinese language, one also needs to distinguish whether someone is his/her mother's brother/sister or father's and choose the exact label accordingly. If it is one's mother's brother, one needs to address him by *jiujiu* (舅舅) while if it is one's father's, *shushu* (叔叔). Then depending on order of birth of the uncles, *da jiu* (大舅; eldest uncle), *er jiu* (二舅; second eldest uncle), and so on. Even younger siblings must not address their older siblings by names. Instead, they need to address them according to the order of birth, for instance, *da ge* (大哥; eldest brother), *er ge* (二哥; second eldest brother), and so on. People are expected to strictly abide by these rules.

Hence, from a very young age, a child receives constant training to help him or her recognize and address each family member by the correct kinship term. The strict kinship address system instills in Chinese people's mind a strong sense of age identity and the realization that they need to act properly based on age differences. That explains the confusion Chinese students who study in the United States might experience when they are asked to address their professors on the first-name basis because this is considered extremely rude or simply wrong according to the Chinese interaction rules.

The value of respect for age is also manifested by other interaction rules. For example, younger people are expected to avoid direct eye contact with elders as a way to show respect. Children are not allowed to stare at their parents when they are disciplined as direct eye gaze in that context means defiance. When an elder person is approaching, the younger one who is seated should stand up. Children should not assert themselves in front of their parents but use hesitation and pauses to indicate uncertainty in what they say. Children should not argue with their parents or talk back. When serving food or drink, one always starts with the oldest member in the family. Thus, age functions as a powerful symbol of interpersonal power and it helps regulate interactions between and among Chinese people.

■ Comparison with the West

So far I have described three core traditional values—filial piety, harmony, and respect for age—that constitute the interpersonal ideology that influences contemporary Chinese family relationships and communication. Such an ideology reveals a highly collectivistic view of personhood (Hofstede, 1980; Triandis, 2000) in China. Within such an ideology, Chinese people view themselves as nodes on various relational nets, and as a result, they emphasize attending to others, fitting in, and establishing and maintaining harmonious connections with them. People are first and foremost family members who are expected to fulfill duties, responsibilities, and obligations in relation to others, especially their parents and other elder members in the family. Thoughts and behaviors that focus on satisfying personal needs or interests, which many younger Chinese favor, are not only discouraged but negatively sanctioned by the society. They will be regarded as selfish or self-centered and are criticized as such. This collectivistic ideology of family relationships is in sharp contrast with the Western ideology that has a different conceptualization of self.

Self is construed differently in the West. While the Chinese interpersonal ideology conceptualizes self as inseparably linked to others in various relationships, the Western ideology views self as independent and self-contained entities who strive to sustain their independence from others by looking after the self and by finding out and communicating their unique inner attributes (Hazel & Shinobu, 1991). Family relationships and communication take on quite different patterns under the influence of the Western individualistic ideology. While collectivistic cultures value community, collaboration, shared interest, harmony, tradition, the public good, and maintaining face, individualistic cultures put stress on personal rights and responsibilities, privacy, voicing one's own opinion, freedom, innovation, and self-expression (Samovar, et al., 2007).

For the sake of comparison with the Chinese family relationships, I will focus on three key components of the individualistic ideology and describe patterns of social interaction that enact the ideology. The three key values of the individualistic ideology are (1) independence, (2) individuality, and (3) equality.

Independence

Within the interpersonal ideology of independence, the Chinese concept of filial piety is out of place. While it is not the case that in the West children do not take care of their parents, the meaning and scope of caretaking are vastly different. The Chinese obligations to provide for their parents financially or to physically look after parents when they are no longer able to care for themselves run counter to the core Western value of independence. On the one hand, the expectation of Chinese filial piety may rob children of their need for independence in that they will feel shackled or chained to family obligations so that they are not free to pursue personal dreams. On the other hand, parents are equally deprived of their sense of independence when they are put under the direct control or care of their children. A viable choice of action is putting parents at nursing homes as this helps satisfy the need for independence by both children and parents. Children get the time, energy, and freedom to focus on their own careers or their own family life whereas parents enjoy their freedom to use their own saved money to support themselves and to be themselves. Children can show love to their parents through visiting them from time to time and providing some financial support. Thus, the individualistic ideology renders what is believed to be an utterly unloving or wrong action from the perspective of the collectivistic ideology, namely, sending aged parents to nursing homes, not only desirable but the right thing to do.

Individuality

As discussed earlier in the chapter, Chinese people choose to conceal their true feelings or thoughts in order to maintain harmonious relationships with others in family. However, striving for harmony in interpersonal relationships might not be a goal in the West where people are expected to express individuality and show unique qualities or attributes

(Hazel & Shinobu, 1991). For example, in the United States, people are encouraged to express their feelings and thoughts freely and openly, and they are taught not to be shy about letting people know that you are upset or annoyed (Samovar, et al., 2007). Within the individualistic ideology, individual action, direct communication, and open confrontation are normative behaviors. Children are encouraged to express their personal emotions and opinions. Parents should listen and not judge what their children say and they should talk with them as they would with any adult. Clear, direct, and straightforward communication is encouraged. The ability to express oneself clearly and persuasively is a skill to be acquired. Though face needs of others are considered (Brown & Levinson, 1987; Goffman, 1959), the need to express oneself freely is highly valued.

Equality

The Chinese concept of respect for age is foreign to the Western ideology that values equality. Within the individualistic ideology, aging is not something to be respected but shunned as it is associated with reduced social value in the West. As a result, older members of a family do not like to be treated as such; they want to be treated equally just as people of younger ages. As much as kinship terms are used to construct age identities and regulate interpersonal interactions in Chinese families, address terms also help construct the equal relationships in Western families. Family members address one another by first names, which might even extend to parents or grandparents. Siblings call each other by name. What is considered rude behavior in Chinese families is thus the norm in the West due to different interpersonal ideologies.

■ Conclusion: Changing Trends in Chinese Family Relationships and Communication

Contemporary Chinese family relationships and communication are shaped by the changed gender roles and an interpersonal ideology that is founded on three core Confucian values, namely, filial piety, harmony, and respect for age. Chinese family relationships thus make Chinese culture unique and, at the same time, they show that Chinese culture is constantly changing and evolving. There are already signs of changing trends in family interaction patterns in China due to globalization. For example, Zhang (2007) found that the present-day Chinese family communication patterns are more conversation oriented than conformity oriented. According to Zhang (2007), in children's eyes, parents have shifted from a conformity orientation to conversation orientation, and this change "might actually reflect the gradual transformation of Chinese culture from a highly hierarchical society to one that endorses equality and freedom" (p. 123).

In addition to globalization, contemporary Chinese families are in a transitional period with traditional family structure still dominant given that those who were born since the One-Child Policy took effect are in their 30s while their parents and grandparents are still alive. Their parents and grandparents were from the traditional multi-children families and have siblings, so the traditional kinship system remains applicable. However, as years go by, the traditional family structure will be completely replaced with the single child family structure. Today, over 90% of all urban children and over 60% of rural children have no brothers or sisters (Chen, 2003).

Western media have also postulated the negative implications of the One-Child Policy, which was amended in October 2015, allowing couples to have two children if either one of them is a single child (formerly, the law permitted two children only if both parents were single child). One major problem with the One-Child Policy is the imbalanced sex ratio in China with 40 million more men than women (Scutti, 2014). It is predicated that 12–15% of young adult men will have no hope of marrying. This will profoundly affect future Chinese family relationships. Among all possible impacts, Settles and her colleagues (Settles, et al., 2013) claim that the One-Child Policy will threaten the basis for Chinese patriarchal family structure as women get more options for marriage and more employment opportunities. Expectations for domestic labor division and everyday interaction norms also will be revised. As they observed, "Even if there were no marked changes in the spousal allocations of domestic responsibility . . . women will have many more options and opportunities to negotiate and renegotiate gender roles and household tasks" (Settles, et al, 2013, p. 641).

As Chen (2003, p. 75) rightly pointed out, at this current stage, "we lack the facility and the necessary parameters to measure the impact of the One-Child Policy on China's new generation" as the single children as a cohort are "still too young to provide a definitive trend." What will Chinese family relationships be like when these single children grow older and start to constitute the main body of the Chinese population? We have to wait and see.

References

Attane, I. (2012). Being a woman in China today: A demography of gender. *China Perspectives, 4*, 5–15. Retrieved on 11/24/2015 from http://chinaperspectives.revues.org/6013?file=1

Brown, P., & Levinson, S. (1987). *Politeness: Some universals in language usage.* Cambridge, MA: Cambridge University Press.

Center for Religion and Civic Culture (September 22, 2009). *Heart & virtue: The revival of Confucian education in contemporary China.* Retrieved on 10/2/2015 from https://crcc.usc.edu/ncs/

Chang, H., & Holt, G. R. (1991). More than relationship: Chinese interaction and the principle of *kuan-hsi. Communication Quarterly, 39*(3), 251–271. DOI: 10.1080/01463379109369802

Chang, Y. (2005, May). Joking, relationships, and culture: Building intimacy through talk. Paper presented at the International Communication Association Annual conference. New York, NY.

Chen, G. M. (2002). The impact of harmony on Chinese conflict management. In G. M. Chen, & R. Ma (Eds.), *Chinese conflict management and resolution* (pp.3–17). Westport, CT: Ablex.

Chen, G. M., & Starosta, W. J. (1997–8). Chinese conflict management and resolution: Overview and implications. *Intercultural Communication Studies, 7*, 1–16.

Chen, X. (2003). The social impact of China's One-Child Policy. *Harvard Asia Pacific Review, 7*(1), 74–76.

Deutsch, F. M. (2006). Filial piety, patrilineality, and China's One-Child Policy. *Journal of Family Issues, 27*, 366–389.

Dicker, L. (2014). 4 grandparents, 2 parents, 1 daughter: The One-Child Policy's restructuring of Chinese families and its positive impact on gender equality. University of Tennessee Honors Thesis Projects. http://trace.tennessee.edu/utk_chanhonoproj/1778

Ding, Q. J., & Hesketh, T (2006). Family size, fertility preferences, and sex ratio in China in the era of the One Child family policy: Results from national family planning and reproductive health survey. *British Medical Journal, 333*(7564), 371–373.

Feng, Y. L., & Derk, B. (1967). *A short history of Chinese philosophy.* New York, NY: Free Press.

Feng, X. T., Poston, D. L., Jr., & Wang, X. T. (2014). China's One-Child Policy and the changing family. *Journal of Comparative Family Studies, 46*(1), 17–29.

Fitch, K. L. (2012). Culture, ideology, and interpersonal communication research. *Communication Yearbook, 17,* 104–135.

Fong, V. L. (2002). China's One-Child Policy and the empowerment of urban daughters. *American Anthropologist, 204*(4), 1098–1109.

Gao, G. (1998). "Don't take my word for it."—understanding Chinese speaking practices. *International Journal of Intercultural Relations, 22*(2), 163–186. DOI: 10.1016/S0147–1767(98)00003–0

Gao, G., & Ting-Toomey, S. (1998). *Communicating effectively with the Chinese.* Thousand Oaks, CA: Sage.

Geertz, C. (1994). Thick description: Toward an interpretive theory of culture. In M. Martin, & L. C. McIntyre (Eds.), *Readings in the philosophy of social science* (pp. 213–232). Cambridge, MA: Massachusetts Institute of Technology.

Goffman, E. (1959). *The presentation of self in everyday life.* New York, NY: Anchor Books.

Hall, B. J. (2005). *Among cultures: The challenge of communication.* Belmont, CA: Thomas Wadsworth.

Hazel, M. R, & Shinobu, K. (1991). Culture and the self: Implications for cognition, emotion, and motivation. *Psychological Review, 98*(2), 224–253. DOI: 10.1037/0033–295X.98.2.224

Hofstede, G. (1980). *Culture's consequences: International differences in work-related values.* Thousand Oaks, CA: Sage

Hu, H. C. (1944). The Chinese concept of "face". *American Anthropologist, 46*(1), 45–64. DOI: 10.1525/aa.1944.46.1.02a00040

Huang, S., & Jia, W. (2000). The cultural connotations and communicative functions of Chinese kinship terms. *American Communication Journal, 3*(3), 1–1.

Jia, W. (2006). The *Wei* (positioning)—*Ming* (naming)—*Lianmian* (face) continuum in contemporary Chinese culture. In L.A. Samovar, R. E. Porter, & E. R. McDaniel (Eds.), *Intercultural communication: A reader (11th ed.)* (pp. 114–122). Belmont, CA: Thomson Wadsworth.

Li, C. (2006). The Confucian ideal of harmony. *Philosophy East and West, 56*(4), 583–603.

Poutiainen, S. (2015). Interpersonal Ideology. *The International Encyclopedia of Language and Social Interaction,* 1–6. DOI: 10.1002/9781118611463.wbielsi173

Reed, G. G. (1995). Moral/political education in the People's Republic of China: Learning through role models. *Journal of Moral Education, 24*(2), 99–111. DOI: 10.1080/0305724950240201

Samovar, L.A., Porter, R. E., & McDaniel, E. R. (2007). *Communication between cultures* (6ᵗʰ ed.). Belmont, CA: Thomson Wadsworth.

Settles, B. H., Sheng, X., Zang, Y., & Zhao, J. (2013). The One-Child Policy and its impact on Chinese families. In K. Chan (Ed.), *International handbook of Chinese families* (pp. 627–646). New York, NY: Springer Science.

Schneider, D. M. (1968/1980). *American kinship: A cultural account.* Chicago, IL: University of Chicago.

Scott, S. (2004). *Fierce conversations: Achieving success at work and in life one conversation at a time.* New York, NY: Berkeley.

Scutti, S. (2014, January 23). One-Child Policy is one big problem for China. *Newsweek.* Retrieved from http://www.newsweek.com/2014/01/24/one-child-policy-one-big- problem-china-245118.html

Soto, J., A., Levenson, R. W., & Ebling, R. (2005). *Emotion, 5*(2), 154–165. Retrieved on 1/18/2016 from http://ist-socrates.berkeley.edu/~ucbpl/docs/84-Cultures%20of%20Moderation05.pdf

Triandis, H. C. (2000). Culture and conflict. *International Journal of Psychology, 35*(2), 145–152. DOI: 10.1080/002075900399448

Upton-McLaughlin, S. (2013). The significance of family in China. Retrieved on 9/30/2015 from http://chinaculturecorner.com/2013/06/21/the-chinese-family/.

Van Dijk, T. A. (1998). *Ideology: A multidisciplinary approach.* Thousand Oaks, CA: Sage.

Wang, J., & Mao, S (1996). Culture and the kindergarten curriculum in the People's Republic of China. *Early Child Development and Care, 123*(1), 143–156. DOI: 10.1080/0300443961230110

Wen, F. (1974) Doctrine of Confucius and Mencius —the shackle that keeps women in bondage. *Peking Review, 10,* 16–18. Retrieved on 10/23/15 from https://www.marxists.org/subject/china/peking-review/1974/PR1974-10c.htm

Yum, J. O. (1988). The impact of Confucianism on interpersonal relationships and communication patterns in East Asia. *Communication Monographs, 55*(4), 374–388. DOI: 10.1080/03637758809376178

Zhan, W., & Ning, W. (2004). The moral education curriculum for junior high schools in 21st century China. *Journal of Moral Education, 33*(4), 511–532. DOI: 10.1080/0305724042000327993

Zhang, L. (2015). China's traditional cultural values and national identity. Retrieved on 9/28/2015 from http://carnegietsinghua.org/publications/?fa=53613.

Zhang, Q. (2007). Family communication patterns and conflict styles in Chinese parent-child relationships. *Communication Quarterly, 55*(1), 113–128. DOI: 10.1080/01463370600998681

Zhu, Y., & Berry, C. (2009). *TV China*. Bloomington, IN: Indiana University Press.

CHAPTER 3
FRIENDSHIP, ROMANTIC RELATIONSHIPS, AND COMMUNICATION IN CHINA

CHIN-CHUNG CHAO, DEXIN TIAN AND MING XIE

Although communication is a global phenomenon, communication research, in the past few decades, has been primarily Western-dominated (Hofstede, 2001). As Hofstede put it, Eurocentrism is still a permeated ideology around the world and among every field of study. Since Eurocentrism has been recognized as a global normal expression of culture and may deny or degrade other cultural perspectives, non-Western views on communication studies are greatly needed (Miike, 2006). This chapter aims to serve as a genuine invitation for more culturally conscious discussions about Chinese interpersonal relationship in general, and friendship and romantic relationships in China in particular. The remainder of the chapter consists of a brief introduction to the impacts of globalization on human relationships and cultural construction of intimate relationships with elaborate discussions about friendships and romantic relationships in China. This chapter also makes consistent conceptual and practical comparisons and contrasts between the East with China as a representative and the West with the United States as a representative for a better understanding of the impacts of the dominant cultural values upon social patterns of behavior in intimate relationships.

■ Impacts of Globalization on Human Relationships

Globalization interconnects all parts of the world. During the past decades, China has arguably placed great importance on reforming and modernizing its culture and traditions. Several key features of Chinese culture have existed in the Chinese societies for thousands of years. Some of them are still valid in modern Chinese societies, whereas others are changing. Because of the pressure from both the collectivistic culture and hierarchical structure, the Chinese people have had a tendency to subordinate their individual goals and interests to the wishes of superiors as well as to those of the group. No wonder it is still widely believed that one's own emancipation can be possible only through the normative and structural changes in the family system (Yang, 1959, p. 168). With the increasing influence of Western individualistic values since the early twentieth century and the inexorably evolving forces resulting from industrialization and urbanization, the Chinese family system emphasizing collectivism has slowly, but definitely, been eroded (Wong, 1975). Moreover, it is not just that the internal family structure has been weakened; the individual's life space has been extended more and more from this primary group into secondary groups. As a result, the Chinese individual is no longer tightly locked in a family structure but finds himself in quite a new social situation where the individual is given a much broader scope for self-expression.

Historically, with the influence of collectivistic culture and Confucianism, any romantic relationship was considered detrimental to the supremacy of filial piety in the family. Given the emphasis on family interests, the mate for marriage was decided by parents or superiors in the family. Because marital relations were considered a filial duty to the family, the choice was more important for parents taking a daughter-in-law to continue the family line and to help out with the household chores than for the son taking a wife (Baker, 1979). Personal emotion and free will based on love were considered not only unnecessary but also harmful. So it was common that many couples did not love each other, but they still stayed together to continue their responsibilities to their families.

Traditionally, the Chinese also emphasized the importance for decent young people not to mingle or fall in love until they were married. However, parents never fully succeeded in keeping boys and girls apart or in eliminating love from their lives. Premarital sex was forbidden for both genders, but the rule was more strictly enforced for girls than for boys. Young men's sexual experimentation was more likely with prostitutes or household servant girls (Levy, 1971). Although most parents and the society still consider premarital sex unacceptable nowadays, more and more young people think it acceptable, especially when two people are in love. In contemporary China, people's conception of mate selection has experienced dramatic changes. When selecting their partners many young people in China tend to emphasize interactions with a strong ethical dimension, rather than family responsibilities.

To sum up, because of the influences of Western values and as a result of the social progress in China, the Chinese cultural values have gradually been changing. In the age of globalization, more and more contradictions and conflicts are apparently reflected in the intimate relationships of the Chinese people, whose social patterns of behavior are under the dual impacts of both traditional and contemporary Chinese cultural values.

■ Cultural Construction of Intimate Relationships in China

As the most important intimate relationships for everybody, friendships and romantic relationships are framed by social and cultural conventions. Researchers have discovered that cultural values exert profound influences on how people think, feel, and behave in intimate relationships. According to Hofstede (1993), cultural patterns of behavior within a group of people can serve as a cognitive guide or blueprint for future actions in building or maintaining interpersonal relationships. Cultural patterns of behavior are determined by cultural values situated at the core of a culture (Hofstede, 1993). Thus, cultural values, which are invisible, untouchable, and usually taken for granted, shape what people say and do on a daily basis. Since there exist substantial differences in the Chinese and American cultural values, it is advisable to interpret the intimate relationships in China by taking into consideration the Chinese cultural values and various cultural contexts.

Cultural Conception of Friendship

Friendship is a universally recognized human need in every society. Yet, friendships in China are generally based more on mutual need than on sincere and simple friendships. That is why one of the five Confucian cardinal relationships explicitly emphasizes the relationship between friends, which is usually established on equal footing and in times of need. Just as the Chinese saying goes, "At home, one turns to his or her parents for help; outside, one seeks help from friends."

All Chinese people live in a web of interpersonal relationships woven around the family. The Chinese familial network is not merely a kinship-based one that works only in a unidirectional way; rather, it can be extended outward many directions through a loosely defined quasi-kinship system. According to Confucius, all types of people such as colleagues, classmates, church members, and playmates can be included into this web and treated as extended members of the family. Once the friendship relationship is established between one family member and another person outside the family, it can be transferred to other family members as well (cited in Yan, 1998). What is probably a distinctive characteristic of Chinese friendship is that its nature is always couched in kinship terms. That is, relations among friends are constructed along the pattern of elder and younger siblings, which means friends treat each other as brothers or sisters. To better understand the Chinese cultural concepts toward friendship, it is essential to understand three significant Chinese concepts of *renqing* (人情; human sentiment), *guanxi* (关系; social network), and *mianzi* (面子; face).

Renqing, Guanxi, and Mianzi

Renqing, guanxi, and *mianzi* are indigenous concepts and fundamental sociocultural factors in the Chinese culture, which are closely related to the Five Constant Virtues of Confucianism, and are embedded in every aspect of the Chinese social life (Chow & Ng, 2004). These are the critical instruments for communication, negotiation, and social interaction in the Chinese context.

There is no equivalent single word in English that can conveniently translate these concepts. The closest translation of *renqing* in English is human sentiment. *Guanxi* refers to "a relationship" between two or more individuals or social network that is implicitly based on reciprocity and mutual interest (Yang, 1994). *Mianzi* literally means face. In the Chinese culture, *renqing* coupled with *bao* (报; reciprocity) is used to manage different types of interpersonal transactions. A person who understands *renqing* knows how to reciprocate (*bao*). Usually, the receiver of *renqing* will not reject the provider's requests because a person who is indebted to *renqing* is expected to pay back. A well-known Chinese saying, "You honor me a plum, and I will in return honor you a peach," attests to this principle of reciprocity. To illustrate, if one were given a favor or a gift, one would immediately be in a double-bind situation: rejecting it would be rude and disruptive to the harmony of the relationship; accepting it, however, would put one in a "yes" only condition, that is, unable to decline any request for a favor. Also, if one fails to reciprocate, one is perceived as heartless.

Renqing is closely related to *guanxi* and *mianzi*. Actually, another word for *renqing* could be favor which is an important element in maintaining *guanxi* in the Chinese society. When one has received a favor from someone, he or she is expected to return the favor to the other person in due time. If not, it could mean you are not giving *mianzi* to that person and hence affect the *guanxi* between you. Moreover, *renqing* can be accomplished through an intermediary who feels obligated to the help seeker and who is able to motivate the help provider. In other words, *renqing* can be expressed and exercised through a particular kind of social exchange relationship, *guanxi*. It is not difficult for someone who has had first-hand experience of Chinese society to note that the Chinese people are extremely sensitive to *guanxi* and make deliberate efforts to establish and maintain it.

Since social interactions in the Chinese culture involve dynamic relationships, *guanxi* or friendship-support relationships are becoming increasingly complex, which are expanding day by day, throughout the lives of all the Chinese. According to Lee (2006), the Chinese form rich, life-long networks of mutual relations, usually involving reciprocal obligations similar to the Confucian rules. For the Chinese, personal relationships often take a long time to develop; therefore, as long as the relationships have been developed, they tend to stay very solid. To the Chinese, it is essential to create links between people and have a mutually dependent relationship in their daily life, which has been defined as "*la guanxi*" (拉关系；establishing connections). To this end, the Chinese may use some strategies such as showing care, giving a gift, or offering a hand (Hwang, 2011). In contrast to the social patterns in Western societies, especially the United States, these relationships persist long after the relationship networks dissolve. Although Americans also have the notion of "networking," the networks involve much fewer obligations than those within "*guanxi*." Within the networks of Americans, people are not expected to provide assistance in a wide range of aspects of life as in *guanxi*; they are expected to take care of themselves (Bond & Hwang, 1986).

The exchange of *guanxi* is mutual but not necessarily symmetrical. In other words, the availability and use of *guanxi* are not equal. The use of social relationships among the Chinese has become part of a cultural art form that requires a certain kind of nurturing process (Yang, 1994). Help seekers and help providers need to have the skills to observe the reciprocity in a delicate and unspecified manner. One of the important criteria is *mianzi* because the degree of preservation and enhancement of *mianzi* will influence people's management of *guanxi*.

According to Gao (1998), Ting-Toomey (2005), and Chang and Holt (1991), people in individualistic (Western) and collectivistic (Eastern) cultures assign different meanings to the content notions of face. Individualistic societies tend to emphasize non-imposition by others and self-presentational facework competence. In contrast, collectivistic cultures (Eastern) tend to emphasize non-imposition of self on others, inclusion of others, and other-directed facework competence. In individualistic cultures, face is mostly associated with self-worth, self-presentation, and self-value, whereas in collectivistic cultures face is concerned more about what others think of one's worth. That is, in many collectivistic cultures such as China and Japan, face is a primary concern in social interaction (Ting-Toomey, 2005). Originally, the concept of the Chinese face consists of two types: *lian* (脸; face) and *mianzi*. According to Chang and Holt (1991), *lian* refers to the moral character of an individual and is a behavioral standard while *mianzi* indicates social status achieved through successes in life. The bigger social success one achieves, the bigger *mianzi* he or she has. In the Chinese culture, one's concern for *mianzi* is not only personally based but also collectively based. As Sueda (1995) pointed out, face in the Chinese society is more a concern to the family than to the person and is a national character, national spirit, and even an honor and dignity. Face-losing and face-gaining acts reflect both on individual persons themselves and on their families which directly influence individuals' daily communication, political involvement, and economic activity (Chang & Holt, 1991). Therefore, one's failure threatens the face of the family, whereas one's accomplishment gains face for the family. Oftentimes, some Chinese may even use face as social capital to ask for favors.

Cultural Construction of Friendship

For most Chinese people, friends are those who can keep company or accompany one another through thick and thin. As friends, people should pay more attention to spiritual togetherness and emotional exchange rather than material things. In addition, friends may show their closeness by physical intimacy as well as spiritual intimacy. When two friends are spiritually intimate, physical distance may mean nothing. Because Chinese people would like to take a long time to build intimate and deep relationships with their in-group members, they tend to have more acquaintances, but fewer friends; yet once they become friends, the friendship will continue even for a lifetime. Therefore, the following expectations are generally held high in the construction of Chinese friendships.

Moral enrichment. Confucius emphasizes that one should associate with friends who are better than oneself for moral enrichment. According to Confucius, there are three types of good friends: one that is direct and honest with you when he/she thinks you are wrong; one that is trustworthy, dependable, and generous when you need help; and one that is knowledgeable and talented to guide you and show you what you cannot see through (*The Analects*, 1998). All this grows out of the Confucian tendency to conceive relationships in the hierarchically structured Chinese society and Confucian belief that people tend to be improved by associating with morally exemplary individuals.

Duties and responsibilities. For the Chinese people, friendship is more about duties and responsibilities, rather than similar or same interests. Thus, many Chinese take it for granted to offer help to their friends, even at financial losses and at the risk of losing their lives in some extreme cases. They often determine who will be their true friends when they need help badly. True friends are always ready to help them out without any hesitation. In return, they will do the same when their friends need assistance.

Honesty, loyalty, and trust. For many Chinese people, friends should be honest and loyal to one another under any circumstances. Sometimes, they offer immediate help without even asking whether or not their friends are right. This happens especially among those very close friends who have sworn oaths of mock-siblinghood, converting themselves from friends to sworn siblings to reach higher levels of loyalty.

Family connections. Due to the influences of Confucian and collectivistic cultural values, friendships develop not just among individual friends but tend to expand to reach the friends' families. Friends often influence one another significantly, and family members, especially the parents, usually have a meaningful input in the whole process of friendship construction. Hence, it is very common for Chinese friends to go to each other's home, meet with their parents, relatives, and other family members.

Development and Maintenance of Friendships

Friendships are fundamental in everyone's life, particularly for the Chinese. Since most Chinese people desire to have long-term, stable, and satisfying friendships, developing and maintaining friendships with others become indispensable. Accordingly, Spitzberg and Cupach (2002) explained that interpersonal skills and social interactions are crucial for the maturity of any social relationships just as they are important to any person's well-being and happiness. In addition, relational development and maintenance rely on relational stability, satisfaction, and such essential characteristics as commitment and involvement (Dindia & Canary, 1993). Nevertheless, behaviors and skills people tend to use to develop or maintain their friendships may be dissimilar due to their different frame of references such as cultural values and concepts.

For instance, the concept of *yuan* (缘; predestined affinity) has been developed in the Chinese culture to describe destiny or luck as conditioned by one's past or natural affinity among friends. When two Chinese people do not initiate a relationship with one another and cannot explain why, more often than not, they may simply say, "We probably did not have the *yuan*." Rather than relying on their abilities to identify causative factors in the relationship that can be "worked on" (such as communication), many Chinese are likely to accept the conditions imposed by the context, even if they do not fully understand those conditions (Chang & Holt, 1991). Consequently, quite a few would-be friends and couples fail to establish their friendships and romantic relationships.

On other occasions, people may happen to strike up an engaging conversation and find that they have common interests—perhaps in a cinema, restaurant, or at a bus stop—which makes their meeting all the more precious and the depth of their *yuan* all the more noteworthy. People affect one another in subtle and complex ways, and it is important to develop the ability to discern the nature of that influence. According to Buddhism, bad friends are those who encourage our weaknesses. A truly good friend is someone with the compassion and courage to tell us about even those things we would prefer not to hear, which we must confront if we are to develop and grow in our lives. In fact, *yuan* is a key concept in Buddhism. Due to the immense transformative powers of Buddhist practice, even "bad" friends can exert positive influences if we make our relationships with them into opportunities to examine, reform, and strengthen our lives.

In actuality, the concept of *yuan* itself is much broader and can refer to any relationship between people under any circumstance. For example, *yuan* can be thought of as the mechanism by which family members have been "placed" in each other's lives. Even two strangers sitting next to each other on a short-haul plane ride are also thought to have a certain amount of *yuan*. There is a proverb in China, "Ten years of meditation or good deeds bring two people to cross a river in the same ferry, and a hundred years of meditation or good deeds bring two people to rest their heads on the same pillow." It conveys the same message that the two specific persons sitting in the same ferry or sleeping on the same pillow have beaten out all odds out of the six billion people living on this planet to end up in those specific situations.

Most Chinese people are very cautious before they initiate and develop a new friendship, and some may have to deal with very challenging psychological barriers at the beginning. It usually takes a considerably long period of time with frequent contacts and sufficient interactions with one another before two people finally become friends. As the saying goes, "Proof of the pudding, time will tell." In the traditional Chinese culture, friendships mean lifetime covenants among friends. Therefore, people without similar interests and personality can hardly become true friends.

Once friendship is identified, friends become interdependent. Due to the interdependent linkages, Chinese friendships reveal a very unique style. To maintain friendships, friends need to constantly interact, such as engaging in small talks and visiting each other's homes. Thus, it is very common for the Chinese people to stop by others' homes for a chat without previous appointments because friends are welcome at any time.

The reason why Chinese people are able to maintain long-term friendships is that many of them live in the same area and interact with a certain group of people for a long time. Their lives are less likely to change. Long-term relationships foster a complementary social reciprocity in which interpersonal relationships are viewed as symmetrical and reciprocal, as mentioned in the previous two sections. Therefore, the Chinese people value stable and long-term relationships and measure the depth of relationships with the length of time. They maintain the relationships in accordance with vertical social status and mutual obligations.

Friendship rituals. A series of studies have demonstrated the function of ritual practices in developing and maintaining friendships. According to Bruess and Pearson (1997), rituals are everyday interactions and behaviors with special, associated symbolic meaning for people. There are different types of friendship rituals: Social/Fellowship Rituals (Enjoyable Activities, Getting Together, Established Events, and Escape Episodes), Idiosyncratic/Symbolic Rituals (Celebration Rituals, Play Rituals, and Favorites), Communication Rituals, Share/Support/Vent Rituals, Tasks/Favors, and

Patterns/Habits/Mannerisms (Duck, Rutt, Hoy-Hurst & Strejc, 1991, p. 23). Rituals help contributing to the feasibility of relationships through special symbols that are constantly recreated through interactions (Baxter, 1988). Most importantly, "rituals provide researchers with a valuable resource for understanding the communication processes that embody relationships" (Bruess & Pearson, 1997, p. 28). Therefore, it is important to introduce the Chinese friendship rituals with a well-known story among the Chinese.

In the Chinese history, there is a famous story about the oath of the Peach Garden from *The Romance of Three Kingdoms*, which is one of the four major Chinese literary classics. At the end of the Eastern Han dynasty (25 AD–220 AD), Liu Bei, Guan Yu, and Zhang Fei took an oath of fraternity in a ceremony in a peach garden and became sworn brothers from then on. Their goal in taking the oath was to protect the Han Empire. The oath bound the three men, who would later play imperative roles in the establishment of the state of Shu Han during the Three Kingdoms (220 AD-280 AD). The ritual is also often alluded to as a symbol of fraternal loyalty. As sworn brothers, they took the oath by saying, "Although we were not born on the same day in the same month and same year, we would rather die on the same day," which inspired generations of followers throughout the Chinese history.

As the three sworn brothers did, it is common even today to conduct a friendship ritual among the Chinese, especially males, to demonstrate one's relationship with another friend as genuine brothers with different surnames. This is a ceremony or action that bonds the friendship and shows commitment to retaining the friendship. Such practice provides friends with a notion of shared experiences, explicit intimacy, and pseudo-kinship bonds (Oring, 1984).

Challenges of intercultural friendships. Although intercultural friendships can benefit our lives in a wide variety of ways, there are many negative stereotypes associated with this type of relationship. Gaines and Liu (2000) have argued that the reason why an intercultural relationship is more likely to be vulnerable is because the dyad's relational identity is not well developed, resulting in the relationship being influenced by self-serving biases and group-serving biases. Relational identity (also termed "relational culture" or "third culture") is an abstract concept that might best be defined as a reality or culture that reflects the values, the rules, and the processes of the friendship and helps the dyad to maintain its relational distinctiveness (Casmir, 1993; Wood, 2000). Just as the culture of a particular country influences the definition and enactment of appropriate behavior within that country, relational identity guides behavior within a relationship. According to Gaines and Liu, if the dyad's relational identity is strong, the relationship tends to last longer. In this sense, relational identity is a critical component in determining the success of an intercultural friendship. Unfortunately, researchers have paid scant attention to the development of relational identity by members in intercultural friendships (Gaines & Agnew, 2003). While Identity Management Theory (IMT) and Third-Culture Building Model were developed in an effort to describe the phases of relational identity construction between members of intercultural relationships, as Gudykunst (2002) noted, very little research has sought to further explore these two theories.

Huang (2008) made a contrastive analysis of the different friendship views between the Chinese and the Americans and noted that friends in China are more familiar with one another in terms of family background, educational background, interests, and even private life than friends in the United States. Scholars have found that members involved in intercultural friendships have to deal with not only the challenges that exist with intracultural friendships (e.g., values, interests, personality traits, and changes) but also the problems emerging from internal and external relational dialectics, cultural differences, and possible language barriers between the interactants (Chen, 2002; Gareis, 1995; Javidi & Javidi, 1991; Martin & Nakayama, 1997). Clearly, positive facilitation of intercultural friendships requires more than simply increasing the possibilities for contact or interaction.

Fortunately, research has indicated that stereotypes, dissimilarities, and insufficient cultural understandings in a relationship can be constructively addressed through communicative activities, such as value sharing and culture learning (Monsour, 1994). Even though intercultural friendships might seem difficult or anxiety provoking in the beginning stages, little research suggests that intercultural relationships fail more easily than intracultural relationships. In effect, if the dyad knows how to patiently embrace differences and identify their shared similarities, intercultural friendships can be as strong and last as long as intracultural friendships (Gaines & Agnew, 2003).

As for the cultural differences in friendships, since collectivists tend to display a high-context communication style, they are more concerned with avoiding hurting others and are likely to end up being seen by others as indirect, vague, and evasive. On the other hand, individualists are more likely to be concerned with clarity of messages and tend to be perceived as direct, open, and expressive of their opinions consistent with feelings (Kim, 1994). Individualists typically view direct requests and outspokenness as the most effective strategy for gaining compliance, whereas people from collectivist cultures are more likely to perceive the same behaviors generally as the least effective interpersonal strategies (Kim & Wilson, 1994).

In contrast with individualists, collectivists tend to be more sensitive to social evaluation by their significant others and, therefore, try to maintain a positive evaluation by their partners so as to maintain harmony within a relationship (Goodwin, 1999). For collectivists, dyadic needs or affiliate and nurturing needs are likely to play a larger part than individual needs (Hui & Villareal, 1989), and this likelihood is displayed in their relationship behaviors. They tend to view relationships to be cherished and tolerated at all costs as manifested in costly accommodations (Chang & Holt, 1991).

Cultural Conception of Romantic Relationships

As Jankowiak (1993) observed, "romantic passion is a complex, multifaceted emotional phenomenon that is a byproduct of an interplay between biology, self, and society" (p. 4). Romantic relationship is a much more complex relationship when cultural differences are involved. Culture affects our capacity to love and to maintain romantic relationships. According to Chao and Tian (2009), from the Western perspective, love is about a person's private wishes and desires, yet Chinese people tend to praise the kind of love, with emotional restraint, cautious behavior, and the goal of marital harmony. Since the United States and China differ greatly in normative cultural values and formative historical events, it is expected that significant differences exist in the social norms and patterns of romantic behaviors in the two countries.

Excessive love/arranged marriage/conserved love in China. Traditionally, love was considered trivial, even a dangerous thing in the Chinese culture. In a patriarchal society with Confucianism as the dominant ideology for thousands of years, the central role of women is caring for the family at home. Women as lovers or romantic objects were another matter, something to either ignore or beware of (Hsieh, 2008). In addition, romantic love was linked to desire, emotions, and passion. Love was understood mainly as referring to the natural emotional and sexual feelings between a male and a female. Excessive love, even between husband and wife, was normally seen as unbecoming and blind infatuation.

Therefore, arranged marriage was a normal way to maintain family social class and economic wealth in China due to the influence of the collectivistic cultural values. Traditionally, sons and daughters of a Chinese family were seen as a kind of commodity to be "exchanged" for greater social and economic benefits for their families. Loyalty, especially to the wider kin group and extended family, dictated decisions people made about entering marriage and whom they shall marry, and individual's preference was not at all important (Strong & Cohen, 2013). It was women's responsibility to subordinate for the sake of their families, and love and passion were considered negative and unrealistic. Although arranged marriages have been almost extinct in contemporary China, many marriage decisions such as partner choice are still strongly influenced by parents and relatives (Pimentel, 2000).

In a collectivistic culture like China, passionate love and marriage based on romantic love are seen negatively as potential threats to the family and are thought to interfere with family closeness and kin obligations (Kim & Hatfield, 2004). Therefore, companionate love tends to be developed and supported in Chinese romantic relationships. Hatfield and Rapson (1993) proposed the concept *companionate love*, which means a kind of emotional relationship where passion is no longer present, but where a deep affection and commitment remain (as cited in Kim & Hatfield, 2004). That is to say, companionate love emphasizes the importance of shared values, commitment, intimacy, and trust. Pimentel (2000) noted, companionate love and romantic love are different systems. Since arranged marriages tend to "start out cold," they can only get "hotter" (p. 34). On the contrary, the romantic and passionate love starts from a high degree but has nowhere to go but down.

Due to the influence of Confucianism on the traditional Chinese culture, expressions of emotion and love are very subtle for the Chinese people. The Chinese society is far more reserved than the Western society when it comes to demonstrating "love" such as kissing, hugging, and saying "I love you." As mentioned before, *li* (礼; propriety) is one of the original elements of Confucianism, which makes the Chinese people restrain their emotional expressions. Even today, many Chinese people are still affected by the traditional concepts of love. Most Chinese people, especially Chinese men, still think that it is a great shame to openly show their love to their lovers, especially in front of the public.

Although China has increasingly adopted Western ways of life, the traditional family structure is still highly valued and holds a prominent position in the Chinese culture. Both traditional and modern Chinese families have similar values and morals, and these have been an important part of daily life for many centuries. Love for Chinese people is about balancing personal feelings with public and family expectations, and it is mostly companionate love, which is somewhat stronger than friendship because of the element of long-term commitment.

As Ashford (2009) noted, "companionate love is observed in long-term marriages where passion is no longer present, but where a deep affection and commitment remain" (p. 498). In this type of love, each knows he or she can count on the other, and the excitement comes from other things such as work and children. Since it may become routine and dutiful, maintaining romance within the context of companionate love becomes the challenge of an enduring relationship (Strong, DeVault, Suid & Reynolds, 1983).

In the Chinese culture, the most important criterion for pursuing love interest or a romantic partner is who is well matched in social and economic status. The Chinese tend to think that only couples from similar classes or family backgrounds can be loyal to each other, honor their elders, and maintain family harmony. In the traditional Chinese society, parents paid much attention to finding the perfect match for their children and to safeguarding the reputation and interest of the family. Today, although there are some differences in spousal selection standards among the young Chinese generations, the family perspectives and societal requirements toward their marriage partners are still crucial for them. Their thoughts and behaviors are continuously affected by the traditional Chinese cultural values, and they still consider factors such as economic condition, family background, and education level. It is clear that the notion of companionate love has been more valued than romantic love in China.

Practical marriage and social pressure. Traditionally, the Chinese did not develop a romantic relationship before marriage. Instead, they endorsed the love of *yuan* and believed that their marriage was based on fated and predestined love, which could be cultivated gradually after getting married. However, according to Chao and Tian (2009), most young Chinese now have supported practical and romantic relationships and felt that dating is a prestage of marriage that provides a way for people to get to know the other person better. Meanwhile, many young Chinese also tend to emphasize the practical needs for marriage, which include parental approval, responsibility, and the importance of appropriate behavior before marriage. In addition, since numerous Chinese people still view marriage as being realistic and practical, when a man is introduced to a girl, it is very possible that the first question the girl, or more likely the girls' parents, may ask is whether or not the male partner has a house. It might be somewhat exaggerated, but it does happen in modern China where material affluence has received top attention in marriage.

Furthermore, Confucianism stresses patriarchy, hierarchy, and subordination, and individuals, therefore, should be subject to the overall needs of family and society. When a Chinese person chooses celibacy or has not gotten married at a certain age, people around him or her will try to figure out the reason and give him or her much pressure due to the influence of Confucianism.

Cultural Construction of Romantic Relationships

Romantic relationships exist in all cultures, and many people assume that there are, if not the same, at least similar ways of establishing romantic relationships, showing passion, and shouldering responsibilities in all cultures. The truth is that different cultures exert impacts upon romantic relationships differently. Therefore, it requires a detailed understanding of the cultural elements in the conception and construction of romantic relationships in the Chinese society.

The notion of dating. Since most Chinese are living in a collectivistic culture, they often initiate a date with more caution than the people in an individualist culture. They tend not to initiate invitations unless they have consulted with their in-group members or they feel confident about the result of the relationship while individualists are less likely to consult their family or friends before initiating a date. Strongly influenced by the Confucian ideas, many Chinese women tend to be dependent on their male partners to initiate a date, pay for the dating expenses, and initiate sexual behavior.

The development of romantic relationships is affected by dating scripts. According to Duck, West, and Acitelli (1997), "dating scripts" or "sexual scripts" have been used to refer to a set of behavioral rules and orders that individuals follow when they are involved in dating situations. Dating scripts, like other types of interaction scripts, are acquired through one's social experience and interaction. An individual constructs his or her scripts either based on previous personal experience or observations of others' behaviors in similar situations. Hence, it is quite natural to understand that scripts "occur in context and reflect the customs and values of both society and subculture in which they occur" (Honeycutt & Cantrill, 2000, p. 24). Chao and Tian (2009) identified the sequences of the Chinese dating behaviors for a first date: A meal (lunch or dinner) and an activity such as a movie, sporting event, bowling, dancing, and having a drink, which allows dating partners to converse and learn about each other. However, neither person is pressed to talk endlessly due to the activity which takes some of the pressure off a first date. Furthermore, some Chinese people would like to go out as a group including other couples to ease the tension/pressure of a first date.

In addition, cultures influence and shape people's dating attitudes and behaviors. As Whyte (1992) observed, although dating is still based on the idea that it provides valuable experience that will help individuals select mates, dating in the United States today is far removed from mate selection and focuses more on enjoyment or pleasure. In contrast, in the Chinese culture, dating is a preface to marriage, a way by which a suitable marital partner can be found. Moreover, because of China's rigorous and competitive college entrance examinations, high school students simply have too much work to do. Therefore, compared with the American counterparts, teenagers in China have less romantic experience before they leave high school (Chao & Tian, 2009). Actually, many young people in China start their serious dating after finishing their secondary education.

In contemporary China, a new kind of dating arranged by parents is becoming popular. Parents are known to be more resourceful and experienced and are seen as individuals with better capabilities of evaluating the quality of marriage (Huang, Jin, & Xu, 2012). Moreover, Chinese parents in general are expected to be more involved in their children's romantic relationships. It is common for parents and grandparents to set their children up on dating with suitable matches they have found. If their children's dating partners cannot get approval from them, it is difficult for their children to continue with the dating relationship.

Blind date. *Xiang qin* (相亲; blind date) is a kind of meeting between a man and a woman for the purpose of determining marriage. Instead of a dinner and a movie for discovering mutual interests, a blind date is a fact-finding mission to see if the other party fulfills one's expectations of what an ideal spouse should be. There are three reasons why blind date is very popular in contemporary China: personal fear of their age; inevitability of marriage; the need of family life. With these three concepts, people begin a linear type of life: adulthood, marriage, children, and parenting at a certain age with generation after generation repeating the cycle, to continue family heritage. Individual values are not important in this process. Everyone should subordinate and even sacrifice his/her own interests for the family interests.

Sex before marriage. In general, sex before marriage in China is less common and taken more seriously than it is in many individualist cultures. Attitudes toward sex are changing, especially in the more cosmopolitan cities like Beijing and Shanghai, but in general many Chinese women see sex as a sign that a relationship is headed toward marriage and many Chinese men say they would prefer to marry a woman who has not had premarital sex. Most Chinese people have the belief that men are more sexually active than women, who are believed to have less strong desires. Women are thus expected to remain virgins. Men who live by this standard want to marry "nice" girls who have not had sex before marriage. However, Reiss (1967) identified a transitional standard, which still applies today: if the woman is in love or engaged, then sex is permissible. In this context, love is the critical factor determining whether or not a woman may engage in premarital intercourse; however, it is not a critical factor for men (Strong, DeVault, Suid, & Reynolds, 1983). It is also found that more and more Chinese people tend to permit or accept the premarital sex experience of their romantic partners because cohabitation among college students and other young people are not uncommon in present-day China. The phenomenon results partially from the ideological emancipation of the Chinese young people under the impacts of globalization and partially from the shortage of housing for dating including even married couples (Chao & Tian, 2009).

■ The Development and Maintenance of Romantic Relationships

Relational maintenance may be seen as a goal for people; that is, most people desire for long-term, stable, and satisfying relationships (Canary & Stafford, 1994). A workable relationship requires the recognition and adjustment of each person's expectations of the other and of the relationship. Researchers have examined various forms of intimate behavior and expressions of love. For instance, Hofstede (1980) confirmed the cross-cultural differences in the expression of love under individualistic and collectivistic contexts. Klein, Horton, and Zhang (2008) found that the most common expression of love is to communicate, to have dinner together, and to engage in physical intimacy for college students both in the United States and East Asia. In contrast, American college students are more likely than East Asian students to show their care for one another and to express love for their partners.

Regarding the commitment to romantic relationship, Hsu (1985) suggested that the Chinese people treat romantic relationships or dating relationships more seriously than Americans. In China, a romantic relationship is often perceived as one step before marriage and contains long-term commitment. While in the United States, a committed relationship is based on strong emotion (Dion & Dion, 1988). Gao (2001) also found that while more passion was found in American couples than their Chinese counterparts, both US and Chinese romantic couples reveal the same tendency of increasing their commitment in their intimate relationships when their romantic relationships became more serious. To most Chinese people, commitment is a practical approach to maintaining romantic relationships. It also reflects obligations or responsibilities of a person involved in the relationship, whereas many Americans are more likely to focus on the emotional aspects of a romantic relationship.

■ Conclusion

Culture is learned and socially shared, and it influences all aspects of an individual's life. These various influences can create challenges in intimate relationships with a person from a different cultural background. Although intercultural relationships share some similarities, they have some unique characteristics that can guide our thinking about communicating in these relationships. By examining Eastern notions of friendships and romantic relationships, readers in the West can broaden their global perspectives, increase their cultural awareness, and become more interculturally ready to communicate with people from the East. Ideally, learning to understand different perspectives toward interpersonal relationships can not only help us to generate more helpful interpersonal strategies to cope with the cross-cultural differences but also facilitate our efforts building a more harmonious multicultural community.

To this end, this chapter has presented a brief introduction to the impacts of globalization on human relationships and cultural conceptions of intimate relationships, with a focus on friendships and romantic relationships. Globalization does shorten the physical and conceptual distances between the East and West, but the deep-rooted Chinese cultural values such as *renqing, guanxi, mianzi, bao,* and *yuan* still shape how the Chinese perceive and behave toward friendships and romantic relationships. To reveal how exactly the Chinese cultural values are communicated in the process of establishing friendships and romantic relationships in China, the chapter has provided a clear-cut, detailed, and meaningful discussion about the cultural conception, cultural construction, development and maintenance of friendships and romantic relationships in China. In addition, the chapter makes consistent conceptual and practical comparisons and contrasts between China and the United States in regard to the cultural construction of friendships and romantic love.

References

Ashford, J. B., & LeCroy, C. W. (2009). *Human behavior in the social environment: A multidimensional perspective* (4th ed.). Belmont, CA: Brooks/Cole, Cengage Learning.

Baker, H. (1979). *Chinese family and kinship.* New York, NY: Columbia University Press.

Baxter, L. A. (1988). A dialectical perspective on communication strategies in relationship development. In S. Duck, D. F. Hay, S. E. Hobfoll, W. Iches & B. Montgomery (Eds.), *Handbook of personal relationships: Theory, research and interventions* (pp. 257–274). London: Wiley.

Bond, M. H., & Hwang, K. (1986). The social psychology of Chinese people. In M. H. Bond (Ed.), *The psychology of the Chinese people* (pp. 213–266). New York, NY: Oxford University Press.

Bruess, C. J. S., & Pearson, J. C. (1997). Interpersonal rituals in marriage and adult friendship. *Communication Monographs, 64*(1), 25–46. doi: 10.1080/03637759709376403.

Canary, D. J., & Stafford, L. (1994). *Communication and relational maintenance.* San Diego, CA: Academic Press.

Casmir, F. L.(1993). Third-culture building: A paradigm shift for international and intercultural communication. In S. A. Deetz (Ed.), *Communication yearbook 16* (pp. 407–428). Newbury Park, CA: Sage.

Chang, H. C., & Holt, R. (1991). More than relationship: Chinese interaction and the principle of kuan-hsi. *Communication Quarterly, 39*(3), 251–271. doi: 10.1080/01463379109369802.

Chao, C. C., & Tian, D (2009). When Mulan meets Romeo: Cultural impact upon the dating scripts, perceptions, and behaviors of college students from the United States and Taiwan in their cross-cultural romantic relationship. *Journal of Chinese Business Review* 8(8), 50–65.

Chen, L.(2002). Communication in intercultural relationships. In W. B. Gudykunst & B. Mody (Eds.), *Handbook of international and intercultural communication* (pp. 241–258). Thousand Oaks, CA: Sage.

Chow, I. H. S., & Ng, I. (2004). The characteristics of Chinese personal ties (guanxi): Evidence from Hong Kong. *Organization Studies, 25*(7), 1075–1093. doi:10.1177/0170840604045092.

Dindia, K., & Canary, D. J. (1993). Definitions and theoretical perspectives on maintaining relationships. *Journal of Social and Personal Relationships, 10*, 163–173.

Dion, K. L., & Dion, K.K. (1988). Romantic love: Individual and cultural perspectives. In R.J. Sternberg & M.L. Barnes (Eds.), *The psychology of love* (pp. 264–289). New Haven: Yale University Press.

Duck, S., Rutt, D. J., Hoy-Hurst, M. H., & Strejc, H. (1991). Some evident truths about conversations in everyday relationships: All communications are not created equal. *Human Communication Research, 18*, 228–237.

Duck, S., West, L., & Acitelli, L. K. (1997). Sewing the field: The tapestry of relationships in life and research. In S. Duck (Ed.), *Handbook of personal relationships: Theory, research and interventions* (pp. 1–28). New York, NY: John Wiley & Sons.

Gaines, S. O., Jr., & Agnew, C. R.(2003). Relationship maintenance in intercultural couples: An interdependence analysis. In D. J. Canary & M. Dainton (Eds.). *Maintaining Relationships through communication* (pp. 231–253). Mahwah, NJ: Lawrence Erlbaum Associates, Inc.

Gaines, S. O., Jr., & Liu, J. H. (2000). Multicultural/multiracial relationships. In C. Hendrick & S. Hendrick (Eds.), *Close relationships: A sourcebook* (pp. 97–108). Thousand Oaks, CA: Sage.

Gao, G. (2001). Intimacy, passion, and commitment in Chinese and US American romantic relationships. *International Journal of Intercultural Relations, 25*(3), 329–342.

Gao, G. (1998). "Don't take my word for it." – Understanding Chinese speaking practices. *International Journal of Intercultural Relations, 22*, 163–186.

Gareis, E.(1995).*Intercultural friendship: A qualitative study*. Lanham, MD: University Press of America.

Goodwin, R. (1999). *Personal Relationships across Cultures*. London: Routledge.

Gudykunst, W. B.(2002). Intercultural communication theories. InW. B. Gudykunst & B. Mody (Eds.), *Handbook of international and intercultural communication* (pp. 183–205). Thousand Oaks, CA: Sage.

Hofstede, G. (1980). *Culture's consequences: International differences in work-related values*. Newbury Park, CA: Sage.

Hofstede, G. (1993). Cultures and organizations: Software of the mind. *Administrative Science Quarterly, 38*(1), 132–134.

Hofstede, G. (2001). *Culture's Consequences: International differences in work-related values* (3rd ed.). Newbury Park, CA: Sage.

Honeycutt, J. M., & Cantrill, J. G. (2000). *Cognition, communication, and romantic relationships*. Mahwah, NY: L. Erlbaum Associates.

Hsieh, D. (2008). *Love and women in early Chinese fiction*. Hong Kong: Chinese University Press.

Hsu, F. (1985). The self in cross-cultural perspective. In A. J. Marsella, G. DeVos & F. L. K. Hsu (Eds.), *Culture and self: Asian and Western perspectives* (pp. 24–55). London: Tavistock.

Huang, Y. (2008). A contrastive analysis of views on friendship of China and U.S.A. *Journal of Nantong Vocational & Technical Shipping College, 7*(3), 31–33.

Huang, F., Jin, G. Z., & Xu, L. C. (2012). Love and money by parental matchmaking: Evidence from urban couples in China. *The American Economic Review, 102*(2), 555–560.

Hui, C. H., & Villareal, M. J. (1989). Individualism-collectivism and psychological needs: Their relationships in two cultures. *Journal of Cross-Cultural Psychology, 20*(3), 310–323. doi: 10.1177/0022022189203005.

Hwang, K. (2011). *Foundations of Chinese psychology: Confucian social relations*. New York, NY: Springer.

Jankowiak, W. R. (1993). *Sex, death, and hierarchy in a Chinese city: An anthropological account*. New York: Columbia University Press.

Javidi, A., & Javidi, M.(1991). Cross-cultural analysis of interpersonal bonding: A look at East and West.*Howard Journal of Communication, 3*, 129–138.

Kim, J., & Hatfield, E. (2004). Love types and subjective well-being: a cross-cultural study. *Social Behavior and Personality: an International Journal, 32*(2), 173–182.

Kim, M. S. (1994). Cross-cultural comparisons of the perceived importance of conversational constraints. *Human Communication Research, 21*, 128–151.

Kim, M. S., & Wilson, S. R. (1994). A cross-cultural comparison of implicit theories of requesting. *Communication Monographs, 61*, 210–235.

Kline, S. L., Horton, B., & Zhang, S. (2008).Communicating love: Comparisons between American and East Asian university students. *International Journal of Intercultural Relations, 32*, 200–214.

Lee, P. (2006) Bridging cultures: Understanding the construction of relational identity in intercultural friendship. *Journal of Intercultural Communication Research, 35*(1), 3–22. doi: 10.1080/17475740600739156

Levy, M. J. Jr. (1971).*The family revolution in modern China.*New York, NY: Octagon Books.

Martin, I. N., & Nakayama, T. K. (1997). *Intercultural communication in contexts.* Mountain View, CA: Mayfield.

Miike, Y. (2006). Non-Western theory in Western research? An Asiacentric agenda for Asian communication studies. *Review of Communication, 6*(1/2), 4–31.

Miike, Y. (2002). Theorizing Culture and Communication in the Asian Context: An assumptive foundation. *Intercultural Communication Studies, XI*, 1–22.

Monsour, M.(1994). Similarities and dissimilarities in personal relationship: Constructing meaning and building intimacy through communication. In S. Duck (Ed.), *Dynamics of relationships* (pp. 112–134). Thousand Oaks, CA: Sage.

Oring, E. (1984). Dyadic traditions. *Journal of Folklore Research, 21*(1), 19–28.

Pimentel, E. E. (2000). Just how do I love thee? Marital relations in urban China. *Journal of Marriage and Family, 62*(1), 32–47. doi: 10.1111/j.1741-3737.2000.00032.x

Reiss, I. (1967). *The social context of premarital sexual permissiveness.* New York, NY: Holt.

Spitzberg, B. H., & Cupach, W. R. (2002). The inappropriateness of relational intrusion. In R. Goodwin & D. Cramer (Eds.), *Inappropriate Relationships* (pp. 191–219). Mahwah, NJ: Lawrence Erlbaum.

Strong, B., & Cohen, T. F. (2013).*The marriage and family experience: Intimate relationships in a changing society* (12th ed.). Belmont, CA: Wadsworth. Strong, B., DeVault, C., Suid, M., & Reynolds, R. (1983). *The marriage and family experience* (2nd ed.). St. Paul, MI: West Publishing Co.

Sueda, K. (1995). Differences in the perception of face: Chinese mien-tzu and Japanese meutsu. *World Communication, 24,* 23–31.

The analects of Confucius. (1998). Beijing: Foreign Language Teaching and Research Press.

Ting-Toomey, S. (2005). The matrix of face: An updated face-negotiation theory. In W. B.Gudykunst (Ed.), *Theorizing about intercultural communication* (pp. 211–234). Thousand Oaks, CA: Sage.

Weaver, G. R. (1986). Understanding and coping with cross-cultural adjustment stress. In R.M. Paige (Ed), *Cross-cultural orientation: New conceptualizations and applications.* Lanham MD: University Press of America.

Whyte, M. K. (1992). Introduction: Rural economic reforms and Chinese family pattern. *China Quarterly, 130,* 317–322.

Wong, F. M. (1975). Industrialization and family structure in Hong Kong. *Journal of Marriage and Family, 37*(4), 985–1000.

Wood, J. T. (2000). *Relational communication: Continuity and change in personal relationships* (2nd ed.). Belmont, CA: Wadsworth.

Yan, M. C. (1998). A social functioning discourse in Chinese context: implication of developing social work in mainland China. *International Social Work, 41*(2), 181–194.

Yang, C. K. (1959). *The Chinese family in the communist revolution.* Boston, MA: Cambridge.

Yang, M.M. (1994). *Gifts, favors, and banquets: The art of social relationships in China.* Ithaca, NY: Cornell University Press.

CHAPTER 4
PROFESSIONAL RELATIONSHIPS AND ORGANIZATIONAL COMMUNICATION IN CHINA

JENSEN CHUNG

A CEO from North America was to visit a branch in an East Asian country. His adviser on overseas relations finished briefing him by saying, "Americans have a good reputation for being informal and equitable."

Taking this advice, he went to a few meetings with higher-echelon East Asian executives. After these meetings, he solicited some "honest feedback" from a local childhood friend of his who attended one of the meetings. The friend conveyed that some local meeting participants had commented that the CEO lacked *chi* (or *qi*) and was not leader-like. Further probed, the friend gave some examples: he (the CEO) remained sitting throughout the meeting; he kept shaking his leg while sitting down; he tilted his head sideways most of the time.

In this narrative, taken from an interview by the author (J. Chung, personal communication, 2015), what the overseas relations expert failed to advise the CEO was that, in some East Asian cultures, sitting while speaking to a group of certain size, particularly at the beginning of the meeting, is not leader-like. It is also considered condescending to other attendees—contrary to the norm in the North American custom. Shaking one's leg while sitting appears frivolous to many Asians. Constantly tilting one's head sideways appears powerless. Diving into tasks without some ritualistic remarks, often praises, shows disrespect or lack of leadership etiquette.

The CEO later joked: "When I heard the critique 'tilting head sideways,' I thought they suspected me of flirting!" These are just a few nonverbal examples reflecting rudimentary social rules for leaders communicating in certain cultures. They are not universal even in the East Asian cultures, often depending on the degree of Western influence. They indicate that in the highly intertwined globalized era, one cannot take a cultural norm for granted. And all problems in these critiques by the CEO's friend are regarding signs of *chi* or vital dynamics.

Why do these seemingly trivial social rules affect professional relationships and organizational communication? And what is *chi*, anyway? In this chapter we will unveil the source of the Chinese concepts that affect professional relationships and organizational communication like in this case.

The Chinese culture has influenced multiple cultures and billions of people, not only in the Eastern countries but also in other continents of the world. It has never ceased to arouse academic curiosity—just as it has never stopped alluring business interest—of outsiders. Three decades after easing its ideological constraints and opening up to the international community, China has emerged as a strong power economically, militarily, and diplomatically. By signing various international and regional agreements, economic deals, and military pacts, China has been knitted much more closely into the globalized networks than before. Interacting with Chinese business and professional people is becoming inevitable for people in other parts of the world. Understanding the communication in Chinese organizational, business, or professional contexts has been increasingly indispensable.

In this chapter, after presenting the field of organizational communication, its cultural roots will be traced back to various ancient Chinese philosophies. Next is a summary of research on characteristics of contemporary Chinese professional relationships and organizational communication. This will include a discussion on an indigenous system and theory of organizational communication developed from the Chinese philosophies. In general, this chapter attempts to bridge knowledge about classical Chinese philosophical traditions with contemporary Chinese organizational communication theory, practices, and research. This effort will be facilitated by historical and contemporary accounts.

■ Roots of Chinese Organizational Communication

Broadly speaking, organizational communication research examines "the various and complex communication practices of humans engaged in collective, coordinated, and goal-oriented behavior" (Mumby, 2007). Taking a communicative lens, scholars in organizational communication investigate a wide range of organizational phenomena or processes, such as leadership, identity, network, power, and conflict, to mention a few (Putnam & Mumby, 2014). Scholars also examine the role of communication in shaping the boundaries and relationships between organizations and the wider society, such as the community in which they are located. Although organizational communication as an academic field of study originated in the West in the twentieth century, we can locate the roots of many communicative concepts and practices in Chinese organizations to several major ancient Chinese schools of thought, which include Confucianism, Classical Legalism, Daoism, and cyclic course concept. More recently, influence has also come from communism in the Mao Zedong era.

Classical Legalism

Classical Legalists such as the renowned Guan Zhong, Shang Yang, and Shen Dao applied their thoughts to managing a nation and even uniting China, demonstrating the exceptional utility of Legalist thought. Han Feizi (circa 280–233 B.C.) integrated the thoughts and, illustrating them with historical narratives, composed the book *Han Feizi*. The book is still broadly read and discussed in contemporary political, administrative, and management studies.

In stark contrast with Confucians, who intensively quoted and cited ancient sages, Legalists opposed modeling after the ancient and following the existing. They criticized and scorned the Confucian rhetoric and promoted innovation. Han Feizi said, as time moves on, the unchanged ruling would cause turmoil.

Classical Legalism contains the following principles:

Centralized authority padded by credibility. Legalists in the Warring States Era used their strategies to help the nation of *Qin* conquer all other feudalist states and built the first unified empire in China. Legalists argue that when power and laws are set by the king, the king generates awe. When the power is centralized and monopolized by the king, the entire nation becomes a political or military machine, and efficiency is maximized until corruption sets in (Liang, 1998). As illustrated in the example of "moving a log and receiving a huge reward,"[1] when padded by the trust subjects placed

---

[1]Adopting the strategies of Classic Legalists, especially Shang Yang, Emperor Qin Shi turned his nation into a military machine, eliminating all other states and unifying ancient China, Continuing the legalist policy, he abolished the feudal system, centralizing the power and authority. Even before the unification of China, the renowned legalist prime minister Shang Yang (商鞅 370–335 B.C.) of the Qin nation ordered his staff to put up a log by the south gate of the market in the capital. A note with the log offered a reward of 10-liang (about 10 grams) of gold for moving the log to the north gate of a market. The reward was so ludicrously high that no one took it seriously. After the reward was raised to 100-liang, a man did it and was rewarded the gold. Historians called this strategy of complementing the stern central authority with the trustworthy law-observing. This strategy was called "a story of moving log to build trust." Even 1,400 years later in the Song Dynasty (宋朝), Premier Wang An Shi (王安石 1021–1084 AD) wrote a poem extolling the Legalist Sang Yang's strategy as "the words heavier than a hundred liang of gold."

in the ruler, the principle of centralized authority gave more credibility to the laws and more power for enforcement.

Equality

Another legalistic principle is that laws must be applied to all with equality according to administrative protocols. This was to disregard kinship or other sources of favoritism. A Legalistic aphorism has famously crystallized in a tenet in the Daoist legacy: "A law-violating prince is to be convicted like a commoner."

Severity

Classical Legalism argues that laws should be enforced with severity. This following well-known story exemplifies this principle: According to tradition, Sunzi, a military strategist and author of the internationally known book *The Art of War* personally demonstrated certain tactics in a military drill. He summoned a dozen royal court maids to play the role of soldiers. Feeling playful, the girls would not stop giggling despite Sunzi's chiding. Sunzi thus ordered the execution of two leaders of the squad maids, despite the emperor's pleading. What a ruthless and abusive way of demonstrating the rule of severity in executing orders!

Manipulation

This refers to the "carrot and stick" approach when playing games with human greed. As the teacher of Classical Legalists Han Fei and Li Si, Xunzi is well known for his philosophy that human nature is inherently evil. Greed is to be legally curbed but justifiably exploited. The log-moving story illustrating the first tenet listed above also illustrates this principle.

Although Classical Legalism lost the favor of the Chinese rulers after the *Qin* empire collapsed, the Legalistic thoughts, accompanied by the legends like the above, have been communicated from generation to generation with books and oratory media, and thus been rooted in the Chinese culture, particularly in the royal administrations.

Daoism

While the Chinese Classical Legalism is mainly administrative/management oriented, the Daoist approach is an anti-establishment perspective, taking a sarcastic but serious attitude toward the contemporary authoritarian rulers and administrations.

Daoism, also known as Taoism, has pervaded numerous areas of Chinese philosophy and daily life—much like the teachings of Confucianism. One of the most well-known Daoist writings is *Dao De Jing* (traditionally spelled as *Tao Te Ching*), with *Dao* (道) meaning "the way" and *De* (德) referring to "virtue." Traditional historical accounts before the twentieth century say that *Dao De Jing*'s authorship is generally attributed to Li Er (circa 500 B.C.), commonly known as Laozi (literally meaning "old master"). However, various pieces of the *Dao De Jing* have been discovered in excavated tombs, suggesting that the text was assembled from multiple like-minded authors.

Dao is the cornerstone concept of Daoism. Although it is interpreted as "the way," Daoism as a whole tells us that its meaning is closest to the English saying, "let nature take its course." It is a key word for understanding the universe. Lu (1998) suggests that *dao* can be approached through *de* and manifested in *wu wei* (无为; nonaction or spontaneity) and *bu zheng* (不争; nonaction).

Wu ming (无名; namelessness)

While Confucians asserted the importance of rectifying naming practices in human interaction and in administration[2], Daoists consider names are artificial or socially constructed. They view naming as virtually a game—breeding misunderstanding, misleading, and deserving no place in rulership. Using the modern day terms, names bolster or perpetuate, if not substitute, positions to uphold the ruling power.

Wu wei (无为; nonaction)

In contrast to Confucius's stressing virtue and upholding moral standard to regulate human behaviors, especially those of government officials, Laozi argued for *nonaction*. Nonaction is not equivalent to "do nothing"; instead,

---

[2]Confucius taught name rectification, but he likely did not expect that 2,000 years later Chinese would hold such strong value on names or naming—so much that many are superstitious about names. In 1949, Chinese Communists banished ex-president Chiang Kai-shek from the Chinese mainland. According to popular legend, while riding a navy ship on his way to Taiwan to build a stronghold there, Chiang chatted with the ship captain. Learning that the commander's name was Li Yu-xi, he was elated, saying, "Now I got the yu-xi (玉 璽)," "which in Chinese means "jade seal" used by the head of a nation like emperor or president as an official symbol of authority. Chiang regained the presidency in Taiwan and later appointed General Li as the commander of the Navy (J. Chung, personal communication, 2015).

it is noninterference with the natural course. Worded differently, let people transform and rectify themselves. With regard to management and leadership, Laozi says in *Dao De Jing*,

> Therefore the Sage:
> Manages affairs without action;
> Preaches the doctrine without words;
> All things take their rise, but he does not turn away from them;
> He gives them life, but does not take possession of them;
> He acts, but does not appropriate;
> Accomplishes; but claims to no credit.
> It is because he lays claim to no credit
> That the credit cannot be taken away from him. (Lin, 2009, p. 7)
>
> By permission of Hsiang Ju Lin, Jill Lai Miller and Larry Lai

Bu zheng (不争; non-contention)

Unlike Confucians, who argued for striving for achievement through competition, Daoists advocated non-contention. As Chen (1977) explains:

> *Lao Tzu's [Laozi] concept of "not contending" does not involve a negation of the self, nor does it imply an escape into the seclusion of some mountain retreat. Rather, it is propounded as a means for dissolving the dissension, which racks human activity. On the contrary, Lao Tzu urges man to "do"—this "doing" being an expression of human endeavor in accordance with what is natural. (as cited in Lu, 1998, p. 233)*

The Cyclic Course Concept

Yi Jing (易经), traditionally spelled as *I-Ching* in English, is also known as *Book of Changes* or *the Canons of Changes*. It has been one of the most influential writings on Chinese thoughts in the past two thousand years. The concept of "cyclic course" has had powerful impact on Chinese thinking, ranging from philosophy and literature to daily life. It also has molded the Chinese way of viewing organizations and behaviors in business. The key concepts of the cyclic course are as follows:

Yin and *yang*

All things contain the nature or quality of *yin* and *yang* opposites. (*Yin* and *yang* are designated to symbolize any pair of contrasting qualities or natures.) *Yin* represents the dark, the weak, the soft, the cool, etc., and *yang* the bright, the strong, the hard, the hot, etc.)

Rotation

Yin and *yang* rotate. Mother Nature provides abundant examples of rotation: the sun (bright, thus *yang*) with the moon (dim, thus *yin*). Similar rotation takes place in biological bodies (as in circulation systems) and the social worlds. The ups (*yang*) and downs (*yin*) of the dynasties in history are often cited as a prominent example of such rotation.

Dynamism

The rotation of the two opposites and the interaction of *yin* and *yang* forces cause change and generate dynamics. The liveliness (or life energy) brought by the cyclic change of the cold/cool (*yin*) and warm/hot (*yang*) seasons is one example and the rotation of tenure and policy in social systems is another.

Circle

Each rotation constitutes its own circle, and thus a boundary enclosing the circulation elements, forming a small universe.

Stability

The *yin* and *yang* opposite forms an interdependent relationship, unlike the Western counterpart concept of dialectics, of which the opposites are often considered mutually exclusive. The *yin–yang* complementary relationship between the elements must be stable, to some extent, to maintain rotation structure.

As Liu (1991) put it, without the worldview of cyclic course, Chinese culture would not be as we see it today. For example, the notion of *yin–yang* interaction generating *qi*/*chi* dynamics has been a topic carried on in philosophy, literature, medicine, and martial arts. However, until the modern time, the cyclic concept may have led the Chinese to view China as a closed system rather than an open one. People have been satisfied with communicating within this system, limiting interactions and missing opportunities for mutual growth with outsiders.

Confucianism

As described in Chapter 1 of this book, Confucianism was one of the most influential schools of thought in the Chinese culture for 2000 years. In addition to the relational concepts of *wulun* (五伦; five relationships), *ren* (仁; human-heartedness), and *harmony* illustrated in Chapter 1, the Confucian virtue of *yi* (义; righteousness) has also influenced the contemporary discourse of power and legitimacy in regard to state and organizational governance. Mengzi (circa 371–289 B.C.), a prominent Confucian scholar, believed that the welfare of the people should be the foundation for good governance, arguing that the interests of Heaven, which sanctions good and bad political regimes, are perfectly aligned with those of ordinary citizens (Tiwald, 2008). He was fond of the expression, "Heaven sees as the people see, and Heaven hears as the people hear" (as cited in Tu, 1993, p. 19). He further championed the right to overthrow any regime when the king is not worthy of the mandate of Heaven. Although he believed that the campaign to overthrow such a king must be led by a member of the ruling class, he nevertheless thought that the people could participate in such a rebellion and that the leader of the rebellion had to base his decisions on what he considered to be in the best interest of the people (Tiwald, 2008).

Confucianism is generally considered "the foundation of Chinese cultural traditions," continuing to "guide the Chinese way of life in the contemporary age" (Chen, in press). Even Mao Zedong, who initiated the Cultural Revolution in the 1960s and tried to eradicate Confucian heritage from the Chinese culture, was himself influenced by Confucianism. According to the analysis of Lin and Clair (2007), Mao's words are rooted in Confucianism when calling upon leaders to "combat selfishness, slacking, corruption, and seeking the limelight" and to "work with an eye toward harmony" (p. 399).

Although the ancient Chinese philosophies have influenced the values, beliefs, behaviors, communication, and organizational communication, scholars such as Chan (2004) and Chamberlain (1987) have suggested that the Chinese Communist Party (CCP), "guided by the political ideology of [Mao Ze Tung], is a major source of influence on Chinese management and subsequently organizational practices" (as cited in Lin & Clair, 2007, p. 397).

Maoism and the CCP's Influence

Lin and Clair (2007) summarize the works of Helburn & Shearer (1984), Warner (1986), Derong & Faure (1995), and Tung (1981) to suggest that Mao's thoughts have "shaped management and organizational communication practices and influenced human resource management, . . . negotiation, . . . and motivation" (p. 429–430). One of Mao's influential ideas is the concept *democratic centralism*. According to Lin and Clair (2007), *democratic centralism* is relevant to authority, power communication, and message direction. It claims to allow decision making to adopt workers' opinions in addition to command from authority.

■ Contemporary Chinese Organizational Communication

The previous section has explained the unique ancient Chinese thoughts and philosophies and modern ideologies that have influenced organizational communication. With this background, the following section turns to a description of several contemporary communication practices in Chinese organizations, including leadership, negotiation, *guanxi* (关系; interpersonal connections), seniority, remonstration system, and the indigenous *chi* theory.

Leadership

Organizational leadership communication studies conducted in China show hallmarks of ancient Chinese philosophical thoughts, especially in transformational leadership, benevolent leadership, and hands-off leadership.

Factors of Transformational Leadership

In the West, transformational leadership theory has been an influential approach to the study of organizational leadership (Antonakis, 2012). As opposed to transactional leaders, who are concerned with satisfying people's physiological, safety, and belonging needs, transformational leaders attempt to satisfy higher levels of needs of followers such as self-esteem and self-actualization. This type of leadership is still considered by many the most potent type of leadership in the new century. Judge and Bono

(2000) found the following personality traits to be powerful predictors of transformational leadership in North America: extraversion, openness to experience, and agreeableness, with the other two factors (conscientiousness and neuroticism) having no predictive value.

A similar study conducted in China by Shao and Webber (2006), however, showed these traits to be nonfactors at best, even negative for certain traits. The study, conducted on the perception of employees at Chinese State-Owned-Enterprises (SOE), found that openness to experience, agreeableness, and conscientiousness had insignificant relationships, while extraversion and neuroticism had negative relationships with transformational leadership. Shao and Webber (2006) suggested that the negative effect of extraversion might be due to China's "cultural tightness society, where active initiators are discouraged and a noncompetitive relationship is favored in a group environment" (p. 941). With China placing especially high value on stability, Shao and Webber (2006) attribute these negative views toward neuroticism in China to the impossibility of "neurotic leaders who lack confidence and are unsure of the future" to effectively create that feeling of dependability (p. 942).

Overall, they attribute the difference in leadership perception between the Chinese and other cultures to "high power distance, high uncertainty avoidance and collectivism," maintaining that these cultural differences reinforce the "hierarchical and conformist attributes of the top-down command structure," one which "emphasizes a centralized authority and leadership, stability and predictability" (Shao & Webber, 2006, p. 943). These attributes apparently results from Confucian teachings and Legalist tenets.

The perception of the traits and practices that constitute effective leadership differs even among college students between Chinese and other cultures. Shafer, Vieregge, and Choi (2005) conducted a study on "preferred leadership qualities of hospitality students" from China, the United States, and several other countries. They found significant differences between students from the United States and students from the People's Republic of China (PRC) in all categories, including physical attributes, personality traits, transformational leadership skills, interpersonal skills, and administrative skills. For example, the US students rated the category, *is constantly learning and changing*, much higher than the students from the PRC did. In the context of leadership qualities, the authors observed, "U.S. students appear to embrace the concept of change and innovative progress, while the Chinese students seem to prefer to maintain the status quo" (Shafer et al., p. 80). These passive attitudes seem to be consistent with Daoist philosophical views and the cyclic course concept mentioned earlier, particularly being satisfied with the Chinese world as a closed system.

Traditions of Benevolent Leadership

The concept of benevolent leadership commonly refers to a leader's activity intended to help or benefit followers. In China, benevolent leadership was first advocated by Confucius 2,500 years ago and Menzi later in the name of *ren zheng* (仁政; benevolent leadership or rulership) (Curzer, 2012). *Ren*'s core meaning is "love." As Chen & Chung (1994) note, loving oneself is manifest by self-restraint and self-discipline, while loving others is by benevolence. Regulated by Confucius' five ethics, a leader exercises benevolent leadership in exchange for loyalty from subordinates. Therefore, mutual love and loyalty travel between the two roles in a two-way street complementarily. The following stories can help illustrate this nature of benevolent leadership.

This author conducted an interview with a company president in Shanghai who was to return home from a business trip in the United States. Before the conversation began, he zipped up his large luggage full of cans of infant formula. He has no children himself, but he said, "I bought them for my colleagues. Despite several nationwide crackdowns on bogus milk formula, there have been frequent news reports about incidences of baby death caused by malnutrition after drinking fake milk. Many of them contain only a minute fraction of the required amount of nutrients. I am going to give my colleagues and family a pleasant surprise."

A leader's carrying baby formula all the way from another continent should already be sufficient to demonstrate benevolent leadership. Chinese benevolent leadership, however, is often accentuated with patriarchal love. In 2015, in Fuzhou, China, the author interviewed a business leader Mr. Zhao, president of seven companies in Southern China. The author asked about how he would deal with leader–associate relationship when an associate committed a serious mistake. Part of his answer was: "Employees are children; when they err, I still treat them as my errant children."

Such patriarchal love is strongly exhibited by mentors in mentor–mentee relationships in Chinese organizations. Leaders often promote their trusted mentees into prominent positions. Even without favoritism, in return for guidance and help, mentees are expected to show loyalty and commitment. Worded differently, benevolent leadership is an extension of patriarchal love;

leaders should not take followers' respect for granted and vise versa. Like love, it is expected (by cultural norm) to be reciprocated in the future.

Hands-off approach

Daoism may not have been the official philosophy, but some of its teachings offer guidance for leaders in many Chinese societies. For example, the Daoist idea of *wu wei*, as discussed earlier, inspires the hands-off approach to leadership.

In the summer of 2012, the author talked to a successful former congressman Mr. Wen who had been under the heavy influence of the Chinese culture. He had been running several chicken farms since he was a high school teacher. He spent most of his off-school hours with thousands of chickens even after being selected to be a middle school—and then high school—principal in various cities. His success in every aspect of his educational leadership was so much appreciated by the public that he was elected congressman. His secret—actually, a public secret—was delegating most of his job to three directors. He told me that he was inspired by chickens: the more crowded the chickens are, the more conflicts arise, and the more furiously they peck each other. "I don't want to be yet another chicken in schools," said he, a Daoist practitioner (J. Chung, personal communication, 2012).

Negotiation

Water can carry boats, but it may also capsize boats. Culture can carry organizational communication flow, but it may also obstruct organizational communication. As Adler (2001) points out, "the greatest barrier in business transaction process is the one embedded in culture" (as cited by Chen, in press). Chen (in press) thus examines those cultural factors that affect business negotiations in the People's Republic of China (PRC). Four factors originating from this communication pattern greatly affect Chinese conflict and negotiation behaviors: harmony, relation (*guanxi*), face, and power. He further illustrates these factors with specific behaviors or traits. Of the four factors, three (harmony, relation, and face) include behaviors such as "avoidance of saying 'no,' bribery, credibility, emotional control, fairness, gift giving, honesty, humility, patience, reciprocity, self-restraint, sincerity, and trick." The fourth factor (power), on the other hand, is manifest in traits such as "authority, expertise, seniority, and status" (Chen, in press).

Chen then suggests guidelines for negotiating with PRC Chinese. The results of his study propose four general principles:

> *(1) try to build relationships before negotiating with PRC Chinese; (2) follow the principle of* li shang wang lai *(courtesy requires reciprocity) by, for example, giving gifts to Chinese negotiators as a gesture of goodwill; (3) be patient, polite, and humble by avoiding aggressive and confrontational behaviors to save their face; and (4) develop a long-term relationship by showing appreciation to them at the end of negotiation and keeping in contact with them after the negotiation."* (Chen, in press)

Guanxi (关系; Interpersonal Connections)

Guanxi, more commonly known as interpersonal connections, is defined by Su, Mitchell, and Surgy (2006) as a "network of resource coalition-based stakeholders sharing resources for survival" (p. 301). There has been a surging research interest in this aspect of Chinese organizational communication since the late twentieth century. Needs for *guanxi* can be classified into two levels: first is at the organizational (unit-centrism), including the departmental levels, and second is at the personal level (harmony, reciprocity), which may consume more time of organizational members.

Unit-centrism

Guanxi is essential to one's organization. Contemporary Chinese organizational communication has long been faulted for a Chinese version of organizational tribalism, *ben wei zhu yi* (本位主義; unit-centrism), which refers to persistently adhering to the position and interest of one's own unit. It is apparently associated with silo mentality, a mindset of being unwilling to share information with others in the organization. Such a mindset obstructs communication flow and causes a defensive communication climate. The study of Sino-foreign joint ventures by Child and Markoczy (1994) reconfirmed this criticism. Their study shows that horizontal communication between functional departments was extremely poor, which is detrimental to horizontal collaboration within organizations. Child and Markoczy (1994) attribute this phenomenon to the vertically oriented loyalties stemming from the five cardinal relationships or *wulun* preached by Confucianism (see Chapter 1). This is reasonable because with imperative loyalty to one's own unit, an organization's members often need to persuade or negotiate with other units or organizations for the benefit of one's own unit. Therefore, job performance often hinges on how one can successfully fight or defend the resources of one's own unit.

Guanxi benefits not only one's own unit, but also individuals; with abundant *guanxi* and opportunity, one can perform better for promotion or side-step personnel rules to expedite one's promotion. *Sheng tian* (升天; rising to the sky) takes its meaning in nonreligious sense to refer to promotion. In some organizations or in some regions, this tactic of skirting the personnel rules is called "taking a bath." This could be a fountainhead of bribery.

Harmony—Double Faceted States

While Child and Markoczy seem to imply that the Confucian—prescribed role relationship is the culprit of what may be called "evils," Hong and Engeström (2004) consider this relationship simply traditional *guanxi*, something contemporary Chinese organizations may promote as a remedy in internal and interdepartmental communication. Connections should be beneficial to performance, either external to the organization (e.g., public relations) or internal to the organization (e.g., interdepartmental communication).

Chen (in press), noting *guanxi* along with harmony, face, and power to be "the predominant factors that influence Chinese business negotiations," goes on to argue that "harmony is achieved via the exercise of relation (*guanxi*) and face." Indeed, Chen's findings on contemporary practices of *guanxi* indicate the continuing influence of Confucianism, which touts benevolence and hierarchical relationships and forms an order of network relationships, ranging from family to teacher–student, friends, and employer–employees. Those values helped people lubricate their relationships, facilitating a long-term relationship. "The emphasis of *ren, yi,* and *li* leads PRC Chinese to develop a belief that harmony is the ultimate goal in social and business encounters, and in business negotiation the pursuit of a harmonious atmosphere is regulated by face saving, relation building, reciprocity, and credibility. These are factors that govern Chinese business persons' negotiation styles and patterns" (Chen, in press).

Strategies

Su et al. (2006) argue that effective *guanxi* "works as a relationship-based cultural mechanism that draws on Chinese cultural ethics of cooperation (e.g., mutual assistance), gathers necessary resources for business performance and better enables the survival of firms . . . *guanxi* management is predicated on identifying and cultivating a network of 'right people' who help to do business in China" (p.302).

Su et al. (2006) identify three *guanxi* management implications from their analysis. The first is an "assessment of hierarchical/salience factors . . . identifying who possess resources that are necessary for firm survival and who possess vital resources that are more important for firm survival in China" (p. 318). Second are regular evaluations of the hierarchical positioning of partners, or what Su et al. (2006) call "*guanxi* audits" (p. 318). This is also important for maintaining *guanxi* relationships, should these relationships turn "stale and need rejuvenation" (Su et al., 2006, p. 318). Third, strategies for developing *guanxi* should be "dynamic, changing along with business timing and location" (Su et al., 2006, p. 318). According to Su et al. (2006), *guanxi* is largely a matter of strategic positioning, and it is especially crucial in China "to know when, where, and with whom you are doing business" (p. 318).

Reciprocity

Reciprocity is the practice of returning favors. Most people expect the *possibility* of reciprocating each other's help and favor in the future. Notice that the *possibility* is emphasized here because they expect a possible moral, not contractual, obligation to return the favor. In other words, the possibility refers to an expectation to have friends like close kinfolks, who are born to be part of relationship networks. From the viewpoint of the cyclic course concept, giving and taking may go in a cycle. Probability and possibility of compensation or reciprocation always looms in the offing.

The Future of *Guanxi*

Some believe that with the marketization of the Chinese economy and Westernization of the Chinese societies, *guanxi* may be slowly but surely on its way out, while others consider it a fundamental resource of an organization. Hoskisson et al. (2000) argue that according to institutional theory, which is based on interorganizational relationships, in the early stages of market emergence, *guanxi* is key to understanding impacts on firm strategies. In this regard, Peng (2003) highlights the trend of relative decline of networks and connections as opposed to these resource-based approaches. Nevertheless, Peng still considers *guanxi* important to doing business with

Chinese. Current research (e.g., Nie & Lämsä, 2015) suggests that *guanxi* remains a crucial concept in understanding relational networks in China.

Seniority

Respecting seniors—those who are older or of higher official position—is highly emphasized in contemporary organizations in the Chinese cultures. Seniors often play a significant role in mediating conflicts. For example, Lee Teng-hui, president of Taiwan at the time, was running for reelection in 1990, but was challenged by several political heavyweights within the Kuomintang (the Nationalist Party). To persuade them to withdraw, Lee enlisted eight so-called great old elderlies to mediate. The "eight great elders" were mostly from the Chinese mainland. Lee's mediators successfully persuaded them to drop out of the race. Chung (1996), in his interviews with some of those "great old elderlies," identified three major conflict resolution instruments: *guanxi*, seniority, and third parties. In business settings, seniority would typically refer to those who have longer tenure, more experience, or hold higher positions, because age would not matter as much as in political organizations.

In many organizations, the phenomenon of *lun zhi pai bei* (論資排輩; counting seniority to rank order) is less striking but still holds true. For example, who is supposed to sit at the head of the table often becomes an issue before negotiating a "real" issue. Then, it requires creativity to settle the secondary issue. Replacing a rectangular table with a round one might solve this issue. Seniority also impacts a company's decision–making process. For example, in a research interview, an American executive, who was a former Hitachi representative to the United States and later the director of the Hitachi Interactive division in the United States, related the following story to the author. In a recent consultation meeting in Tainan, he and his colleagues spent days to reach a decision. A few days later at the next meeting, to his surprise, the decision reached at the previous meeting was completely scratched. The reasons he surmised ranged from "their boss did not favor the decision" to "a senior advisor had some opinions" and to "there came a new boss."

Inadequate Upward Communication

Organizational communication in China has hit strides in recent decades. Scholarship within the field of organizational communication, however, can still make tremendous contributions, elevating the organizational communication practices to a new horizon. This is especially true in view of the Chinese philosophical roots and cultural heritage. The following is an overall survey according to a research conducted by Nin Chen (2008):

Chinese corporations tend to have no internal mechanism to ensure that workers' complaints and suggestions reach top management. In specific, 77% of respondents to a mail survey noted that there were no people or departments/offices in their organizations designated to be in charge of corporate communication in general and internal/ employee communication *in particular*. Chinese corporations with participative culture, as compared to those with authoritarian culture, do tend to communicate more with two-way models, *and* participative culture tends to lead to higher level of trust and openness between management and employees, as well as employee job satisfaction. Chinese corporate staff in charge of internal or employee communication, identified as "corporate communicators" in the research, spend more time on distributing information out from management to employees and other internal constituencies and do less on seeking input and feedback from them.

This finding regarding lack of upward communication in the Chinese corporations is ironic, because the 2,500 years of Chinese organizational communication boasts a unique upward communication system that is worthy of investigation and modeling by the contemporary world. That is the remonstration system to be discussed below.

Remonstration System

To be a leader or a manager, seeking, choosing, and taking advice has been essential and challenging to leadership and management. It involves not only reasoning capability but also emotion management. The following famous historical account has rich implications to organizational communication with respect to both the reasoning and emotional aspects.

Emperor Taizong of the Tang dynasty (618–907) once received a cute sparrow-hawk. He let it play on his arm. Seeing Wei Zheng approaching, he hid it in his robe. As usual, Wei Zheng's remonstration went on very long—so long that the bird was smothered to death in the emperor's robe (Sima, 1992).

In that authoritarian era, an emperor was so powerful as to be able to put anyone to death without trial, especially when the emperor's ego was bruised. Why would this emperor be so afraid of an expostulation (remonstration) official, his subordinate? Furthermore, Taizong was a heroic emperor whose armies conquered neighboring countries and became the emperor of the "middle kingdom." This was a very capable emperor who led the country to unprecedented prosperity.[3] Why would he need to hide a pet bird?

In view of the context of the official's relationship with the emperor, one answer might be: "Just because the emperor cared enough about his own behavior in the eyes of an expostulatory official, he grew to be an emperor of military exploits outside the borders and economic boom inside it."

This is a famous story illustrating Emperor Taizong's attitude toward his subordinate who gave him negative feedback. This also shows his model leadership in terms of employing a system of remonstration. *Jian* (諫; remonstration or expostulation) is defined as a presentation of disagreement to one's leader over formulating or enacted policy, law, or what the remonstrator considers leader's mistake or wrongdoing.

Taizong's reputation of taking *jian* and advice reached out all over the map and attracted a great deal of useful suggestions, which earned him the praise as the best emperor to receive *jian* (Fan, 1941) and one of the most successful emperors in Chinese history. How did he do it? According to Chao (1993), Emperor Taizong employed the following methods:

First, read sagacious books extensively to enhance his own judgment; second, learn from subordinates and government officials; third, praise or reward those who remonstrate; fourth, yield his own opinion to those of his subordinates; fifth, promote remonstrators; sixth, listen to remonstration with kind look and intonation; seventh, confess his own mistakes; eighth, institutionalize the expostulation to protect remonstrators; ninth, elevate the legal status of the remonstrators. In addition, a collection of 36 remonstration manuscripts selected from Chinese history shows a common strategy used by the remonstrators: deprecate themselves first to exhibit modesty before condemning (Xia, 1997).

---

[3]The success of Tang dynasty earned Chinese a name "Tang people." Till today Chinatowns around the world are still known as "Tang people streets."

The remonstration system was adopted by Japanese[4] and Dr. Sun Yat-sen. Dr. Sun injected the remonstration idea into his proposed constitution for China's new republic after overthrowing the Qing Dynasty (1644–1911). Instead of the mechanism of counterbalances among the three powers of administration, legislature, and justice popular in the West, Sun proposed additional two branches: control and examination (for selecting public functionaries). He attributed his "control" idea to the Chinese *jian* system. The idea of five-power constitution was fulfilled in Taiwan and has exercised the control power to impeach officials at all echelons of government, including a premier appointed by Chiang Kai-shek, then president.

Contemporary organizational leaders or managers may benefit from pondering this Chinese mechanism of upward communication; advice or condemnation from subordinates may be hard to swallow, but communication techniques from both superior and subordinate can pad a criticism to avoid bruising egos. Institutionalizing remonstration coupled with communication training may make the implementation more feasible. *The Wall Street Journal* reports several companies formally encouraging employees to mold a culture of radical candor—known as "front stabbing" (Fentzeig, 2015). Employees are to drop the polite workplace veneer to give each other blunt feedback. "People are expected to defend themselves or change when confronted by coworkers about bad strategy or subpar work" (Fentzeig, 2015). *Jian* should be less brutal to practice than this modern practice. The discussion of remonstration system indicates the centrality of communication in advice seeking, taking, and decision–making. It also reveals the criticality of emotion management. The following introduction to the concept of *qi du* (氣度; emotional magnitude) in *chi* (*qi*) theory may remind us of revisiting the wisdom in the Chinese heritage, particularly amid the frenzy of pursuing the Western leadership and management communication techniques.

Chi (Qi) Theory

Chi theory emerged around the turn of the twenty-first century. It is the first communication theory developed from East Asian cultural milieu. It is based on Lao Zi's renowned adage, which Mair (1990) literally translated as "The myriad creatures bear *yin* on their backs and embrace *yang* in their

---

[4]Japan adopted this remonstration system from China and entitled the remonstration official "big receiving word " or "big word receptionist" (Wang, 2005).

bosoms. They neutralize these vapors and thereby achieve harmony." (For the purpose of this research, the second sentence is tersely translated as "They interplay to generate *chi/qi* for harmony.")

As discussed earlier in the topic of cyclic course concept in the philosophical root section, *yin* and *yang* are symbols of any pair of relative opposite, *yin* standing for the quieter, the smaller, the weaker, the suppler, the darker, the emotional, the negative, etc. and the *yang* for the more raucous, the larger, the stronger, the more rigid, the brighter, the rational, the positive, etc. For explaining *yin* and *yang*, organizational communication provides very useful examples. In an organization and organizational communication, there are plenty of dialectics or simply opposites, which can be represented by the symbols *yin* and *yang*. For example, subordinate (lower organizational status, thus *yin*) vs. superior (with higher status, thus *yang*), staff (relatively invisible, thus *yin*) vs. line (relatively active and visible, thus *yang*), labor (*yin*) vs. management (*yang*), socioemotional functions (traditionally viewed by many as the "soft" dimension of work, thus *yin*) vs. task activities (the "hard" dimension, thus *yang*), organizational constraint (*yin*) vs. organizational creativity (*yang*), and praising (normally amiable and soft, thus *yin*) vs. threatening (normally harsh, thus *yang*). *Yin* and *yang* are arbitrary emblems; therefore, what each represents may be exchanged depending on the perspective or context.

How do *yin* and *yang* interplay? *Yin* and *yang* constitute a *shi* (勢) structure, which can interplay to generate *chi*. Ames (1994) defines *shi* as "strategic advantage" (p. 15). Jullien (1995) also calls *shi* "propensity emanating from a particular configuration of reality" (p. 15). He defines it as "a particular deployment or arrangement of things to be relied on and worked to one's advantage" (p. 15). According to Chung and Busby (2002), there are primarily four kinds of *shi*: suck (riding others' or driving one's own) *shi*, duck (avoiding) *shi*, buck (defying) *shi*, and construct (creating) *shi*. Take buck *shi* as an example—when an employee stands up to argue with the company president (*yin* vs. *yang*), this defiance virtually sets up a *shi* structure of David (*yin*) vs. Goliath (*yang*) situation. This person will appear to be full of *chi* and, applauded by a crowd, may be motivated to be full of courageous *chi/qi* due to the emergence of a power difference. If the president humbles herself to reconcile with the employee, thus reduces the (*yin–yang*) power difference, she will produce a breeze-like atmosphere or energy flow (*yin chi/qi*). If the president fires the employee because of the defiance, she, the president, displays her ultimate power and enlarges the *yin* (employee)–*yang* (the president) power distance, creating a storm-like vibe or dynamic (*yang chi/qi*). This example shows that *chi/qi* can procreate.

The major assumption of the *chi/qi* theory is that all communications and their elements (communicators, messages, media, and so on.) carry *yin* and *yang* aspects, with which their interaction may generate energy flow called *chi* (*qi*). Other assumptions include "*yin* in *yang*, and *yang* in *yin*." Some of the principles of *chi* theory can be explained with *yin–yang* interplay and are indispensible for leadership and organizational communication. For example, *qi du* (氣度; emotional magnitude), focus, change, and so on are essential themes of leadership and organizational communication. From an epistemological point of view, they are developed from *yin–yang* interplay. In the story told above, examples of *yin–yang* interplay include: Emperor Taizong's hiding the bird with which he was playing, remonstrator Wei's long presentation, Taizong's displaying emotional magnitude, and remonstrator Wei's techniques not shown here. In general, organizational change results from a fundamental need to evolve from a lifeless state to a lively state. To that end, *yin* and *yang* interplay becomes pivotal.

In this chapter, Confucianism is classified as *yin* because it is relatively supple compared with Legalism (which is relatively harsh, and thus *yang*). When paired up with Daoism, Daoism is *yin* (more passive tenets), while Confucianism is *yang* (more assertive or even aggressive in attitude toward human relationships). Individuals can play *yin–yang* with the two philosophies. For example, it is said that when a Chinese is in power, she embraces Confucianism (to conform to the position). But she turns to Daoism (to seek comfort) when losing favor of the boss. Conflict resolution style is another example of interplay between *yin* (avoidance) vs. aggression (*yang*) or accommodation (*yin*) vs. problem-solving (*yang*). The resolution process thus yields various kinds of *chi/qi*.

Chi aids effective communication by adding energy (through words of enlarged or reduced contrast or by strengthening a communicator's presence), which in turn strengthens *chi* in a reinforcing cycle. The effects of *chi* are manifest throughout an organization and through a variety of channels. Thus, there are numerous potential practical applications of *chi/qi* theory in organizations. For instance, organizations can strategically manage their communication styles (*yin* and *yang*) to create the right atmosphere (*chi/qi*) and facilitate negotiation and conflict resolution. This theory has been applied to research in several fields, such as Chinese investor relations (Ho, in press) and public relations, which is also known as external organizational communication (Chung, 2011). Opportunities and challenges for demonstrating the explanatory, descriptive, and predictive power of the theory seem to be lying ahead.

■ Conclusion

Bringing the Chinese philosophical roots to light, we are able to observe the Chinese legacy of Classical Legalism, Confucianism, Daoism, and the cyclic course concept. The legacy has left its mark on Chinese professional relationships and organizational communication. The marks are reflected in contemporary relational and communication values and practices. Those values and practices include centralized decision–making (a remnant of Classical Legalism), harmony maintenance, seniority respecting, and hierarchy structuring (rooted in Confucianism), hands-off approach to leadership (a hallmark of the Daoist philosophy of nonaction), and reciprocation of favor (closely tied to a cyclic course mindset).

Though brief, this review surfaces an ample implication to research and practice of Chinese professional relationships and organizational communication: an emerging fertile ground in practice, research, and theory. Such an outlook is based on two phenomena found in this research: First, contemporary Chinese organizational communication has arrived at the confluence of the Eastern influences (by the ancient Chinese philosophies) and the Western impacts (from communism and capitalism); the second phenomenon is the dawn of the identity of Chinese organizational communication studies. This rise is first shown by the indigenous vertical organizational communication system—the remonstration (reflected upon in this chapter) and second, the *chi/qi* theory of organizational communication (introduced toward the end of the chapter). These are just a few examples of the prospect of new features and theories from their ancient cultural roots. A frontier is lying ahead.

References

Adler, N. J. (2001). *International dimensions of organizational behavior*. Belmont, CA: Wadsworth.

Ames, R. (1994). *The art of rulership*. Albany, NY: State University of New York Press.

Antonakis, J. (2012). Transformational and charismatic leadership. In D. V. Day, & J. Antonakis (Eds.), *The nature of leadership* (2nd ed.) (pp. 256–288). Thousand Oaks, CA: Sage.

Chamberlain, H. B. (1987). Party-management relations in Chinese industries: Some political dimensions of economic reform. *China Quarterly, 112*, 631–661.

Chan, H. S. (2004). Cadre personnel management in China: The nomenklatura system, 1990–1998. *China Quarterly, 179*, 703–734.

Chao, W. (1993). *Zhi zai de ren* (Exhilarated to get talents). Taipei: New News Culture.

Chen, G. M. (*in-press*). An examination of People's Republic of China business negotiating behaviors. *China Media Research.* Manuscript submitted for publication.

Chen, G. & Chung, J. (1994a). The impact of Confucianism on organizational communication. *Communication Quarterly,* Vol. 42, No. 2, Spring. 93–105.

Chen, K. (1977). *Lao Tzu text, notes, and comments.* San Francisco: Chinese Material Center.

Chen, N. (2008). Internal/Employee communication and organizational effectiveness: A study of Chinese corporations in transition. *Journal of Contemporary China,* 17(54), 167–189.

Child, J., & Markoczy, L. (1994). Host country managerial behavior in Chinese and Hungarian joint ventures: Assessment of competing explanations. *East-West Business Collaboration. London: Routledge.*

Chung, J. (1996). Avoiding a "Bull Moose" rebellion: particularistic ties, seniority, and third-party mediation. *International and Intercultural Communication Annual, 20,* 166–185.

Chung, J. (2011). *Chi*-based strategies for public relations in globalizing world. In N. Bardhan & K. Weaver (Eds.) *Public Relations in Global Cultural Contexts: Multiparadigmatic Perspectives.* 226–247. New York: Routledge.

Chung, J. & Busby, R. (2002). Naming strategies for organizational communication: The *ch'i-shih* approach. *Intercultural Communication Studies.* Vol. 11, No. 1, 77–95.

Curzer, H. B. (2012). Benevolent government now. *Comparative Philosophy,* 3 (1), 74–85.

Derong, C., & Faure, G. O. (1995). When Chinese companies negotiate with their government. *Organization Studies,* 16(1), 27–54.

Fan, W. (1941). *Zhong Guo Tong Shi* (Chinese General History).

Fentzeig, R. (2015, December 30). "Nice" is a four-letter word at companies practicing radical candor. *The Wall Street Journal*. Retrieved March 22, 2016, from http://www.wsj.com/articles/nice-is-a-four-letter-word-at-companies-practicing-radical-candor-1451498192

Helburn, I. B., & Shearer, J. C. (1984). Human resources and industrial relations in China: A time of ferment. *Industrial & Labor Relations Review*, 38(1), 3–15.

Hong, J., & Engeström, Y. (2004). Changing principles of communication between Chinese managers and workers Confucian authority chains and guanxi as social networking. *Management Communication Quarterly*, 17(4), 552–585.

Hoskisson, R. E., Eden, L., Lau, C. M., & Wright, M. (2000). Strategy in emerging economies. *Academy of Management Journal*, 43(3), 249–267.

Judge, T. A., & Bono, J. E. (2000). Five-factor model of personality and transformational leadership. *Journal of Applied Psychology, 85(5)*, 751.

Jullien, F. (1995). *The propensity of things*. New York: Zone Books.

Liang, Q. (1998). *Xian qin zheng zhi si xiang shi* (Pre-Qin political thoughts). Hang Zhou, Zhejiang: People's Press.

Lin, C. & Clair, R. (2007). Measuring Mao Zedong thought and interpreting organizational communication in China. *Management Communication Quarterly, 20* (4), 395–429.

Lin, Y. (2009). *The wisdom of Laotse*. Beijing: Foreign Language Teaching and Research Press.

Liu, C. (1991). *Zhong Guo zhihui yu xitong si wei* (Chinese wisdom and the system thinking). Hong Kong: Commerce Press.

Lu, X. (1998). *Rhetoric in ancient China fifth to third century B.C.E.: A comparison with classical Greek rhetoric*. Columbia, S. C.: University of South Carolina Press.

Mair, V. (1990). *Tao Te Ching: The classic book of integrity and the way*. New York: Bantam Books.

Mumby, D. K. (2007). Organizational communication. In G. Ritzer (Ed.), *The Encyclopedia of Sociology* (pp. 3290–3299). London: Blackwell.

Nie, D., & Lämsä, A-M. (2015). The leader-member exchange theory in the Chinese context and the ethical challenge of guanxi. *Journal of Business Ethics, 128*, 851–861. doi 10.1007/s10551-013-1983-9

Peng, M. W. 2003. Institutional transitions and strategic choices. *Academy of Management Review*, 28: 275–296.

Putnam, L. L., & Mumby, D. K. (2014). Introduction: Advancing theory and research in organizational communication. In L. L. Putnam, & D. K., Mumby (Eds.), *The Sage handbook of organizational communication* (3rd ed.). (pp. 1–18). Thousand Oaks, CA: Sage.

Shafer, E. L., Vieregge, M., & Choi, Y. (2005). Cultural differences in perceived leadership styles. *International Journal of Hospitality & Tourism Administration, 6*(3), 65–88.

Shao, L., & Webber, S. (2006). A cross-cultural test of the "five-factor model of personality and transformational leadership". *Journal of Business Research, 59*(8), 936–944.

Sima, G. (1992). *Zizhi tongjian,* 20 vols. Beijing: Zhonghua Shuju, 3281(6).

Su, C., Mitchell, R. K., & Sirgy, M. J. (2006). Enabling guanxi management in China: A hierarchical stakeholder model of effective guanxi. *Journal of Business Ethics, 71*(3), 301–319.

Tiwald, J. (2008). A right of rebellion in the Menzi? *Dao, 7,* 269–282.

Tu, W. (1993). *Way, learning, and politics: Essays on the Confucian intellectual.* Albany: State University of New York Press.

Tung, R. L. (1981). Patterns of motivation in Chinese industrial enterprises. *Academy of Management Review, 6*(3), 481–489.

Wang, G. (2005). Ru Ben Shi Hua-Jin Dai Pien. (Japanese Historical Talk—Modern Volume). Taipei: Lien Jing.

Warner, M. (1986). Managing human resources in China: An empirical study. *Organization Studies, 7*(4), 353–366.

Xia, B. (1997). *Zhong Guo Li Dai Ming Chen Ming Jian* (Famous Chinese Remonstrations). Hefei, Anhui: Anhui People's Press.

CHAPTER 5
FAMILY RELATIONSHIPS AND COMMUNICATION IN JAPAN
SACHIYO M. SHEARMAN

■ Introduction

Sazae-san (サザエさん; Ms. Sazae) as a Traditional Japanese Family Archetype

Sazae-san can be considered one of the most famous families in Japan. *Sazae-san* started as a comic strip written for a local newspaper by Machiko Hasegawa in 1946 (Hasegawa Machiko Art Museum, 2015). In 1969, *Sazae-san* become an animated television series, aired by one of Japan's major networks, Fuji Television, and has been aired until now at 6:30–7:00 p.m. prime time on every Sunday. *Sazae-san* now holds the Guinness World Record for *Longest Running Animated Television Series* (Fuji Television, 2015).

Sazae-san depicts the daily lives and the occurrences of the Isono family, centering around fun, silly, and lovable *Sazae* who is a daughter and a mother. Sazae lives with her father, Namihei, and mother, Fune, younger brother, Katsuo, and younger sister, Wakame. Sazae's husband, Masuo, is adopted into the Isono Family. Sazae, Masuo, and their son (Tara) live with Sazae's parents and siblings. The show depicts a happy three-generational household dealing with rather trivial family issues. When it was first aired, and in the 1970s, Sazae was seen as more of a forward-thinking female, one who can overpower her husband, Masuo, who chose to be adopted into and live with Sazae's family. Nowadays, she is seen as a rather traditional stay-at-home mother who lives in a generational family and is viewed with nostalgia.

Sazae-san depicts a traditional three-generational household, which used to be common in Japan, yet is on the decline in the past several decades. *Sazae-san* gives us some important insights as we review Japanese family relationships and communication in this chapter. This chapter reviews Japan's changing family demographics, dating and marriage, family communication, elderly in the family, and the role of individuals who remain single. With an in-depth look at the changing family structure in Japan, it reveals duality, entailing both traditional and modern cultural values in various ways.

Traditional Family vs. Modern Family

Japanese people could relate to the silly family matters that *Sazae-san* depicts from different perspectives, such as those of a grandmother, a grandfather, a mother, an eldest son, and an eldest daughter. *Sazae-san* has been a popular animation, partly because many Japanese people value *Ie* (家; family, family system, and family lineage) and feel a sense of comfort viewing a traditional family that mirrors their own.

Ie, or traditional family system, and *dozoku* (同族; groups composed of several families, often with same last name) have been emphasized both in agrarian and in feudalistic periods in Japan (Nakano, 1962). *Ie*, or the patrilineal family system (often times called feudalistic family system), was institutionalized and legally enforced by the Meiji government (established in 1868) in the late nineteenth century. With the revision of the Civil Law in 1947, however, the *Ie* system is no longer enforced by the Japanese government. Although feudalistic family systems may not be in place any longer in current Japanese society, the familial values and basic principle of life governed by familial values continue at some level.

As we review Japan's family relationship structure and communication styles it becomes crucial for us to know household structures in Japan, and its trends, and continuity. It used to be that family structures in Japan were more uniform, where most individuals got married and reproduced in a rather timely manner, living with or living close to their parents. Three-generational households were predominant, often with the first-born son succeeding the family name, or eldest daughter welcoming her partner into her family. With the economic and cultural shifts in Japan after WWII, Japanese society started to welcome individual freedom away from traditional family values, and hence Japanese society now enjoys diverse family types. An increasing number of males and females choose not to marry in favor of staying single, and the sociologist Masahiro Yamada called some of those singles, *parasite singles*, since those individuals often end up staying at home and living with their parents (Yamada, 1999). It is also true that the divorce rate has gone up in Japan (Nonoyama, 2000). As the divorce rate went up in Japan, the poverty of single mothers in Japan has been discussed in depth as a societal issue by a Japanese poet and sociologist, Kiriu Minashida (2014). Although same-sex marriage is not currently legal in Japan, Nobuto Hosaka, head of the Setagaya-ku ward in Tokyo, issued the *Proof of Acceptance of the Partnership* oath to same-sex couples (Sasakawa, 2015).

Noting the above examples, you can begin to see the changing family structure in Japan. These nontraditional family types may not show up in *Sazae-san* programs where nostalgia is being sold, but it is the reality of the modern Japanese family. Now, Japanese society enjoys significantly more varieties of family types besides the traditional three-generational household including the nuclear household, single-parent household, LGBT partnership, cohabitation, and the increasing rate of the *never-married singles*. Although these nontraditional family types may not be very prevalent in Japan, some of these nonconventional family types have become more visible and accepted today.

■ Japan's Changing Family Demography

Aging Society

After WWII, Japanese society went through a drastic change both economically and culturally. Along with it came changes in population and family demographics. The most notable changes in Japanese family demographics are the rapidly aging population and low fertility rate. With a stable economy, low crime rate, and reputable national healthcare system, Japan now enjoys a long life expectancy. In comparison to the rest of the world, Japanese females enjoy the longest life expectancy at a rate of 87 years, and Japanese males rank eighth in the world at 80 years (WHO, 2015).

The National Institute of Population and Social Security Research (IPSSR) reported that the ratio of people aged 65 years or older in Japan was 4.95% in 1950, which ranked Japan 58th out of 158 nations with an older population. In 2010, Japan was ranked number one out of those 158 nations, having 22.96% of its population being 65 years or older.

Low Fertility Rate

In 1997, the proportion of the elderly population (15.65%) exceeded that of the child population (13.1%), and in 2013, the elderly population increased to 25.1% of the total population, while the proportion of children decreased to 13.1%. It is projected that the trend will continue to 11.7% and 9.1% for the child population and 29.1% and 39.9% for the elderly population (MIAC 2014, cited in Kumagai, 2015).

According to IPSSR's report of 2015, the total fertility rate in Japan has been on the decline. Japan's total fertility rate was 3.65 in 1950 and continued to decline and reached its lowest level ever, 1.26, in 2006. It has shown a slight increase since then, but the total fertility rate in Japan remains low, 1.43 in 2013. Going back to *Sazae-san* as a family example: Sazae is the oldest daughter of three kids, while she has only one son, Tara. This is consistent with the statistics on fertility rate and the decline of family size.

Stem Family vs. Nuclear Family

Typically, a nuclear family is defined as either a couple only, a couple with unmarried children, or a single parent with unmarried children. With this definition, the IPSSR of 2015 reports that the rate of nuclear families was 56.7% in 1970 and 56.3% in 2010, with the highest rate being 59.5% in 1990. Although nuclear families are often associated with industrialization, it seems that there has not been a sharp increase in the rate of nuclear households in Japan. The stem family, or the generational household (where there are three or more generations that live in a single household), is on the decline, as the rate of a stem family in Japan was 54.4% in 1975, 39.5% in 1990, 26.5% in 2000, and, most recently, 13.2% in 2013 (IPSSR, 2015).

Smaller Family Size

Along with the significant decline of the generational household, the average family size in Japan has also been declining. In 1970, almost half (48.3%) of households in Japan consisted of more than four family members. In 2010, however, the ratio was cut in half: 22.3% of the families consisted of more than four family members. The average family size was 3.41 in 1970, yet decreased to 2.42 in 2010 (IPSSR, 2015). Family size in Japan has been declining, and the family type that is showing the most significant increase is the single household. Single household has increased from 20.3% of the population in 1970 to 23.1% in 1990, 27.6% in 2000, and then to 32.4% in 2010 (IPSSR, 2015).

Regional Difference within Japan

Kumagai (2015) examined how Japanese family demographics and household structures have changed after WWII. She reported not only the general trends (significant decrease in three-generational households and a sharp increase in single households) but also the significant regional variations. For instance, she reported that the Yamagata prefecture enjoys the highest ratio of three-generational households (21.5%). The national average for three-generational households is only slightly more than 7%, while Kagoshima, the southernmost prefecture on the Kyushu Island, comprises less than half of the national average (3.2%) (Kumagai, 2015). Also, Kumagai (2015) noted that "the Tohoku and Hokuriku regions (Northern and Northeastern parts of mainland Japan) are reported to have kept relatively larger family sizes, while prefectures in urban areas such as Tokyo, Osaka, and those of rural Hokkaido, Kagoshima, and Kochi are reported to have a relatively small family size" (p. 16). She also mentioned that the average "family size in Tokyo will become less than two (1.90) by 2025," indicating that a significantly large proportion of the households in Tokyo will be those of singles, either young people or senior citizens (Kumagai, 2015, p. 16). Kumagai (2015) also notes that Japanese family demographics indicate a dual structural mode, where both elements of modern family values and traditional family values coexist.

■ Dating and Marriage

Getting Married Later

Sakai (2003) wrote a best-selling essay titled "an underdog's howl" about herself and other career-focused women in Japan who have failed to marry and have children by certain age. Sakai (2003) sarcastically referred to these successful Japanese women as *makeinu* (負け犬; underdogs) who are lost in a game of finding a right marriage partner and having children, despite enjoying their lives, having a great success in their careers, and having fun casual relationships and friendships.

Going back to *Sazae-san* as an example, it was typical for people like Sazae, who was in her early twentieth, to get married and have kids soon after getting married. It has been said that Japanese females are like a Christmas cake. Christmas cake is valuable before the 25th of December. Yet, if a cake is not sold before the 25th (implying a woman failing to marry before the age of 25), it loses its value or has no use after that. Naturally, this metaphor has met with sharp criticism. Regardless, it is often cited in television dramas and in various places such as matchmaking agencies to warn women not to take too much time to think about marriage, or else it may be too late (Marriage, 2015). This *Christmas cake theory* for women's marriage was criticized as too obsolete; however it was simply replaced with the *Toshikoshi Soba Theory*, referring to the Soba Noodles that Japanese people eat for good luck on December 31, indicating that the age limit is now prolonged to 31, since more and more females and males are getting married later in life (Garukekimania, 2015).

Japanese women may have a little bit more freedom and a longer timeframe to decide on marriage or finding a partner, yet the use of these metaphors demonstrates how the Japanese society overemphasizes the reproductive ability of women. The reality is that more and more Japanese people are getting married later in life. According to the Vital Statistics Report of Population Dynamics by the Japanese Ministry of Health, Labor, and Welfare of 2013, both males and females are getting married later in life with the initial age of marriage at 30.9 years for males and 29.3 years for females. In 1947, the average initial ages of marriage were only 26.1 for males and 22.9 for females. The average age of remarriage in 1947 was 36.5 for males and 29.3 for females, while the average age of remarriage in 2013 was 42.4 for males and 39.4 for females.

Arranged Marriage vs. Romantic Love Marriage

The above statistics indicate that later marriage is more commonplace and that Japanese people have more time to engage in dating and marriage-seeking activities before actually choosing to marry. The 2010 demographic report by the IPSSR showed that arrangement marriage consisted of almost 70% of all marriages in 1935 but less than 10% of marriages after 1995. Sometime in the late 1960s, romantic love marriage surpassed the ratio of arranged marriages.

This indicates that Japanese people have adopted the romantic love marriage ideology while rejecting the previous notion to marry for a family lineage or a family business any longer. Hirakiuchi (2010) claimed that Japanese individuals tend to have both traditional and westernized romantic-love-based view of marriage. Many Japanese individuals have adopted the western style romantic love ideology, and individual freedom to choose a partner, while appreciating traditional, rather practical views of marriage, or marring for family and family lineage at some level. She claimed that the recent popularity of *marriage-seeking activity* indicates the continued emphasis on practical aspects of marriage while hoping for romantic love elements.

In *Sazae-san*, Sazae met her husband, Masuo, through an arranged marriage. It is said that they fell in love at first sight during the arranged marriage. It can be said that their marriage embodies the combination of romantic love and traditional marriage, as they fell in love by their own will within the structure of an arranged marriage, where families are also valued. Even in this narrative, we can clearly see the duality of Japanese cultural values, where individual will for romantic love is beginning to gain respect to some extent, while traditional values are cherished.

Kon-katsu (婚活・結婚活動; Marriage-Seeking Activity)

A Japanese sociologist, Masahiro Yamada, and a journalist, Momoko Shirakawa (2008), cowrote a book titled *Kon-katsu Jidai* [Era of Marriage-seeking activity] and popularized the term *Kon-katsu*, short for marriage-seeking activity. This stemmed from the term *Shu-katsu* (就活・就職活動) as in job-seeking activity. They pointed out that the low fertility rate in Japan is not only due to the lack of social support for working females which has often been argued in various places and reflected in recent policy changes in Japan but also due to the choice of Japanese people who choose to stay single and those who failed to get married. They argued that in the past, when arranged marriages were more common than romantic love marriages, many Japanese people got married without thinking too much about their romantic interest. It was more so a norm for them to marry a partner that was selected by their parents, and it was said that all individuals form attachments to one another through the partnership. Now, young Japanese men and women have more options—whom to marry and when to marry and whether to stay single. They are no longer encouraged to marry for a family. With that freedom came the risk of not being able to find the right marriage partner; hence, *kon-katsu* is now recommended for many Japanese young adults (Yamada & Shirakawa, 2008). They argue that Japanese males and females need to change their old era views of traditional family roles, where the husband is a breadwinner, and the wife a homemaker, and actively engage in *Kon-katsu* to find a partner.

Herbivore-Type Japanese Males

For many Japanese people, dating and marriage are often viewed as being intertwined. So, it may be harder for Japanese young adults to choose a partner if dating is viewed as a concrete precursor of marriage. Ishii-Kuntz (2010) claimed that the Japanese tend to presume that dating equals marriage more so than those in the United States. According to a survey study, 52% of American couples do not feel obligated to marry even if they have a child together, while 59% of Japanese couples stated that it is preferable to get married before having a child (Iranamiyori, 2005, cited in Ishii-Kuntz, 2010).

Ushikubo (2015) interviewed many Japanese young adults and reported that an increasing number of them seem to be rather passive about dating. Ushikubo (2015) used the term *sousyokukei* (草食系; herbivore-type males), referring to Japanese males who are passive in dating, as opposed to *nikushokukei* (肉食系; carnivore-type males, who are aggressively pursuing females). She claims that there were more carnivore-type males when the Japanese economy was going strong, but now there are more and more reticent herbivore-type males. This is partly due to the fact that young Japanese males and females are struggling to balance traditional and modern gender roles in marriage. Both males and females are expected to be equal at home and at the workplace per the modern view, yet in a persistent traditional view, males are expected to take the lead in pursuing, paying for dates, and being decisive within the various aspects of dating. Young males and females struggle to maintain their individual role orientations in light of these two diverging expectations. More and more males want their partners to work, yet many females indicate that they want to stay at home to take care of children. This is partly due to Japanese corporations expecting all of their workers (both males and females) to work long hours, regardless of their family situation. The Japanese society is not yet fully accommodating of families with working parents to have a healthy work–life balance.

Staying Single

The concept of *Ie* and valuing family lineage was traditionally emphasized in Japanese society. Yet, more and more Japanese people are choosing to stay single for their lifetime. Those who stay single are called *Ohitori-sama* (おひとり様; Mr. or Ms. Single), showing politeness and acceptance for those who are alone when they dine, travel, or during various life events. According to the news article in Excite Bit News titled *Mr. or Ms. Single Data* (Teranishi, 2012), various establishments are starting to target singles as their customers in such places as karaoke (typically a room is reserved for more than two customers) or shabu shabu restaurants (しゃぶしゃぶ; hot pot foods typically served for two or more customers). More and more individuals are now welcomed to be going out and eating out by themselves. Although contrasts between Japanese collectivism and Western individualism are often discussed, these singles markets can be viewed as an evidence for Japanese youth valuing individualism.

Yamada (2014) mentioned that 71.4% of males and 59% of females between ages 25 to 29 are not married, and 47.1% of males and 31% of females between ages 30 and 34 are not married, according to the 2005 Japanese census data. He pointed out that only 2–3% of the 1975 population were never married, but in 2005, 15.4% have never been married by the age of 50, and it is projected that over 25% of those males and females are going to stay single for their lifetime. Yamada (2014) claimed that this is partly because of the increased rate of contractual employment due to deregulation in the 1980s. In the past, most employees in Japan were regular full-time employees, and were protected with relatively high (and stable) salaries with generous benefits. Nonregular and contractual workers have lower pay grades and receive more modest benefits. Given the traditional views of marriage, many Japanese females are still not willing to marry someone who has limited job prospects, despite the trends toward romantic love marriages.

■ Family Relations and Communication

Parasite Singles—Singles Living with Parents

Yamada (1999; 2013) pointed out that there are an increasing number of not-married Japanese individuals who live with their parents and labels them *parasite singles* (パラサイトシングル; parasite single). He claimed that these Japanese people stay single partly because they are living contentedly with the economic assistance of their parents. He explained that these parasite singles (both males and females) are not compelled to be independent and find a marriage partner, because they are comfortable living with parents. He claimed that this is partly the reason why so many Japanese people are getting married late in life or not at all, and contributing to the low fertility rate. Ushikubo (2015) noted that the apathy or unwillingness to date and marry among young Japanese people is partly due to the close tie of these young adults to the generation of postwar baby boomer parents in Japan. In addition, parents wanted their children to stay at home and under their control, so that they could be together. Many parents of this generation are so attached that some are having a hard time being independent from their children.

Maeda and Hecht (2012) examined the identity of single Japanese women's identity through in-depth longitudinal interviews. They reported that *always-single* Japanese women think about family responsibility, parents' dependency, and their position in their respective *Ie* (family) systems, when they consider the possibility of marriages. They also reported that the always-single Japanese women seem to be able to accept their non-normative identity, as there are more and more 'always-single' women in Japan. With the continued rise of parasite singles in Japan, we can see the signs of both individualism and collectivism. These persistently single individuals are choosing not to marry, indicating that they value their own space and needs and are not being compelled to marry and carry on a traditional role of maintaining family and continuing family lineage. At the same time, these always-single individuals are showing collectivism, valuing family ties and family events with their parents. It can also be said that these singles are too dependent on family to be away from the comfort of their parents' homes and be independent. This also shows a duality of identity for Japanese young adults, where they would want to value individuality while maintaining their strong ties and relationship with their parents.

Absent Fathers and Codependent Mothers

Ishii-Kuntz (1994) reported that Japanese fathers (37.4%) do not have enough time to spend with their children, compared to German fathers (19.5%) and American fathers (14.7%). Ishii-Kuntz (1993) claimed that the sense of fatherhood is intertwined with the role of main provider for the family, and mothers project the image of an absent yet authoritative father figure to their children. Fathers in Japan have been expected to work long hours to be loyal to the company that they work for, and with the pressure to not just work long hours but to hang out with their coworkers and customers after hours, they do not have much time left for their family.

Oftentimes, mothers are responsible for all the family and household tasks, and many mothers have completely devoted their lives to their children. Due to the father's absenteeism and mother's strong attachment to children, overly controlling, dependent, and almost 'poisonous' mothers can ruin the individuality of their daughters, according to a Japanese clinical psychologist and counselor, Sayoko Nobuta (Nobuta, 2008; 2011). Also in analyzing the Japanese male hermit, or *hikikomori* (引きこもり; social withdrawal), who is withdrawn from any social interaction for an extended period, Adam (2012) claimed that Japanese mothers' strong codependency and poisonous relation with their sons have caused them to not being able to be independent from their parents.

Japan as Maternal Society

As the Japanese psychologist Hayao Kawai claimed in his book titled *The Pathology of Japan as a Maternal Society*, Japanese society maintains strong maternal elements while the paternal element is enacted only superficially and not strongly enough in reality (1976; 2003). Kawai (2003) claims that maternal principles are characterized with being nurturing and accepting, as if a mother loves all her children equally. In contrast, he claims that the paternal principles are characterized with being divisive and strict, as if a father brings in societal reality and standards to the household. He claims that Japanese individuals' identity is heavily intertwined with the maternal principle, where context is valued more so than individuals, suggests that individualism in Western society cannot be recreated in the same way in Japanese society.

Doi (1973) explained the concept of *amae* (甘え; dependency), or the interpersonal dependency. This notion of interpersonal dependency can be said as the core concept that underlies Japanese relationships, where people would be respectful with the intentions of the other. It is also a key underlying concept to understand high-context communication, where one expects others to read between the lines instead of explicitly speaking ones' intentions. Doi claimed that *amae* can be seen as if imitating one's inseparable relation with one's mother and also mentioned that the Japanese families have been mostly fatherless, thereby strengthening the dependency between children and mothers. This analysis, taken together with the high masculinity score reported by Hofstede (1980; 2010), indicates yet another duality of Japanese society.

Changing Gender Roles in the Japanese Family

Sazae and her mother Fune embody the stereotypical female gender roles. They both take care of things at home, while taking care of their children. In one recent episode, Sazae goes out to work at a supermarket but then quits her job within two days, saying that the job is too physically demanding and that her son wants her stay at home. Koshiba (2015) criticized this episode as being outdated when about 56% of females in married couples are reportedly employed, yet noted that it may be good that at least Sazae actually worked rather than simply staying at home.

Japanese households used to enjoy the division of labor where the fathers worked as breadwinners while the mothers stayed at home and took care of children and household chores. As more and more women started to gain an education and join in the workforce over the last several decades, more and more families are moving away from this typical division of labor based on gender. Ishii-Kuntz (2013) examined the changing views of gender roles in Japan. She reported that in 1976, 75.6% of males and 70.1% of females agreed with the statement: Husbands should work and earn money, while wives should stay at home and protect the family. In 2009, however, 50% of both males and females disagreed with the above statement regarding the division of labor by gender. This indicates that many Japanese males and females have been changing their traditional views of the division of labor within families in the past several decades. However, when this figure is contrasted with other countries such as Korea, France, Sweden, and the United States, Japanese males and females supported this traditional view of the division of labor more frequently than those in other countries. It is possible that many Japanese people still adhere to persistent gender roles.

Due to the economic crises and restructuralization of the Japanese economy and organizations in the 1990s, Japanese people started to question their lifestyle, where too much emphasis is placed on their professional lives (especially for men). Together with low fertility rates and the increasingly aging society, life–work balance issues have been discussed more seriously. In Japan, each year, several popularized terms that demonstrate the trend of each year are selected and awarded. In 2010, the word *Iku-men* (育メン; child-rearing men) was one of the top 10 most popular new terms. The term *Iku-men* is a play on words from *ikemen* (イケメン; good-looking guy, and *iku ji* (育児; child rearing), referring to the males/partners who can participate child rearing as an ideal male.

This *Iku-men* boom has been featured in various popular magazines targeting both males and females. Many baby and child-rearing items targeting males (such as baby carriages and diaper bags that have more of masculine designs) are being sold in various places. Ishii-Kuntz (2013) reported that more and more Japanese males are participating in child-rearing and household chores than ever before. Numerous suggestions (i.e., flexible work hours, supportive work and community environments, visibility of male role models) have been offered in support of the *iku-men* generation of males.

Family Communication Patterns and Conflict

As mentioned earlier, the concept of *amae*, or interpersonal dependency discussed by Doi (1973), can play its role in the in-group communication such as in a family context. This concept of amae, the interpersonal dependency, together with the kindness and sensitivities to infer what the other person is implying, can be stated as the key values causing Japanese people's preference for high context communication. Bresnahan, Shearman, Lee, Ohashi and Mosher (2002) examined communication preferences and perception for indirect and direct communication among friends by the Japanese, Korean, and American participants. In their study, Japanese participants indicated high preference for high-context communication than American participants. It is also reported that Japanese tend to view nonassertive communication more so likable and socially appropriate, compared to Americans (Bresnahan, et al., 2002). These communication preferences and their underling perceptions, which were examined in friendship contexts, could also be applied and examined in family contexts.

Matsunaga and Imahori (2009) examined conflict communication in relation to family communication standards (FCS) or beliefs about the ideal ways of family interactions among Japanese and American participants in regard to conflict interaction. Matsunaga and Imahori (2009) emphasized the individual differences within each culture, Japan and the United States. In regards to the overall perception of ideal FCS or ideals, they reported that Americans preferred laissez-fair (characterized with detached and blunt interactions, low openness with modest levels of family regularities and traditional values) and open-affectionate FCS (characterized with high openness, expression of affection, and emotional instrumental support and low avoidance), while majority of Japanese put its emphasis on high-context FCS (characterized with high mind reading and avoidance, coupled with modest levels of openness and expression of affection) (Matsunaga & Imahori, 2009).

Shearman, Dumlao, and Kagawa (2011) analyzed memorable parent–child conflict episodes reported by the young adults in Japan and in the United States. They reported that Japanese young adults used distributive (assertive) strategies with their parents followed by integrative (problem solving) and avoidance (withdrawal) strategies, indicating that Japanese young adults act assertively and confront their parents more so than they would avoid a conflict with their parents. The reported conflict strategies by the Japanese young adults' and their parents' were matched significantly more than American young adults/parents, indicating possible reciprocal sequencing (meaning they used same type of conflict strategies such as a young adults' use of distributive strategies met by parents' use of distributive strategies) among Japanese family members (Shearman, et al., 2011).

Shearman and Dumlao (2008) examined family communication patterns in Japan and in the United States. Family communication patterns theory claims that family members create unique family communication environment (Koerner & Fitzpatrik, 1997; 2006). Family communication environments can be examined through the combinations of the extent to which family members' emphasize open communication climate (i.e., conversation orientation) and the extent to which family members emphasize shared attitudes, beliefs, and values (i.e., conformity orientations). Shearman and Dumlao (2008) reported that Japanese families scored low in conversation orientation relative to American families, indicating that Japanese family has less emphasis on open communication than American families. Japanese family also reported low conformity orientation score compared to Americans families.

By intersecting two family communication orientations (conversation orientation and conformity orientation), four family types emerge: consensual family (high in conversation and conformity), protective family (high in conformity but low in conversation), pluralistic family (high in conformity but low in conversation), and laissez-fair family (low in both conversation and conformity). When family types were examined, laissez-fair and protective family types were two most common family types in Japan while consensual and pluralistic family types were two most common family types in the United States (Shearman & Dumlao, 2008).

Regardless of culture, open communication orientation within family was positively associated with perceived family communication satisfaction (Shearman & Dumlao, 2008). Members in Sazae's family engage in open and lively conflict communication exchanges. Although Sazae-san's episodes are for an animated television program and some of the conflict interactions are made to be entertaining and obvious to viewers, yet, it does give us insights as to how Japanese individuals in in-group communication context, as in family (as opposed to out-group communication context) can be played out.

Elderly in Japanese Families

Let us imagine what *Sazae-san* would be like when it comes to the time that her parents, Fune and Namihei, get sick and are in need of care. It is very likely that Sazae would take care of her parents at home. A typical Japanese family expects the daughter or eldest son's wife to look after parents who are in need of care. Like Sazae, many Japanese families still choose to live with their parents in multigenerational co-residences or live close by, so in case that parents need any assistance, they are available. Some even quit their job or choose to relocate closer to the parents in case parents become sick or are in need of care. However, as reviewed earlier in this chapter, Japan's family demography has shifted and now displays an aging population, low fertility rates, late marriage or non-marriage (or staying single), and fewer three-generational households.

With these shifts, Japanese women started to change their attitudes toward filial care of elderly parents. Now fewer people believe that children caring for their elderly parents is "good custom" and "natural duty," while more people now think of filial care as "unavoidable" and "not good custom" (Ogawa & Retherford, 1993, p.588). Ogawa and Retherford (1993) also reported that education, age, and living condition (living with parents or not and urban area vs. rural area) also impact their attitudes and predicted that more Japanese women will become psychologically comfortable not following culturally prescribed stem-family living conditions and filial duties to care for their and their husband's parents. The rate of three-generation families has declined and the proportion of elderly couples and/or elderly persons living alone has increased. The rate of three-generational households with family members 60 or older is still high at 32% in Japan, compared to 1% in the United Kingdom and in the United States and 3% in

Germany (Ogawa and Retherford, 1997). The decline in multigenerational co-residence happened with with the increase in women's education and full time employment, which has been associated with the weakening values of filial piety (Ogawa & Retherford, 1993; 1997).

Ota, Giles, and Somora (2007) examined cross-cultural intra- and intergenerational communication in Japan, the Philippines, and the United States. They reported that young respondents across three different cultures perceived their communication with younger individuals more positively than with older individuals. Interestingly, Japanese younger adults felt a greater obligatory respect toward the elderly and claimed to avoid older people more than American younger adults. Due to the changing family structure of not being physically close to their grandparents, Japanese young adults may enjoy less chance to be with the elderly in and outside of their own home.

■ Conclusion

This chapter has reviewed family demographics, dating and marriage, family communication, family and gender roles, and the elderly in Japan. Since WWII, Japan has gone through drastic cultural and economic changes. In contrast to traditional three-generational households as portrayed in a popular animation about a family, *Sazae-san*, Japan now enjoys a variety of family types now—the nuclear family, single mother/single father family, LGBT family, and always-single individuals. With its long life expectancy, Japanese society is aging rapidly.

Together with a rapidly aging society, Japanese people are getting married later and having fewer children. There are more nuclear families and significantly fewer three-generational households. Family size in Japan is significantly smaller now than in the past. Not only Japanese people are getting married later and having fewer children but also many Japanese people are choosing to stay single for their lifetime.

The changing patterns of family relationships and communication reveal that Japanese individuals exhibit duality in various aspects of their lives. For instance, Japanese family structures and demographic changes indicate that both elements of traditional family values and modern cultural values coexist. In terms of dating and marriage, Japanese young adults have adopted the Western style romantic love ideology as an individual freedom and choice, while maintaining traditional, practical views of marriage, with implications for family structure and family lineage. Parasite singles value individual freedom to some extent, while maintaining ties with their parents and family members. Japanese people may value high-context communication while members in family may engage in distributive conflict interactions. Japanese males may have been expected to act aggressively and lead females in dating, yet some of them may just want to be more passive herbivore-type males. There may be an image of an authoritative traditional Japanese father, yet fathers today may want to play with their children regardless of the level of social or cultural support for them. It seems as if Japanese individuals have been attempting to achieve an ambivalent balance between traditional values and modern values in various aspects of their lives as they maintain family relationships.

References

Bresnahan, M. J., Shearman, S. M., Lee, S. Y., Ohashi, R., Mosher, D. (2002). Personal and cultural differences in responding to criticism in three countries. *Asian Journal of Social Psychology 5(2)*, 93–105.

Doi, T. (1973). *The anatomy of dependence. [Amae no kouzou.]* Tokyo: Koudansha International.

Fuji Television (2015) *Sazae-san forty fifth anniversary exhibition.* Retrieved from http://www.sazaesan45.com/UserPage/Detail/6

Garukekimania (2015, Nov 5). *Summary—What's Christmas cake theory? [Matome: Kurisumasu ke-ki riron towa?]* Retrieved from http://matome.naver.jp/odai/2143623135656835901

Ishii-Kuntz, M. (1994). The Japanese father: Work demands and family roles. In J. C. Hood (Ed.). *Men, work, and family (pp. 454–67).* Newbury Park, CA: Sage.

Ishii-Kuntz, M. (2013). *The sociology of Iku-men phenomena. [Iku-men gensyo no shakaigaku.]* Tokyo: Minerva.

Hasegawa Machiko Art Museum (2015) *About Hasagawa Machiko.* Retrieved from http://www.hasegawamachiko.jp/

Hofstede, G. (1980). *Culture's consequences.* Beverly Hills, CA: Sage.

Hofstede, G. (2010). *Culture's consequence: Comparing values, behaviors, institutions, and organizations across nations (2nd ed.).* Thousand Oaks, CA: Sage.

Institute of Population and Social Security Research [IPSSR]. (2014). *Jinko Toukei Shiryoushuu:2014 [Demographic Statistics—2014 Table 2-19].*

Retrieved from http://www.ipss.go.jp/syoushika/tohkei/Popular/P_
Detail2014.asp?fname=T02-19.htm on Oct 12, 2015.

Institute of Population and Social Security Research [IPSSR]. (2015). *Jinko
Toukei Shiryoushuu:2015 [Demographic Statistics—2015 Table 4–5].*
Retrieved from http://www.ipss.go.jp/syoushika/tohkei/Popular/P_
Detail2015.asp?fname=T04-05.htm on Oct 12, 2015.

Institute of Population and Social Security Research [IPSSR]. (2015). *Jinko
Toukei Shiryoushuu:2015 [Demographic Statistics—2015 Table 7–10]*
Household types and ratio between 1970 to 2010]. Retrieved from
http://www.ipss.go.jp/syoushika/tohkei/Popular/P_Detail2015.asp?
fname=T07-10.htm on Oct 12, 2015.

Institute of Population and Social Security Research [IPSSR]. (2015). *Jinko
Toukei Shiryoushuu: 2015 [Demographic Statistics—2015 Table 7–9]*
Single Household and ratio between 1970 to 2010]. Retrieved from
http://www.ipss.go.jp/syoushika/tohkei/Popular/P_Detail2015.asp?
fname=T07-09.htm on Oct 12, 2015.

Kawai, H. (1976; 2003). *The pathology of Japan as a maternal society.* Tokyo:
Chuo Koronsha.

Koerner, A., & Fitzpatrick, M. (1997). Family type and conflict: The impact
of conversation orientation and conformity orientation in the family.
Communication Studies, 48, 59–75.

Koerner, A., & Fitspatrick, M. (2006). Family communication patterns
theory: A social cognitive approach. In D. Braithwaite & L. Baxter
(Eds.), *Engaging theories in family communication: Multiple perspectives*
(pp. 50–65). Thousand Oaks: Sage.

Koshiba, E. (2015). *Why Sazae-san quit her job in two days?* (Huffington
Post). Retrieved from http://www.huffingtonpost.jp/sharescafe-online/
sazaesan_b_7781284.htmls

Kumagai, F. (2015). *Family issues on marriage, divorce, and older adults in
Japan: with special attention to regional variations.* Springer Science and
Business Media: Singapore.

Marriage, A. (2015, March 10). *How not to fail marriage-seeking-activity*
[Sippai Shinai Konkatu no susume.] Retrieved from http://konkatsu-
nomiss.info/equivalent-exchange/

Maeda, E. & Hecht, M. L. (2012). Identity search: Interpersonal relationships and relational identities of always-single Japanese women over
time. *Western Journal of Communication, 76(1),* 44–64.

Minashida, K. (2014). *Poverty of the single mothers.* Koubunsha. Tokyo.

Ministry of Health, Labor, and Welfare [MHLW]. (2014a, February). *Heisei 26-nenn Wagakuni no Jinkou Doutai: Heisei 24-nenn made no Doukou* [Vital statistics of Japan: Trends up to 2012]. http://www.mhlw.go.jp/toukei/list/dl/81-1a2.pdf. Accessed 15 Apr 2014.

NHK Web News. (2015, Oct 28). Starting to accept the application for the proof of partnership to same-sex couples [Dousei kappuru ni shoumeisho uketuke kaishi]. Retrieved from http://www3.nhk.or.jp/news/html/20151028/k10010285281000.html

Nakano, T. (1962). Recent studies of change in the Japanese family. *International Social Science Journal, 14*(3), 527–539.

Nonoyama, H. (2000). The family and family sociology in Japan. *American Sociologist, 31*(3), 27–41.

Nobuta, S. (2008). *Cannot bear 'heavy' mothers: when daughters deplore. [Haha ga omokute tamaranai.]* Tokyo, Shunjyusya.

Nobuta, S. (2011). *Good-by mother: when daughters decide [Sayonara Okasan, hakri musume ga ketsudansuru toki.]* Tokyo, Shunjyusya.

Ogawa, N. & Retherford, R. D. (1993). Care of the elderly in Japan: Changing norms and expectations. *Journal of Marriage and Family, 55*, 585–597.

Ogawa, N. & Retherford, R. D. (1997). Shifting costs of caring for the elderly back to families in Japan: Will it work? *Population and Development Review, 23*(1), 59–94.

Ota, H., Giles, H. & Somera, L. P. (2007). Beliefs about intra-and inter-generational communication in Japan, the Philippines, and the United States: Implication for older adults' subjective well-being. *Communication Studies, 58(2),* 173–188.

Sakai, J. (2003). *An underdog's howl. [Make inu no toboe.]* Kodansya. Tokyo.

Sasakawa, K. (2015, June 14). *Society for LGBT—Thinking about same-sex marriage with Higashi Koyuki and Matsuhara Yuko.* The Huffington Post. Retrieved from http://www.huffingtonpost.jp/2015/06/13/lgbt-higasi-koyuki-masuhara_n_7577964.html

Shearman, S. M. & Dumlao, R. (2008). A cross-cultural comparison of communication patterns and conflict between young adults and parents. *Journal of Family Communication, 8*, 186–211.

Shearman, S. M., Dumlao, R., & Kagawa, N. (2011). Cultural variations in accounts by American and Japanese young adults: Recalling a major conflict with parents. *Journal of Family Communication,* 11(2), 105–125.

Teranishi, J. (2012, July 6). Female ohitorisama information data. [Jyosei Ohitorisama jijyo data-ka]. Retrieved from http://www.excite.co.jp/News/bit/E1341404898238.html?_p=2

Yamada, M. (2014). The future of the family in Japan: The impact of the social transformation on the family. (Nihon no kazuku no korekara: Shakai no kozotenkan ga Nihon kazoku ni ataeta inpakuto.) *Japanese Sociological Review (Shakaigaku Hyoron)*, 64(4), 649–662

World Health Organization (2015). *World health statistics 2015: Large gains in life expectancy.* Retrieved from http://www.who.int/mediacentre/news/releases/2014/world-health-statistics-2014/en/

CHAPTER 6
FRIENDSHIP AND COMMUNICATION IN JAPAN

LINDA SEWARD AND SUSAN LONG

Rudyard Kipling's poem, "The Thousandth Man" extols the virtues of a true friend: someone who accepts you as you are, without pretense or wealth; someone who will remain at your side through difficult times as well as those filled with laughter; and someone who would take your side in any dispute. While the specific attributes of what one desires in a friend may vary, acceptance and steadfastness in the face of difficulty would surely make many people's lists of valued qualities. Yet, how often do we stop to really reflect upon the many functions friends serve in our lives? Research reveals that they contribute to our lives in many ways, ranging from the obvious (an improved social life; moral support when we encounter setbacks) to the less thought about functions of improving our self-esteem and keeping us healthy (Adler & Proctor, 2011, pp. 5–8).

But what happens when friendships develop across cultural lines? Developing a friendship with someone from another culture can be rewarding and beneficial in many ways—but it can also be more challenging if the people involved have different expectations about behaviors, values, and communication norms. Consider the reflections of a student from the United States who spent eight months overseas and made friends from a variety of cultures:

> In developing those friends, we definitely encountered issues related to the fact we had very different cultural lenses and there are still instances sometimes when talking to a friend from a foreign country when I realize I've said something in a manner confusing or offensive

Contributed by Linda Seward and Susan Long. Copyright © Kendall Hunt Publishing Company *to them. Working through those mistakes can take a lot of time and effort, but the result, a lot of amazing friends from so many parts of the world, has definitely been worth it!*

Joy Rogers, Fall 2015

In this chapter, we will compare what friendship means in Japan and the United States. This exploration will examine how differing understandings of the meaning and significance of social relationships outside the family can impact the development of intercultural friendships with people who have grown up in different cultural settings. To begin, we will consider the nature of "culture" and its general effects on friendship. From there we will delve into some of the Japanese assumptions and categories of social relationships that overlap with American categories of friendship. Finally, we will complete our exploration by drawing from the fields of anthropology and intercultural communication to consider a variety of issues that may arise in cross-cultural friendships between people from Japan and the United States.

■ Understanding Cultural Assumptions and Variations

When you meet and make friends with someone from another culture, we typically begin by noticing what we have in common; we may like the same music, love the same movies, enjoy the same hobbies, etc. But as you spend more time together and learn more about each other, you begin to notice differences that may involve deeply held values or cultural norms of behavior and perceptions. Consider, for example, something we all do: getting clean. In Japan many people take long, relaxing baths at the end of the day, not only to get clean in a practical sense, but also to symbolically separate the time and space of the daily grind from the intimacy and cleanliness of home. When one of the authors used this as an example of hidden cultural assumptions in class, most of the American students, who generally took showers in the morning or after working out, did not imagine taking a long soak in the tub after work as "normal" or "natural." Yet they had never consciously thought about their own assumptions about the timing of cleaning their bodies either. When asked, they could articulate why they want to shower in the morning (to wake up, for example, or to look and smell nice as they go out into the public realm). Yet the Japanese students in the class admitted that although they had been showering every morning in the dorm since coming to the United States, they had never felt *really* clean. The long evening bath was one of the things they missed most about home. (Of course, there are exceptions in both countries: some Japanese shower in the mornings and some Americans do enjoy a leisurely bath at the end of the day).

When considering cultural variations, it's important to remember that there are different *levels* of culture. Ting-Toomey and Chung (2012) use the analogy of an iceberg to distinguish between easily observed aspects of a culture (fashion, music, food, etc.) and deeper, underlying values and beliefs (p. 16). Thus, an American might point to a shared love of anime or sushi while a person from Japan might be a big fan of American movies and love McDonald's hamburgers. However, people who visit other cultures and return declaring that "we're all alike" are people who have not penetrated the deeper levels of the culture. Thus, while everyone values family, cherishes friends, believes in politeness, and wants to succeed in life, what those phrases *mean* can vary greatly depending on the culture. In cross-cultural relationships, being able to identify and understand important cultural patterns can help you reach that deeper level of understanding of a culture, which, in turn, helps you understand what to expect when interacting with someone from that culture (Nydell, 2012, p. 2). An American consultant in Japan points out that:

> [T]he typical American only notices the obvious differences [like] driving on the left . . . [but] in almost everything in Japan there is some unseen or unstated meaning which is usually not pointed out but which everybody is supposed to know. So my advice is to look for the underlying meanings. [For example] look at what people do at parties, how people talk to each other and how kids are taught.
> (Condon, 1984, pp. 5–6).

With greater understanding of the deeper levels of a culture, we increase our chances of understanding how people analyze information, gain insights into the rationale for their behavior, and clarify what they hold dear as core values.

While this chapter will contrast key Japanese and American cultural values that might raise challenges or misunderstandings in a cross-cultural friendship, we do recognize that there are variations within each culture. These may be due to positionality (a person's relative ability to access social and cultural capital needed to achieve what is culturally desirable such as education or the purchase of the latest cell phone) or to the gap between the stated *ideals* of a culture and the *reality* of what occurs within a culture. You may be thinking: if there is variety within a culture and if individuals don't always live up to the ideals of their culture, why should we learn about cultural norms and values? The answer is that while diversity exists, knowing what someone has been taught—explicitly and implicitly—about various norms and values can help you understand someone's behavior or thought processes when you do encounter differences. For example, consider these two actual situations:

> **Example #1:** *Michael moved to Japan to work as a teaching assistant for English classes at a middle school. Once he made friends, he decided to host a party at his apartment. As is common with Americans in their 20s, he did not expect his Japanese friends to arrive at the stated time. Thus, when he heard a knock at his door, he was still getting dressed! So he frantically threw on his clothes and opened the door to see not one but <u>everyone</u> he had invited.*

> **Example #2:** *When Hannah answered the phone, Hideshi asked her if she could take him to the airport. He explained that he had left a message with Sarah but she didn't respond to his call so he knew she couldn't take him to the airport. The next day as Hannah drove Hideshi to the airport she commented that Hideshi's interpretation about what it meant when Sarah didn't respond to his message was very Japanese. [And, in fact, Sarah had been in the shower when he called.] Hannah explained that in the United States if we can't do something for someone we usually just tell them directly. "I know," said Hideshi, "and it sounds **so rude!**"*

In the first example, the issue was how time is viewed. According to Edward Hall, cultures are predominately either monochronic or polychronic (Hall, 1977). In monochronic cultures (like Japan and the United States), schedules and being prompt are important. Time is discussed as if it is something concrete that can be used, wasted, saved, or lost. According to this concept, time should not have been a problem for friends from the United States and Japan. But the example illustrates exceptions that can occur due to age. In the United States, people in their 20s often dread arriving first to a party. Thus, we have the phenomenon of Americans in their 20s arriving one to two hours after the stated time. So while Michael would be on time, even early, for a job interview he would never go to a party at the stated time—and did not expect the Japanese people to either. The longer he lived in Japan, the more he realized that the Japanese, like the Germans, value promptness and smooth running schedules even more than we do in the United States. In fact, Japan is famous for keeping their trains on schedule.

The example with time is relatively straightforward and easy to adapt to. Other cultural values and norms may be more difficult to adjust to or employ. To understand unexpected issues that might arise in an intercultural friendship between people from Japan and the United States, we will examine three important concepts: (1) high-context vs. low-context communication, (2) collectivism vs. individualism, and (3) approaches to conflict resolution. Before we explore these concepts in American–Japanese relationships, however, we need to examine Japanese cultural definitions of friendship.

■ Who Is a Friend? Categories of Relationships

We all have categories provided by our language and culture into which we classify our relationships with other people. For example, in the United States, when we refer to "family," we generally mean our nuclear family. Yet we know that we also have cousins, aunts, and uncles who in some contexts fit into "family" as well. Likewise, we might call or refer to people who are not relatives by blood or marriage "brother" or "auntie" to indicate that for us, for that situation at least, they fall into the category of "brother" or "aunt."

It might be useful to think about the category of "friendship" in a similar way. In the United States, many people draw a sharp distinction between themselves as individuals and people in social categories such as family and friends. The boundary between family and friends exists clearly in our English terminology, but in reality cousins may be as close as siblings and a neighbor who teaches a child to ride a bike may be a more significant figure in his/her life than an uncle who lives in a distant city. For many Americans, boundaries that distinguish between family, friends, and acquaintances are more fluid and easier to penetrate than in other countries.

In Japan, for example, society stresses a more formal structure in relationships than is found in the United States. Anthropologist Toshinao Yoneyama (1973) suggests that the structure of social relationships in Japan can be conceptualized as a set of concentric circles (Figure 1) with the self in the center. The second circle encloses the people closest to the self, generally immediate family but possibly including a few very close friends, while the third circle comprises other ongoing social relationships such as friends, colleagues, classmates, and acquaintances. Those outside the circles are strangers, people with whom there is no ongoing relationship.

The inner circle of relationships is called *miuchi* (身内), those so close that they are "of the body" of the self, almost a part of the person. Within this circle, you can completely relax and be yourself. You can depend on miuchi to care for and about you. In an emotional sense, miuchi is "home." Homes are considered cleaner, perhaps even more "pure" than the outside

Figure 6.1 *Yoneyama's Concentric Circles of Japanese Social Relationships*

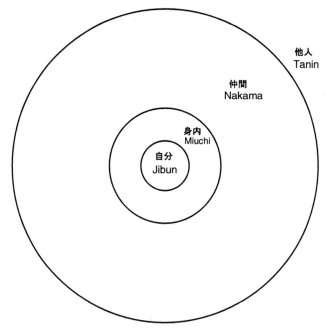

world, and thus the meaningful custom mentioned earlier of bathing when people return home at the end of the day to clean off the "outside dirt" of the world. Taking shoes off in the entryway similarly provides a symbolic separation of miuchi from the rest of the world and its pressures. A close friend who is miuchi may sometimes join in a family meal, whereas people outside this circle would rarely be invited to the home, and even then it would be a more formal and stressful event.

Greater formality characterizes Yoneyama's next circle of relationships; those who, while not in the inner circle, make up a network of people important to the person's life: other family members such as aunts, uncles, and cousins, colleagues at the workplace, friends, and acquaintances. Yoneyama adopts the common term *nakama* (仲間) to describe this part of his model, literally "the space of relationships." With nakama (the friendship level), established relationships need to be maintained through behavior. You cannot assume, as in the miuchi circle, that you will be accepted as you are, so there is great concern for how others see you, for "face." In fact, nakama relationships require the kind of "facework" described in the introduction to this volume. This facework toward nakama requires conscious consideration of the relative status of the other, such as the seating arrangement at a business meeting in which the highest status person sits in the middle seat rather than at the end of a table and faces outward toward the room. Adopting the proper level of formality in dress (as when a businessman wears a typical blue suit) indicates the person's concern that the group be well regarded. Using the proper forms of speech to distinguish between those of equal, greater, or lesser status is also important in Japan.

In Japan, people keep track of gifts and favors received so that they can repay them at an appropriate time. In the past, for example, some families kept registries of donations made at the time of a death in the family, the amount largely being determined by the closeness of the relationship. An equivalent amount would be expected in return upon the death of a member of those families, but that might not happen in the lifetime of the senior members of the household. Thus the registries were passed down through the generations so that the debt between the families could be repaid at the right level. Nakama contributes to a sense of personal identity and belonging. Yet, the facework required to maintain these relationships can also be a source of stress because of the continuous need to be concerned with doing things appropriately and being aware of other people's perspectives and needs even if they are not voiced.

Beyond the friendship/colleagues circle is the rest of society, *tanin* (他人, others, strangers). These people are different from friends or coworkers because a person does not have an ongoing relationship with them. The line between tanin (others) and nakama is not as penetrable as Americans might expect; getting through this social boundary often necessitates an introduction by someone in the nakama of both parties. Cold-calling someone with a request would be considered rude and would be ineffective at best. Even in the middle of the twentieth century, potential marriage partners were identified and approached in this way through (*nakōdo* 仲人, go-betweens). Such introductions created an obligation for repayment that might last a lifetime. In the short run, a gift to the introducer is appropriate. Over the course of a marriage created in this way, a couple would formally visit the nakōdo each year at the New Year's holiday, bringing a substantial thank you gift each time. The go-betweens, on their part, were expected to maintain an interest in the couple and to provide advice or other assistance if needed.

Friendships are a sign of the maturity needed to balance consideration of the other with care of the self. What matters is not the *number* of close friends, but rather their *quality*. It is also important as a member of society, however, to maintain a wider social network of relationships through participation in group activities such as workplace sociality, alumni groups, PTA, and other civic organizations. People maintain nakama relationships through gift giving, exchange of New Year's cards, or doing favors such as introducing nakama to others in their social network.

Relationships with people in the same program or club, who are a bit older or a bit younger, referred to as *sempai* and *kohai*, respectively, are also maintained and valued through the years. Even when people meet years later and discover they attended the same school, they immediately define themselves relative to the other as sempai, kohai, or classmates based on graduation dates. Even as they exchange memories of former teachers or club activities they are conscious of their relative status. On the positive side, sempai may be mentors or provide guidance or support for kohai. The more difficult side of this unequal status relationship, however, can be serious teasing that is similar to fraternity hazing in the United States, in which kohai may be given the worst chores of a middle school sports team, or forced to drink more than they normally would to prove themselves as they join a college club.

In contrast, relationships among classmates who are the same year or workers who join a company at the same time are based on social equality.

Members of civic organizations are equals in principle, such as mothers who are active in the child's school PTA. Those who come in at the same time (generally based on when the child enters the school) are in a sense on the same level in contrast to the more experienced members of the group. They form a group which develops its own history and relationships; these, too, can continue well beyond the years the group is together.

All of these relationships belong to the realm of nakama, in which there is concern about how others perceive you. These relationships provide support, a sense of belonging, and also pleasure and fun. But what about closer personal relationships?

While the general term used to translate the English "friend" is *tomodachi* (友達), there is another word used to distinguish best friends or very close friends, *shinyū* (親友). The first character of tomodachi is the same as the second character of shinyū, indicating friend, even though the reading of the character is different. The character shin (親) makes the difference since it means intimacy. While English does not afford these linguistic distinctions, Maeda and Ritchie (2003) were interested in learning if Japanese college students would respond similarly to American college students when it came to noting what was desirable in best friend relationships. They replicated the approach taken by Cole and Bradac, two researchers who had investigated what American students thought were important qualities of a best friend (1996). They found that college students in both cultures valued a best friend relationship with someone who shared their interests, was enjoyable to be with, and was reliable. Differences between the two groups appeared when the students were asked to rank order qualities of communication they desired in a friendship. While American college students placed importance on frankness and spontaneity, Japanese students emphasized comfort and self-control. Keep in mind, however, that the characteristics desired in a friendship change over time. What a child values in a playmate is not always what he/she desires as a young adult (Sherman, de Vries and Lansford, 2005). As both parties to a close friendship change and mature, the relationship may become less intense over time, but it may deepen as well. For many Japanese adults, their closest friendships are those formed in their school years. Although they may enjoy socializing with workmates, those relationships rarely achieve the intimacy of shinyū, due to the stresses and competition of the workplace.

What about romantic relationships? Romance and sex may be found within these circles of relationships, but sometimes are found outside of these. In the days when an arranged marriage was the norm, people who provided introductions to appropriate partners were generally nakama who nominated someone in their own network but not previously known to the other potential partner. Now, most marriages are not arranged. Instead, companionship and physical attraction have come to be seen as the most important factors in deciding on a spouse. Living together before marriage was virtually unheard of several decades ago, but such partner relationships have increased rapidly in recent years and social judgment against it is declining. For most of these couples, living together is not a decision to have an alternative lifestyle, but rather a step toward marriage, especially for people with limited social and financial capital (Raymo, Iwasawa, & Bumpass, 2009).

With the decline of traditional ways to meet a spouse, new methods of establishing romantic and/or premarital relationships have come into existence. National and local governments are concerned about the declining rates of marriage of people in their 20s and the related issue of the ongoing decline in the birth rate. This has led local governments to sponsor singles events and outings to encourage young people to socialize together. Some private companies also provide matchmaking services and online dating sites. We might expect that in high-tech Japan with high levels of media saturation, these would be extremely popular. However, some of these companies have been involved in well-publicized scandals, and individuals are widely reported to use these sites dishonestly by misrepresenting themselves (Akimoto, 2013; Kumagai, 2015). Given the resulting distrust of these services, it makes more sense to most people to rely on friends for introductions (Ishida, 2013).

Commercial sex has also been widely available in urban Japan for centuries. In the Edo period (1600–1868) sex workers lived in licensed entertainment districts, and movement in and out of those parts of the city were regulated and policed. For men in the modern era, visiting prostitutes or having a concubine was legal and concubines even had equal status to wives under the law until 1898. For men, there were no consequences for sex and romance outside of marriage, but adultery for women was a crime and grounds for divorce. Women, who had few opportunities for economic independence in the twentieth century Japan, had little choice but to tolerate their husband's extramarital affairs. At the same time, the Japanese government had an interest in presenting itself as a modern nation equal to the nations of Europe and North America, and so made efforts to eliminate the most objectionable aspects of the brothel business. On the other hand, licensed prostitution was also seen as a way to control venereal disease through medical inspections and to maintain social order by providing sexual outlets for the large number of young men coming to the cities for new industrial jobs and for education (Sheldon, 1993).

An antiprostitution law was not passed in Japan until 1956, several years after the end of the post-World War II Allied Occupation (1945–1952). The law makes coital sex for pay illegal. It did not, however, lead to the disappearance of a thriving industry around paid sex, flirtation, and romance. Large Japanese cities have colorful districts and cozy corners containing numerous clubs in which women act as "hostesses" who flirt with and flatter male customers on behalf of their employer's bottom line. These relationships might be for an hour of light conversation over many drinks or may develop into ongoing relationships without, or sometimes with, some form of sex (see Allison, 1994). A more recent development of "host clubs," in contrast, provides romance and attention to single and married women in contemporary Japan at high prices (Takeyama, 2005). But regardless of the frequency or depth of interpersonal relationships created in this way, they are mainly considered problematical when they interfere with the real-life consequential relationships of the nakama and miuchi spheres.

This discussion of sex and romance has reflected the heteronormative assumptions of Japanese society today. Yet homosexual and bisexual relationships have had an accepted place in Japanese society for hundreds of years among Buddhist monks, samurai, and in the entertainment districts. As in ancient Greece, it was in some cases institutionalized and well accepted in society (Leupp, 1995; Pflugfelder, 1999). Sexuality was not perceived as sinful or through a homosexual–heterosexual binary lens. Thus, as with adulterous heterosexual relationships, the tolerance was high, but reached its limits if such relationships interfered with work and family responsibilities. That qualified tolerance continues today in that there are no laws in Japan against same sex relationships or transgender behavior. In fact, a 2013 Pew Research Center cross-national opinion poll found that 54 percent of the Japanese people included in the poll agreed that society should accept homosexuality (with only 36% opposing). In reviewing the responses in all of the countries included in the poll, it is clear that there is a trend in affluent societies toward acceptance of homosexuality. Many adults who in the United States might categorize themselves as LGBTQ in Japan marry someone of the opposite sex and remain closeted. But at least in larger urban centers, as socioeconomic change has driven a broad reconsideration of the late twentieth century businessman-style masculinity, alternative lifestyles and communities have become more prominent (McLelland & Dasgupta, 2005).

The underlying value behind all of the relationships we have discussed is the human capacity to develop and maintain ties with others and to know and act appropriately on the expectation of those ties. In numerous speeches at a wedding reception recently attended by one of the authors, for example, much was said about the bride's and groom's relationships with others, emphasizing the loyalty they showed to friends. They were complimented on the way they had maintained the special relationship between the two of them while remaining committed to their friends and mentors. They were thus praised as having accomplished this developmental task of growing up. Those who cannot maintain friendships are pitied, stigmatized, and/or given a diagnostic label such as *hikikomori* (social withdrawal), and not perceived as mature human beings. A popular early twenty-first century feature film *Train Man* is the story of such a young man who is drawn out of his isolation by his online acquaintances who become his cheerleaders and an attractive young woman who motivates and guides him gently into adulthood (Shōsuke, 2005).

■ Analyzing the Differences in Expectations of Friends

Thus far we have examined how the meaning of friendship can be affected by the larger set of social expectations and cultural norms, such as the face-work and unequal obligations expected in nakama relationships, the social space in which friendship is located. Friends are clearly not tanin strangers, but it is also rare that friends achieve the intimacy of the miuchi sphere, so when we interact with Japanese friends, we should understand that their expectations and behaviors are likely to be those of nakama. Cross-cultural friendships may thus encounter challenges due to differing views on what is expected from a friend. For people from Japan and the United States, there are significant variations in three primary areas: (1) high-context vs. low-context communication, (2) individualism vs. collectivism, and (3) conflict resolution.

High-Context/Low-Context Cultures

Context refers to the environment, conditions, or setting in which something is located. In the field of Communication, then, we ask about the context of a message or statement as clues to properly interpret it. For example, consider a comment in an e-mail message that might be a joke or a snide remark. Without being able to see the writer's face or know the person's motivation, we might not know unless the comment is followed by an emoticon. At its heart, then, context is what allows us to understand the communication of another. In low-context cultures, the focus is on what is actually said or written. Details are included and connections are made explicit. In high-context cultures, however, more is needed to decipher the true meaning of a statement, story, or poem. Low-context communicators often have a difficult time understanding why anyone would want to communicate indirectly while high-context communicators do not understand why low-context communicators regularly employ a communication style that they perceive as rude. Before providing examples of how this concept could affect a friendship between someone from Japan and someone from the United States, consider what happened when two Americans—one familiar with the Japanese culture and one not—discuss a traditional haiku poem:

"Parting"
For me who go,
For you who stay–
Two autumns
Taniguchi Buson, 1716–1783
Translated by Harold G. Henderson

The first time I read the English translation of this Japanese haiku I was immediately, and deeply, moved. So, when a friend came over, I shared it with him and here is a recreation of our conversation:

Jim: "I don't get it."

Katrina: "It's a beautiful poem about two good friends. One is getting ready to move and the two are sad because they will miss each other."

Jim: "Why doesn't it say that?"

Katrina: "It does say it!"

Jim: "But I love autumn. All the yellow and red leaves - they're great!"

Katrina: "But it isn't that part of autumn. It's the time in autumn when all the leaves have dropped and the trees are bare."

*Jim: "How do you know that? It doesn't **say** that."*

Katrina: "In haiku poems, the readers would understand the meaning by knowing the context. In this situation, it would be talking about the dreary looking bare trees at the end of autumn

Jim: "Well, they should just say it. It's a stupid poem."

Two years later when he moved to Florida, I put the poem in his going-away card - and we had a good laugh.

The traditional Japanese haiku, a form of poetry that often requires an understanding of symbolism or contextual elements to understand its meaning, might be clear to someone from a high-context culture, like Japan, but confusing to someone from a low-context culture like the United States where we are encouraged to express ideas directly and completely. Thus, a more subtle form of communication (from the low-context view) can result in missed messages. While we do not know why cultures vary on the degree of directness preferred in their culture, we do know that cultural values and norms are deeply rooted and slow to change.

Consider, for example, the conclusions of Inazo Nitobe (1862–1933) about the source of cultural values in Japan. In one of his visits to Belgium in the early part of the twentieth century, his European hosts were shocked to learn that religion was not taught in Japanese schools. Upon reflection, Nitobe concluded that moral education for the Japanese was found in the many stories told about samurai behavior and ideals. His 1905 book (Nitobe, 1969) *Bushido, The Soul of Japan* explains the ideals of the samurai code of conduct with the goal of explaining Japanese cultural values and behavior in a way that Westerners could understand. While much has changed since Nitobe lived, many of the values he explained remain relevant background for understanding Japan today.

For example, Nitobe's discussion of core values includes a norm in which people are more concerned with politeness and harmony than in stating true feelings or thoughts. According to Nitobe: "To give in so many articulate words one's inmost thoughts and feelings . . . is taken among us as an unmistakable sign that they are neither very profound nor very sincere. Only a pomegranate is he who, when he gapes his mouth, displays the contents of his heart" (p. 107).

Approximately 80 years later, when Condon (1984) contrasted American and Japanese communication patterns in his book *With Respect to the Japanese,* he compared the Japanese words *tatemae* (建て前, the politeness needed in nakama relationships) and *honne* (本音, one's true self, what you might never express publicly) (pp. 25–26). In the United States, we also have this contrast between politeness and truth. Consider, for example, what you say to someone who has fixed you a special dinner which you didn't particularly enjoy. When they ask, "Did you like it?" do you not respond with praise (even as you mentally make a note to stop at a fast food restaurant on the way home)?

This raises an important question: if both cultures have times when people say what is polite rather than what they truly feel or believe, why would Condon take time to explain and discuss these concepts in a book for Westerners trying to understand Japanese norms and values? The answer lies in *how frequently* and *when* the norms are applied. From the standpoint of an American, the Japanese present their public face (tatemae) almost exclusively within the nakama circle, and in situations where Americans would not, making it hard to know how they truly feel. From the standpoint of the Japanese, Americans rarely employ their public face and are unnervingly direct. As Nishida (1996) pointed out, for the Japanese:

> *Understanding is often left up to the listener's sasshi (*察し*, guessing what someone means) ability. The concept of sasshi is defined as conjecture, surmise, or guessing what someone means. In its verb form (sassuru), its meaning is expanded to mean to imagine, to suppose, to empathize with, or to make allowances for others (p. 114).*

Okabe (1983) describes this process as "point/dot/space" and a "stepping-stone mode" which is in contrast to the U.S. communication pattern of a straight line (p. 28).

Difficult topics (criticisms, saying no, etc.) are often conveyed nonverbally through facial expressions, pauses, and even silence (Nishida, 1996, p. 115). Japanese conversations may include long moments of silence, with gaps that Americans may find uncomfortable because silence is generally avoided in the United States (Ishii and Bruneau, 1994; Lebra 1987).

The meaning of these subtle responses must then be inferred by the listener. "For example, when a person who is requested to do something wishes to refuse the request, he or she will pause and not respond within an appropriate time period" (Nishida, p. 115). Thinking back to Example #2 earlier in this chapter, we can now better understand why Hideshi assumed Sarah could not take him to the airport and why he would find the direct communication style in the United States rude.

In contrast to the restrained, indirect communication that is common among Japanese people, American communication patterns reflect "informality, ease with strangers, infectious exhibitionism, spontaneity, and a propensity for argument" (Barnlund, 1975, pp. 61–62). The differences revealed in Barnlund's studies led him to wonder if we could identify members of each culture if our observation blurred physical characteristics. In his view, we would be able to tell who was Japanese and who was American because our styles are so distinctive from each other.

Differences in communication styles were confirmed by Toyosaki when she asked Japanese students studying in the United States to discuss their relationships with American university students and found that communication differences played a significant role (2004, p. 163). Comments of the Japanese students focused on the tendency of Americans to talk a lot (from their perspective) and to make statements that might—or might not—be sincere (honne). For example, they stated:

- "Americans seem to verbalize their thoughts as they emerge. . . . Americans talk a lot. . . . Americans speak about everything just like they are [a computer that has] to [constantly] update and update." (p. 165)
- One student referred to the style of communication used by Americans as "option-talk" where they constantly talked about options as if they represented true feelings or were definite courses of action that the person intended to take. "Americans say things too often without thinking very hard, so what is said [as a definite statement is, in fact,]. . . . just an option in [the American's] mind." (p. 163).

While Americans may not view themselves as overly talkative or be bothered if someone "thinks out loud," a Japanese friend might be confused since Japanese people tend to listen completely to what another person says before even beginning to develop what they will say (Toyosaki, p. 165). To use an analogy, American conversation is often closer to a quick text—what we think immediately, without refinement or adjustment to our audience—while Japanese conversation is closer to a final version of a document.

The Japanese language itself reflects the cultural expectation of close listening. The main verb comes at the end of the sentence, and perhaps a more significant example of high context is that the subject of the sentence is often assumed and other details vague. For example, if someone asks where Atsuko is, in the United States, we might reply that she just ran out to the store for bread. In Japan, the response would perhaps be, "*chotto dekakimashita*" (ちょっと出かけました, went out for a bit), or even "*sugu modorimasu*" (直ぐ戻ります, will return soon, to address the questioner's intent). The "she" is omitted since everyone in the conversation knows they are talking about Atsuko. The fact that Atsuko had run out of bread is not relevant to the intent of the questioner in asking, and the speaker might not want to reveal something that might reflect badly on Atsuko's homemaking skills, so the details are just left out.

While the Japanese may find our habit of "thinking out loud" confusing, Americans may feel frustrated at the silence and tentative nature of Japanese communication styles. "Say what you think," "speak up," and "tell it like it is" are common expressions in the United States. Additionally, while Americans are often comfortable with a fast-paced conversational style that includes interrupting another person to make their point, or completing another persons comments to help the person express their ideas, Japanese find these styles rude (Condon, 1984, pp. 36–37).

Having different norms on how much we should talk and how direct that communication should be, it is perhaps not surprising that Japanese and Americans can also differ in how much of themselves they reveal to others. In Barnlund's studies, he found that Americans self-disclosed significantly more than the Japanese both on personal opinions and feelings (1975, p. 64). Thirty years later, Kito examined self-disclosure between friends and in love relationships and she, too, found that American college students self-disclosed more than Japanese college students in each of the relationship categories (cross-sex friends, same-sex friends, passionate love relationships, and companionate love relationships) (2005, p. 136).

Since "self-clarification" and "self-validation" have been noted as two benefits (among others) of self-disclosure (Adler & Proctor, 2011, p. 318),

Asai and Barnlund suggested that Americans might use self-disclosure as a way to learn about themselves and others (1998, p. 445, 450). This raises an interesting question: if self-disclosure can result in increased self-knowledge, why wouldn't the Japanese culture encourage it as a norm? That answer can be found in the next section that examines Hofstede's concept of individualism.

Individualism vs. Collectivism

How would you respond if you were asked this question: "Whose needs are more important: the group or the individual?" According to Hofstede, your answer would be influenced by the culture(s) in which you were raised, because cultures vary in which values and norms are given precedence. Hofstede, who was able to collect data from employees from 70 countries around the world, analyzed the data and concluded that cultures could be compared by how they were rated in categories that he called "Cultural Dimensions." The cultural dimension that could be particularly relevant to a cross-cultural relationship with friends from Japan and the United States is the one identified as individualism. According to his research, the United States is rated as the most individualistic culture in the world and, as such, a variety of American ideals encourage Americans to focus on meeting personal goals and desires (Hofstede, 2001). Hofstede argues that in collectivistic cultures like Japan, however, social norms encourage people to sublimate personal goals and desires to the needs of the group (family, friends, coworkers, etc.), a conclusion reached by other researchers as well (Cathcart & Cathcart, 1994, p. 293; Lustig & Koester, 2000, p. 199; Markus & Kitayama, 1991, p. 226–227). If you are from the United States, you might find the concept of giving precedence to group needs difficult to accept but Barnlund pointed out that Americans often overlook the fact that collectivistic cultures reward cooperation, making the behavior of sublimating personal goals to those of the group a rational choice that is also often desirable (Barnlund, 1989, p. 163).

Given the priority of groups in the social structure of collectivistic cultures like Japan, Gudykunst and Matsumoto contend that people tend to belong to fewer social groups, but those groups are seen as affecting their behavior more than is typical in individualistic cultures (1996, p. 23). For example, Gudykunst and Matsumoto have pointed out that in the United States, our behavior might be influenced by the university we attend when we are on campus or at an alumni event, but in Japan, the university that students attend affects their behavior regardless of where they are or how long ago they graduated from the university because they see their actions as potentially reflecting on the university and all of its students and alumni.

Additionally, as noted earlier in this chapter with Yoneyama's concentric circle model of social relationships, people in collectivistic cultures pay more attention to in-group (nakama) or out-group (tanin) status than those from individualistic cultures because it can take a longer time to become part of a group. In the United States, we do have a few examples of this, such as when a college student pledges a fraternity or sorority. In general, however, it is more common for Americans to join several clubs or groups and skip meetings or drop out altogether if the group interferes with other commitments or desires. For people in collectivistic cultures, however, such behavior is viewed negatively as a lack of commitment to the greater good.

Decisions about the extent of participation in group activities and the degree to which consideration for others should override one's own wishes are not merely arbitrary personal decisions, but are likely to be based on the society's "rules of the game." Since college admissions in Japan are based almost entirely on a single test score, Japanese high school students are not concerned about appearing well rounded, but as studious. For the Japanese, joining only one club or pursuing a single sport or musical instrument shows a commitment to personal skill development and to others, both of which are valued by employers.

Not surprisingly, in collectivistic cultures like Japan where groups are an integral part of a person's identity, group harmony is a key value—and part of maintaining harmony is being able to ascertain what another person wants without that person explicitly expressing that person views (Ishii & Bruneau, 1994, p. 249; Okabe, 1983, p. 27; Ramsey, 1985, p. 312). The result is that people from interdependent cultures like Japan are viewed as more attuned to, and knowledgeable about, people in their social relationships than those who live in independent cultures like the United States (Condon, 1984, p. 45; Markus & Kitayama, 1991, p. 231). The term *ishin-denshin* (以心伝心) is used in Japanese to refer to a supposedly traditional style of communication in which wishes are not expressed directly, but rather are inferred by others. Ishin-denshin is sometimes translated as "silent understanding," reached without any direct communication, so it can be thought of as a form of mental or heart-to-heart transmission.

This occurs even regarding sensitive topics about health. While many Americans have come to talk more openly to family members and doctors about living wills, do-not-resuscitate orders, or how they would want to be treated if they became terminally ill, for many Japanese patients, especially elderly ones, such a direct discussion sounds like they are being given a death sentence when their admission might be for something like a joint replacement. Thus, some Japanese patients would prefer that the family be consulted since they would already intuitively know what their relative would want, or that their communication with their doctor is ishin-denshin, achieving a heart-to-heart but silent understanding.

In addition to valuing harmony and being experienced at figuring out what others want or need, Japanese culture stresses the importance of fitting in with others. Almost any book or article on Japanese culture will include a translation of the saying *deru kugi wa utareru* (出る釘は打たれる, "the nail that stands up will be pounded down") (Cathcart & Cathcart, 1985, p. 190; Condon, 1984, p. 11; Markus & Kitayama, 1991, p. 224). This affects everything from how decisions are made to how one dresses.

Group harmony and identity have been so central to the Japanese culture that Cathcart and Cathcart (1985) argue that individuals find fulfillment by "finding and maintaining one's place within the group" (p. 191). Anthropologists have pointed out that this norm of harmony (*wa*) helps to maintain the status quo in the workplace. Thus, people who are assertive and obviously acting in their own self-interest are sanctioned while those who act collaboratively, seeming to put the interest of the group or company ahead of their own, are rewarded (Rohlen, 1974; Kondo, 1990). With changes in employment practices resulting from an economic downturn that began in the 1990s, this norm may not be as strong as it was in the past and there has been more questioning of who reaps the benefits of group harmony.

Americans would likely be surprised to learn, however, that in Japan, it is common—and sometimes the law—that a group may make restitution for the misdeeds of an individual (Cathcart & Cathcart, 1985, p. 191). The head of a company or other unit will frequently resign as a way to take responsibility for the failure of its members (suggesting a deficit in the person's leadership). Understanding this explains why a baseball team competing in a national high school tournament was eliminated from the competition when one player was caught violating the no smoking rule during training

(*Young Baseball Heroes, 1986*). In the United States, this would be an inconceivable decision, but in Japan, where the needs of the group trump the desires of the individual, it is entirely logical.

Now think back to the issues of self-disclosure. If you live in a culture where group harmony is vital, where members of a group make decisions by consensus, and individuals often subdue their personal desires to the desires or needs of the group—do you see how you might limit your self-disclosure? Harmony and fitting in with a group are easier to accomplish if you keep your thoughts and views to yourself. Even in the United States, we may do this with family members, particularly parents and grandparents and at family gatherings that occur only once or twice a year. So, like tatamae and honne, it is not that the two cultures lack similar concepts; rather it is a matter of frequency, situation, degree, and interpretation. Differences between the two cultures on this issue, however, affect yet another important issue for friendship relationships: conflict resolution.

Conflict Resolution

In the United States, communication textbooks typically present five basic conflict strategies (or styles) as typical in interpersonal or group interactions. Explanations of the five conflict strategies center on the benefits and drawbacks to the various styles as well as discussions of when one style might be more productive than another (e.g., Adler & Proctor, 2011, pp. 381–389; Engleberg & Wynn, 2010, pp. 216–219; Hamilton & Parker, 1993, pp. 311–316).

Those five approaches are:

Obliging/Accommodating/Smoothing: people who use this are more concerned with the feelings of others than with anything else; they will give in to what the others want to do in order to avoid conflict.

Avoiding/Withdrawal: views conflict as a negative experience that must be avoided at all costs; people who use this may avoid meetings or discussing a topic.

Compromising: no one gets exactly what they want, but everyone gets something that they do want and everyone can live with the decision.

Dominating/Forcing/Competing: for people who use this, results (usually their goals) are more important than anyone's feelings, conflict is a test of power, and there is a definite winner and a loser—and they are determined to be the winner!

Integrating/Problem Solving/Collaborating: gives equal consideration to people and results; views conflict as beneficial if it is handled well; values consensus.

While the terms for the five conflict styles vary, the concepts are so well established in the United States that they are assumed to be universal. Moreover, as you read these descriptions in American texts, the integrating approach is often presented as the most productive and valuable style for dealing with conflict, while avoiding and obliging are presented as generally counterproductive, even destructive, conflict styles.

When researchers began collecting data from countries around the world, however, they discovered three new categories: Emotional Expression, Passive Aggressive, and Third Party Help (Griffin, 2012; Ting-Toomey & Oetzel, 2001; Ting-Toomey, et al., 1991). Two of the newly identified strategies were found to be associated specifically with people in individualistic cultures:

Emotional Expression: a spontaneous emotional reaction that would help a person know how to respond to a conflict situation; respondents described it as "going with your gut reaction."
Passive Aggressive: someone who resents what is being decided but, generally, lacks the power to affect change so the person will go along but secretly hope the decision/policy/process fails; common examples include using sarcasm, not doing something they are assigned, and even sabotaging the project/decision.

The third category discovered by the researchers was named **Third Party Help**. An important distinction between this category and previous categories, however, is that while people in both individualistic and collectivistic cultures use Third Party Help, it is *implemented differently*. In collectivistic cultures like Japan, the preference is to have the assistance of a person of high status, someone who is respected and known to all parties involved in the conflict. Given our earlier discussions on the importance of nakama to tanin to go from being on the outer circle (a stranger or distant acquaintance) to the circle of friends and colleagues, it should not be surprising to learn that someone in that position might also take steps to prevent conflict or to soothe it when it begins to occur. Thus, the idea is that the people involved in the conflict will work hard to reach a solution and to respect the advice given by the third party so that that person can maintain their high standing in the community with their "face" intact. In individualistic cultures, however, third party help is more likely to involve using a lawyer or a mandated mediator; in these cases, the conflicted parties are not concerned with the "face" of the mediator and may even be using a third party because it was mandated by law (Griffin, 2012, p. 415).

When researchers examined who used which of the eight conflict strategies, they could identify patterns based on the type of face that predominated in the culture. Thus, dominating, passive aggressive or emotional expression styles in conflict were most commonly used by people who lived in individualistic cultures while people in collectivistic cultures were more likely to use avoiding, obliging, integrating, or compromising when involved in conflict (Ting-Toomey & Oetzel, 2001, p. 37, 48–49; Griffin, 2012, p. 414). This finding is particularly important because members of individualistic cultures are taught that avoiding conflict and obliging (giving in) are unproductive conflict strategies while compromising is presented as a partial "lose–lose" option (Adler & Proctor, 2011, p. 385). Yet, these strategies are preferred by people raised in collectivistic cultures. Thus, in an intercultural friendship, problems may occur not only with the issue that created the conflict but also with *how* the conflict is handled.

For Americans raised on the cultural value of being direct, it is difficult to understand that avoiding an issue is actually considered a beneficial reaction to a conflict. On the other hand, a Japanese person may not be just uncomfortable, but confused by an American who insists that "we talk it out" when an issue has developed. For example, a Japanese exchange student approached one of the authors to ask about a situation involving her American roommate. The Japanese student explained that her roommate had had an argument with her boyfriend and rather than avoiding talking about it and letting time take care of the issue, her roommate and boyfriend kept talking about the issue at the center of their argument every time they talked. In the Japanese student's view, the Americans were handling this problem in a destructive way and she had approached the professor to try to understand why Americans thought continually talking about a contested issue was productive.

■ Who Adjusts?

These differences in communication norms may present a hurdle in developing intercultural relationships because members of each culture find their style of communication natural and they may not understand why members of the other culture can't just adapt to *their* cultural norms. This raises the question of *who makes adjustments.* While developing a dual perspective that considers the face needs of people from other cultures is desirable, it can be difficult to achieve (Lustig & Koester, 2000, p. 200; Wood, 2002, p. 45). Consider, for example, the difference between the "Golden Rule" (which admonishes us to treat others as *we* would like to be treated) and the "Platinum Rule" (which states that we should treat others as *they* would like to be treated) (Adler & Procter, 2011, p. 111). The first approach is definitely easier for us to implement but can also lead to ethnocentric interactions and views while the second approach develops empathy and openness to the views and practices of others.

In some cases, an easier place to start when considering the question of who should make adjustments in intercultural relationships might be to focus on pragmatic issues. Questions to ask yourself could include how important is it for the relationship to work (either for personal or work reasons) or which person is better able to adapt their style of communication? For some, intercultural relationships might develop more naturally either because they communicate in similar patterns found in another culture and/or they can successfully moderate their communication patterns to be more sensitive to, and accepting of, other communication styles and norms.

■ Reflections on Cultural Change

Cultural differences sometimes stand in the way of people's comfort in developing relationships with those raised with values and styles of communication different from their own. This chapter has explored the ways that Japanese and Americans perceive friendship in order to help better understand how intercultural friendships can both expand horizons and present communication challenges. We first clarified that culture is a set of meanings established through interaction within a group. At the individual level, our own culture is the invisible lens through which we see the world. We do not notice that lens is there until we find people whose lens is shaped and colored differently. We recognized that a person's position in society as well as their personal idiosyncrasies make it difficult to generalize about a culture without stereotyping. There is always a gap between what people say they do or should do and what they actually do; moreover, all cultures change over time. Nonetheless, we argue that it is worthwhile to ask questions and to learn how to better communicate with those whose cultural lens is different from our own.

Learning how to communicate with a Japanese friend may be especially challenging for both people because the Japanese friend's underlying expectations of different levels of intimacy may not match that of someone from the United States. By considering the model of concentric circles of relationships going outward from the self, we can recognize common ground for building relationships and identify ways that our relationship might be differently interpreted by me and by my Japanese friend. This ethnographic approach helps us to bring to light some of the hidden assumptions we each bring to our relationship, things we ourselves might not be aware of until we meet someone who does not share them.

Of particular help in understanding friendships between Japanese and Americans were the oppositional notions of high- and low-context cultures, individualistic and collectivistic societies, and approaches to conflict management. Although the contrasts can be overdrawn, they are helpful in bringing our attention to areas in which we might expect misunderstanding. All of these assume that being made aware of background values and assumptions will allow us to adapt our own style of communication when dealing with those from other cultural backgrounds and to understand better the motivations of our intercultural friends.

But can we count on awareness to overcome the challenges to an intercultural relationship? We argue that it helps us not so much to predict but to stop ourselves from assuming anything and, thus, to ask questions. Knowledge of Japanese culture and elements of intercultural communication help us frame those questions. Earlier we discussed how individual characteristics and position in society lead to variation in the way norms are interpreted and acted upon. As we conclude this chapter, we wish to briefly consider the ways that norms can change.

One factor may be generational change. Sometimes differences by age cohort reflect life stages; we expect increasingly more mature judgment and interpersonal skills as people age, for example. Yet there is more to what we call the "generation gap." Each generation grows up in a particular era and understands the historical events and technology of the times differently than those who were not there. This issue has been raised in one study where, contrary to previous research, the authors found that the Japanese were more direct than Americans in expressing how they felt about each other when talking with friends of the same sex (Matsumoto, Matsumoto, & Imahori, 2002). When the authors realized what their results showed, they suggested that part of the reason for this unexpected result might be found in a changing youth culture in Japan. This concept of a generational change has been widely noted in the United States as well. Much of this change may be driven by new technologies, so that the nature of friendship and self-disclosure might be expected to change with widespread use of social media in the future. The change will not happen overnight, nor will it look exactly like the United States, but it will also not be the same as it was in the past. Old ways may be maintained, such as traditional dress or the celebration of traditional holidays with special foods, but they take on new meaning in light of the broader range of possibilities in the modern world. Thus, traditions may become markers of ethnic pride and, in some places, of political resistance to a dominant culture.

Another approach that raises the issue of cultural change focuses on elements of globalization, especially increases in world travel and immigration as well as by the diffusion of technology and other cultural artifacts such as popular film and music. We live in a time where you could (metaphorically) never leave your front porch yet you can read British news articles online, watch YouTube videos on the Japanese tea ceremony, and use free Internet phone services to converse with people around the world. These aspects of our contemporary world raise an interesting question: As people increase their knowledge of and interactions with people around the world, will we all become more similar?

We may think the answer is obviously yes. Yet, we continue to grab on to things we know about other cultures as though they are stable handles for knowing the way others think and live. At many times in human history, cultures change because new ways are forced upon people in circumstances of conquest and colonialism. Yet cultures also change as social–economic conditions modify behavior and as attractive ideas and material goods are introduced from outside. Cultures change as people change, passing on partial versions, new adaptations, and new interpretations of traditional values and lifeways. In this sense, the development of intercultural friendships not only contributes to expanding opportunities for the individuals involved for meaningful relationships and new understandings of the world but alsocontributes to the broader cultures of both by introducing new patterns of relationships and new responses to the dilemmas of intercultural communication.

References

Adler, R. B., & Proctor II, R. F. (2011). *Looking out, Looking in* (13th ed.). Boston, M.A.: Wadsworth Cengage Learning.

Akimoto, A. (2013, October 15). Japan's social-networking pioneer turns matchmaker. *The Japan Times Digital*, p. 2. Retrieved from www.japantimes.co.jp/life/2013/10/15/digital/japans-social-networking-pioneer-turns-matchmaker/#.Vij9gX6rTIU .

Allison, A. (1994). *Nightwork: Sexuality, pleasure, and corporate masculinity in a Tokyo hostess club*. Chicago: University of Chicago Press.

Asai, A., & Barnlund, D. C. (1998). Boundaries of the unconscious, private, and public self in Japanese and Americans: A cross-cultural comparison. *International Journal of Intercultural Relations, 22* (4), 431–452.

Barnlund, D. C. (1975). *Public and private self in Japan and the United States, Communicative styles of two cultures*. Tokyo, Japan: Simul Press.

Barnlund, D. C. (1989). *Communicative styles of Japanese and Americans, Images and realities*. Belmont, CA: Wadsworth Publishing Co.

Cathcart, D., & Cathcart R. (1985). Japanese social experience and concept of groups. In L. A. Samovar, & R. E. Porter (Eds.), *Intercultural communication: A reader* (4th ed., pp. 190–199). Belmont, CA: Wadsworth Publishing Co.

Cathcart, D., & Cathcart, R. (1994). The group: A Japanese context. In L. A. Samovar, & R. E. Porter (Eds.), *Intercultural communication: A reader* (7th ed., pp. 293–304). Belmont, CA: Wadsworth Publishing Co.

Cole, T., & Bradac, J. J. (1996). A lay theory of relational satisfaction with best friends. *Journal of Social and Personal Relationships, 13* (1), 57–83.

Condon, J. C. (1984). *With respect to the Japanese: A guide for Americans*. Yarmouth, M.E.: Intercultural Press, Inc.

Engleberg, I. N., & Wynn, D. R. (2010). *Working in groups* (5th ed.). Boston, MA: Allyn & Bacon.

Griffin, E. (2012). *A first look at communication theory* (8th ed.). New York: McGraw Hill Companies, Inc.

Gudykunst, W. B., & Matsumoto, Y. (1996). Cross cultural variability of communication in personal relationships. In W. B. Gudykunst, S. Ting-Toomey, & T. Nishida (Eds.), *Communication in personal relationships across cultures* (pp. 19–56) London: Sage Press.

Hall, E. T. (1977). *Beyond culture*. Garden City, N.Y.: Anchor Books.

Hamilton, C., & Parker, C. (1987). *Communicating for results: A guide for business and the professions* (2nd ed.). Belmont: CA: Wadsworth Publishing Co.

Hofstede, G. (2001). *Culture's consequences, comparing values, behaviors, institutions, and organizations across nations.* Thousand Oaks, CA: Sage Publications.

Ishida, H. (2013). The transition to adulthood among Japanese youths: Understanding courtship in Japan. *The Annals of the American Academy of Political and Social Science, 646*(1), 86–106.

Ishii, S., & Bruneau, T. (1994). Silence and silences in cross-cultural perspective: Japan and the United States. In L. A. Samovar, & R. E. Porter (Eds.), *Intercultural communication: A reader* (7th ed., pp. 246–251). Belmont, CA: Wadsworth Publishing Co.

Kito, M. (2005). Self-disclosure in romantic relationships and friendships among American and Japanese college students. *Journal of Social Psychology, 145*(2), 127–140.

Kondo, D. K. (1990). *Crafting selves: Power, gender, and discourses of identity in a Japanese workplace.* Chicago: University of Chicago Press.

Kumagai, F. (2015). History of courtship and marriage in Japan. In *Family issues on marriage, divorce and older adults in Japan,* (Chapter 3). Singapore: Springer Science.

Lebra, T. S. (1987). The cultural significance of silence in Japanese communication *Multilingua: Journal of Cross-Cultural and Interlanguage Communication, 6*(4), 343–358.

Leupp, G. P. (1995). *Male colors: The construction of homosexuality in Tokugawa Japan.* Berkeley: University of California Press.

Lustig, M., & Koester, J. (2000). Negotiating intercultural competence. In M. W. Lustig, & J. Koester (Eds.), *Among us: Essays on identity, belonging, and intercultural competence* (pp. 197–202). New York: Addison Wesley Longman, Inc.

Maeda, E., & Ritchie, L. D. (2003). The concept of *shinyū* in Japan: A replication to Cole and Bradac's study of U.S. Friendship. *Journal of Social and Personal Relationships, 20*(5), 579–598.

Markus, H. R., & Kitayama, S. (April 1991). Cross cultural differences: Self perception; Social perception. *Psychological Review,* 98(2), 224-253.

Matsumoto, S. K. D., Matsumoto, D., & Imahori, T. T. (2002). The conceptualization and expression of intimacy in Japan and the United States. *Journal of Cross Cultural Psychology, 33*(3), 303–319.

McLelland, M., & Dasgupta, R. (2005). Introduction. In M. McLelland, & R. Dasgupta (Eds.), *Genders, Transgenders and Sexualities in Japan* (pp. 1–14). London: Routledge.

Nishida, T. (1996). Communication in personal relationships in Japan. In W. B. Gudykunst, S. Ting-Toomey, & T. Nishida (Eds.), *Communication in personal relationships across cultures,* (pp. 102–121). Thousand Oaks, CA: Sage Publications.

Nitobe, I. (1969). *Bushido, the soul of Japan* (Revised and Enlarged ed.). Rutland, VT: Charles E. Tuttle Co. [Note: this book was first published in 1905 and can be downloaded for free on the internet.]

Nydell, M. K. (2012). *Understanding Arabs, A contemporary guide to Arab society* (5th ed.). Boston, M.A.: Intercultural Press.

Okabe, R. (1983). Cultural assumptions of east and west, Japan and the United States. In W. B. Gudykunst (Ed.), *Intercultural communication theory, current perspectives* (pp. 21–44). Beverly Hills, CA: Sage Publications.

Pew Research Center. (2013). The global divide on homosexuality. Retrieved from http://www.pewglobal.org/2013/06/04/the-global-divide-on-homosexuality/

Plugfelder, G. M. (1999). *Cartographies of desire: Male-male sexuality in Japanese discourse, 1600–1950.* Berkeley: University of California Press.

Ramsey, S. (1985). To hear one and understand ten: Nonverbal behavior in Japan. In L. A. Samovar, & R. E. Porter (Eds.), *Intercultural communication: A reader* (4th ed., pp. 307–325). Belmont, CA: Wadsworth Publishing Co.

Sheldon, G. (1993). The world's oldest debate: Prostitution and the state in imperial Japan, 1900–1945. *American Historical Review, 98*(3), 710–733.

Sherman, A.M., de Vries, B., & Lansford, J.E. (2005). Friendship in childhood and adulthood: Lessons across the life span. *International Journal of Aging and Human Development.* 51(1), 31-51.

Shōsuke, M. (Dir.) (2005). *Densha Otoko (Train man).* Toho.

Raymo, J. M., Iwasawa, M., & Bumpass, L. (2009). Cohabilitation and family formation in Japan. *Demography, 46*(4), 785–803.

Rohlen, T. P. (1974). *For harmony and strength.* Berkeley: University of California Press.

Takeyama, A. (2005). Commodified romance in a Tokyo host club. In M. McLelland, & R. Dasgupta (Eds.), *Genders, Transgenders and Sexualities in Japan* (pp. 200–215). London: Routledge.

Ting-Toomey, S., Gao, G., Trubisky, P., Yang, Z., Kim, H. S., Lin, S.-L., et al. (1991). Culture, face maintenance, and styles of handling interpersonal conflict: A study in five cultures. *International Journal of Conflict Management, 2*(4) 275–296.

Ting-Toomey, S., & Oetzel, J. (2001). *Managing Intercultural Conflict Effectively*. Thousand Oaks, CA: Sage Publications, Inc.

Ting-Toomey, S., & Chung, L. C. (2012). *Understanding Intercultural Communication* (2nd ed.). New York: Oxford University Press.

Toyosaki, S. (2004). Ethnography of cross-cultural communication: Japanese international students' accounts of US-American culture and communication. *Journal of Intercultural Communication Research. 33*(3).

White, M. (1994). *The material child: Coming of age in Japan and America.* Berkeley: University of California Press.

Wood, J. T. (2002). *Interpersonal communication, Everyday encounters* (3rd ed.). Belmont, CA: Wadsworth/Thomson Learning.

Yoneyama, T. (1973). Basic notions in Japanese social relations. In J. H. Bailey (Ed.), *Listening to Japan: A Japanese anthology,* (pp. 91–110). New York: Praeger.

Young Baseball Heroes. (1986). *Faces of Japan,* Produced by TeleJapan USA, Inc. Distributed by Pacific Mountain Network. Season 1, Episode 3, 30 minutes.

CHAPTER 7
PROFESSIONAL RELATIONSHIPS AND ORGANIZATIONAL COMMUNICATION IN JAPAN

REIKO NEBASHI-NAKAHARA AND YOUQI YE

I n our daily life, we encounter many different types of professional rela-tionships. Based on the norms of large Japanese corporations, this chap-ter focuses on professional relationships and communication practices in Japanese business settings. Although the working population employed in such large organizations is quite small (Matanle, 2006; Watanabe, 2015), large Japanese corporations tend to set the norms and standards of employ-ment practices, including relational and communicative practices, which small- and medium-sized enterprises follow.

◼ The Changing Context in Japan

Japanese corporations are known all over the world for their unique man-agement style, *nihonteki keiei* (日本的経営; Japanese style management), introduced by Abegglen (1958). An understanding of *nihonteki keiei* is a prerequisite for comprehending the way Japanese people acquire and main-tain their professional relationships. This section starts with a review of Abegglen's observations about Japanese management styles and then exam-ines how these aspects have changed across three periods: (1) postwar eco-nomic growth years, (2) the post-bubble economy years, and (3) after 2000. The discussion then considers a new perspective: *nihongata koyo shisutemu* (日本型雇用システム; Japanese employment system) (Hamaguchi, 2009, 2011, 2014).

Postwar Economic Growth Years

Abegglen (2006) described three main features of *nihonteki keiei* as follows: (1) a social contract between the firm and employee, (2) the seniority system, and (3) trade union organizations. Although these three features appeared in Japanese firms established after the First World War, they became normative models only from the 1960s (Hamaguchi, 2011).

The first pillar, the social contract between the firm and employee, refers to "a commitment to work as a community to achieve economic security for all members of the workforce" (Abegglen, 2006, p. 73), which is the so-called *shushinkoyo* (終身雇用; lifetime employment). Most employees in the system are directly recruited from school, *shinsotsu ikkatsu saiyo* (新卒一括採用; simultaneous recruitment of new graduates), rather than from an open market. Therefore, they are not expected to possess any particular technical skills; rather, companies are focused on general characteristics and the employees' skill development potential (Abegglen & Stalk, 1985). The employees are expected to remain at the company all their working life, and, in turn, they expect that they will not be easily laid off (Chen, 2004). It is not an explicit contract, but is based on unspoken rules between the employees and the employer (McCann, Hassard, & Morris, 2006; Watanabe, 2015). Due to this long-term employment agreement, commitment is a strong cultural norm and employees develop firm-specific skills through *haichitenkan* (配置転換; job rotation) (Shimizu, 2014).

The second pillar is *nenkojoretsu* (年功序列; seniority system), whereby pay and promotion are determined according to an employee's tenure in the company. The seniority system is closely linked to the aforementioned lifetime employment. When employees are directly hired from school, their age and tenure for the company become parallel, thus the seniority system becomes a natural basis for reward. Since the company is responsible for the employees' careers, the compensation increases as the employees' responsibilities increase (Abegglen & Stalk, 1985). Hence, the seniority system is a major motivation to stay in one company for a lifetime (Chen, 2004). This system goes back to the postwar collective system of pay and promotion, which reduced the salary gap between employees in institutional hierarchies. This system provides greater compensation to older employees because of the needs of their life stage, such as buying a house and children's education, and less compensation to younger employees, thus overall minimizing the total wage expenditure (Watanabe, 2015).

The third pillar is *kigyonai kumiai* (企業内組合; trade union organization), in which all employees of a given enterprise are members of a single union (Abegglen, 2006). This is also known as *kigyo-betsu kumiai* (企業別組合; the enterprise trade unions), which encompasses all employees in the firm with no distinctions made between occupation and job status, such as between white-collar and blue-collar workers. The firm and the union are interdependent, in that the "union does not exist as an entity separate from the company, while the company regards the union experience as valuable training for efficient management rather than merely treating it as an adversary" (Chen, 2004, p. 161). Therefore, the union and company are both considered to be part of the same primary group.

Although other management aspects, such as group decision making, have been added by other scholars over time (Chen, 2004; Kono, 2012; Watanabe, 2015), these three pillars illustrate the distinct features of the Japanese management style originally documented by Abegglen (1958). These three pillars have been considered the Japanese management system's primary source of stability and were the driving force behind Japan's economic growth before the collapse of the bubble economy.[1]

Post-bubble Economy

Since the bubble economy burst in the beginning of the 1990s, Japan has experienced prolonged economic stagnation, and, as a result, several changes have taken place within Japanese corporations. Two aspects of the Japanese management style, *nihonteki keiei*, lifetime employment, and the pay and seniority promotion system are more closely examined in the following.

Although *nihonteki keiei* had been seen as an efficient practice in enhancing group spirit and promoting employee loyalty and organizational harmony for several decades, its baneful influence began to be recognized as the economic recession deepened in the 1990s, so organizational reconstruction took place to modify the traditional *nihonteki keiei* (Higashimura, 1997). Some changes were made such as downsizing, restructuring, management layer reduction, section mergers, and changes in the grading of the pay and promotion systems (McCann, Hassard, & Morris, 2006). When *seikashugi* (成果主義; merit/performance-based pay and romotion system)

[1]The bubble economy here refers to Japanese economic growth led by an increase in asset prices after the Plaza Accord of 1985. Property prices peaked in 1990 followed by a decline, which ended in 1992 when real GDP growth suddenly slowed (Yoshino, 2010).

was introduced, it was hailed as a new model for the coming age. The traditional seniority pay and promotion system that evaluated employees based on years of service to the company was found to discourage highly motivated employees. *Seikashugi*, therefore, was expected to motivate employees and enhance organizational performance, but, in fact, many new problems arose. Watanabe (2015) summarized these into five categories: (1) losing a long-term perspective, (2) demotivation due to unfair evaluations, (3) a worsening in teamwork, (4) neglecting employee training, and (5) resistance to change.

First, *seikashugi* requires outcomes in a relatively short period of time, so employees tended to set goals that were easier to achieve rather than aiming at long-term product development, which diluted their motivation to complete new projects. Second, although most employees assumed a fair assessment under *seikashugi*, in reality, uncertain evaluation criteria because of blurred job descriptions increased frustrations. Third, employees often prioritized their individual work over that of the organization, which led to less work sharing and weakened solidarity and teamwork within the organization. Fourth, senior and experienced employees gave precedence to their own achievements and neglected to educate the young or new employees. Finally, to increase an employee's remuneration, the organizations needed to reduce the rewards given to others. Familiarity with the seniority system in Japanese managers made it more difficult for them to change their minds regarding the giving of differential treatment to subordinates.

Dysfunctional management practices at that point led to restructuring in many companies, but some aspects of *nihonteki keiei* such as *haichitekan* (配置転換; job rotation system) and cutting overtime work mitigated the effects to some degree. According to the Statistics Bureau (2015b), the labor participation rate in Japan between 1970 and 2014 showed no significant economic deterioration effects in the 1990s, just after the bubble economy. The practices of *nihonteki keiei*, including the seniority pay and promotion system, persist and are unlikely to disappear in the near future (Toyokeizai, 2015).

After 2000

Reports of the end of *nihonteki keiei* or lifetime employment and the seniority pay and promotion system became a standard feature in newspaper and magazine articles, yet evidence pointed to the persistent nature of these practices (Abegglen, 2006). Abegglen argued that even during the economic crisis between 1992 and 2000, employment tenure in Japan was considerably longer than in the United States and the 14 countries of the European Union (Auer & Cazes, 2003) and long-term employment was generally maintained. Table 7.1 and Figure 7.1 both show the low turnover rate of Japanese employees during the economic recession (Statistics Bureau, 2009, 2015a; Cabinet Office, 1998, 2003, 2008). Although the turnover rate of the younger group was high in Japan, it was still very

Table 7.1 *Labor Turnover Rate in Japan, 1990–2013*

1990	1995	2000	2005	2010	(%) 2013
16.8	13.5	16.0	17.5	14.5	15.6

Adopted from the Statistics Bureau (2009, 2015a)

Figure 7.1 *Career Change Experience*

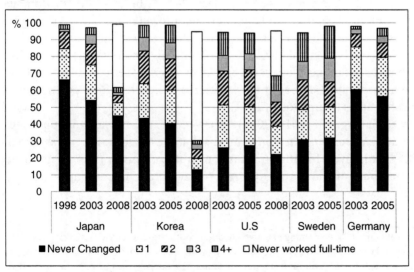

Adapted from the World census of youth (Cabinet Office, 1998; 2003; 2008)

low compared to other countries. Figure 7.1 shows the job change ratio in young people aged between 19 and 24 in five countries: Japan, Korea, the United States, Sweden, and Germany. Many young Japanese and Germans, however, had never changed jobs, while young people in other countries had had at least one if not two job changes (Cabinet Office, 1998, 2003, 2008).[2]

The introduction of *seikashugi* was often cited as a replacement for the seniority pay and promotion system, but actual practice indicated that this was not the case (Itagaki, 2011). In fact, Japanese companies began exploring a combination of several methods so the formulas changed over time; however, the basic idea behind the compensation calculation had four main elements: *nenreikyu* (年齢給; age/length of service), *shokunokyu* (職能給; ability), *yakuwarikyu* (役割給; job classification), and *seikakyu* (成果給; merit/performance) (Nippon Keidanren Jigyo Service Personnel and Wage Center, 2010). Some companies paid more attention to *yakuwarikyu* and some paid more attention to *nenreikyu*. Each company sought its own combination for its own payment systems.

A New Perspective

There have been some changes to Japanese management styles since the 1990s; however, the three main features observed by Abegglen have remained the basic management ideas. This is because *nihongata koyo shisutemu* has been the fundamental system for *nihonteki keiei*. *Nihongata koyo shisutemu*, which is also known as the *membership system*, was first observed by Hamaguchi (2009, 2011, 2014). This membership system refers to the practice in most Japanese companies where the employment contract is as a corporate member of the workforce rather than for a position with specific duties (Hamaguchi, 2011).

As Hamaguchi (2011, 2014) observed, the recruitment of employees through *shinsotsu ikkatsu saiyo* means that these people are not *shushoku* (就職; employed for their profession) but are *shusha* (就社; employed as members of the company). After they enter the company, they are

---

[2]The category of "never changed career" included both those who had never changed their career and those who had never worked. Along with the real situation in which many young people at this age are still undertaking education, the category was broken down into two different groups from 2008.

engaged in individual jobs. However, the employment contracts are not explicit, so sometimes companies transfer employees to other jobs if a position is no longer necessary. At the same time, *haichitenkan* is also often practiced in Japanese companies. However, since employees are treated as members of the workforce, they cannot be easily laid off. As a result, employees are able to have a long-term job (Hamaguchi, 2014). Although in most societies, it is common to outline the professional duties in an employment contract, the employment contract in Japan is based on hiring new graduates as members of the company rather than for a specific set of skills.

As mentioned above, Japanese companies hire employees with an employment contract that does not outline specific professional duties. This leads to the need for a unique scale to determine salaries. As previously stated, although there are other methods, most Japanese companies use (1) length of service and (2) age as the most important indicators when determining salaries, which usually has annual increase. Therefore, Japanese companies continue to use a salary system based on seniority. However, salary increases are not the same for everyone, as companies still determine differences through personnel assessments. The objective element in these assessments is based on visible results, but there are also subjective elements assessed such as (1) job performance skills, (2) willingness to do individual duties, and (3) the degree of effort put into the job. These subjective elements are determined by the Human Resource departments in each company. Hamaguchi (2011) speculated that company loyalty plays a greater role in salary assessment than skill levels. Moreover, in conjunction with this system, significant bonuses which are proportional to the length of service are often paid twice yearly. In addition, benefits such as retirement plans (favoring long-service workers) and welfare costs for residences, meals, and entertainment are based on company membership (Hamaguchi, 2009).

When employees are forced to switch duties due to technological innovations and/or when there is a corporate restructuring caused by a deterioration in business conditions, the enterprise trade unions obtain information from both the management and the employees, and then information exchange takes place, with the main purpose being to maintain employee membership. In other words, the goal is to minimize the possibility of laying off employees or forcing employees to compromise on working conditions or salary (Hamaguchi, 2009).

■ Effects of the Japanese Employment System

Effect on the "Employees"

As mentioned above, the essence of the Japanese employment system, such as employment contracts without specific duties, supports the following: (1) lifetime employment, (2) seniority, and (3) enterprise trade unions. Therefore, this makes it possible for employees to stay in a position for the long term (Hamaguchi, 2009, 2014). If an employee does not move to another company (which breaks the loyalty to the original company), salary increases and promotions are given based on years of service.

In such a system, the employees are unable to acquire any specific skills in advance because they are unsure about which job they will be assigned to. This system is therefore also understood by those seeking a job. As job seekers are not expected to have any specific skill set, they are assessed based on the qualities required to fit with the company ethos. Employees receive education and training within the company after they enter the organization (Hamaguchi, 2014). The so-called Off-JT (off-the-job training) and OJT (on-the-job training) are used for job education and training, with Off-JT used for introductory basic training through lectures. OJT is used to learn the skills needed for gathering real work experience under the guidance of a boss or senior employee in the workplace. In these cases, the boss or senior employee is responsible for leading and training the new staff on specific work assignments (Hamaguchi, 2014).

Further, under this operating system, it is difficult for employees to take a new position with another company. From the corporate side, companies do not welcome people who switch job(s) as each company often has its own graduate recruitment system. Moreover, from the employee side, such a move represents a betrayal of the original company. Therefore, if people move to another company, their salary and years of service status are reset and restarted from zero. Therefore, it is very disadvantageous for employees to move from their original company.

After new graduates are hired, they are required to work long hours until they retire and have no right to refuse a transfer to another position as the Japanese emphasis on membership is not limited to a certain time or place (Hamaguchi, 2014). In most Japanese companies, a person's work is not clearly differentiated from another person's work and, as all employees are company members, many tasks are completed through collaboration and cooperation.

Assisting colleagues with their work after one's own work is completed shows that the employee is a good member of the company. Leaving work after finishing all the assigned work without helping others is interpreted as being unfaithful to the company and also to colleagues. As a result, employees have long working hours. In addition, as Japanese companies avoid laying off employees through job rotation systems, employees are obliged to respond to any company order. Even if employees are transferred to another branch of the company far away, they are expected to accept the assignment without complaint.

"Temporary Employees": Female Employees

This membership agreement with the company until retirement is granted mainly to male employees. In contrast, many female employees have a shorter membership agreement, which ceases at marriage and/or childbirth, although this is not explicitly stated (Hamaguchi, 2011). The Ministry of Health, Labour and Welfare (2009) reported that women's labor participation rate declined at marriage, childbirth, and child care ages (in their late 20s and early 30s) (Iwai, 2013), primarily because of the clear gender labor division in work assignments. Moreover, the Japanese system was created for male employees, placing female employees in a very disadvantageous position. Female employees who are married or have children are expected to be responsible for housework and child care, so it is therefore difficult for them to work overtime every day or accept transfers, meaning they are unable to devote themselves to their work in the same way as the male employees. Therefore, Japanese female employees are more likely to work over a shorter period of time than male employees, with many employed in assistant positions, the so-called *ippannshoku* (一般職; support and/or clerical staff) (Ehara & Yamada, 2003; Yamaguchi, 2007).

In recent years, when Japanese female employees leave their jobs, many tend to return after child rearing (Ministry of Health, Labour and Welfare, 2009). However, as described above, if a person leaves the workplace for a while, it is very difficult to return as a full-time employee, so many women often work part time.

Nonregular Employees

Currently, the number of people working as "nonregular employees" has increased for both men and women (Iwai, 2010, 2013). Employees who sign an employment contract for nonregular employment usually work for a fixed period of time. After the fixed period expires, the workers renew their employment contracts. However, as they are not considered to have a membership contract with the company, they are excluded from the Japanese-style employment system, so this type of employment tends to be unstable and has few welfare benefits.

■ Features of Professional Relationships and Communication Practices in Japan

Through the membership contract as discussed above, the Japanese management system is based on a Japanese employment system in which companies bind workers through an employment contract to be a corporate member of the workforce with no specific duties (Hamaguchi, 2009, 2011, 2013, 2014). The influence of the Japanese employment system on professional relationships and communication in terms of decision making, leadership, and teamwork is illustrated in Figure 7.2. Details of this figure are clarified in the following sections.

Decision Making

Generally, there are two decision making styles in Japan. The first is a top-down style, in which the leader gathers as much information as possible, makes decisions based on the information, and then informs subordinates about the decisions. The second is a bottom-up style, in which the subordinates collect the required information, make decisions, and then send these to the leader, after which the leader makes revisions or additions if necessary (Kuwada & Tao, 1998). Most Japanese companies use the bottom-up style in a typical system known as *ringi seido* (稟議制度; reaching a decision by circulating *ringi-sho*) and *nemawashi* (根回し; consensus building) (Abegglen & Stalk, 1985; Chen, 2004; Ishiguro, 2012; Zhou, 2007).

Most Japanese companies practice *ringi seido*. A *ringi-sho* (稟議書; request for approval) is developed for a certain issue and is then circulated to all relevant middle managers who make changes and improvements if

Figure 7.2 *Features of the Japanese Employment System and Communication*

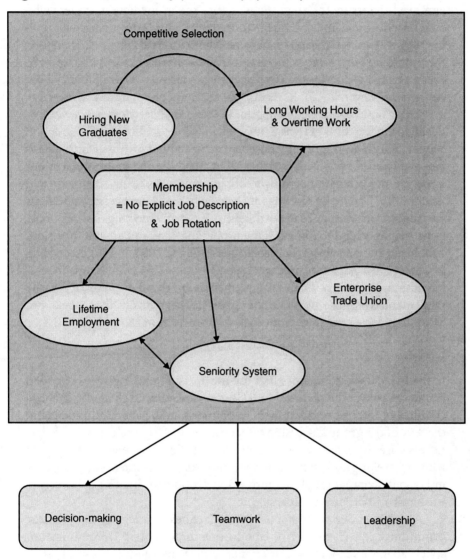

necessary, and give their stamp of approval. When all middle managers have approved the issue, the *ringi-sho* is sent to the immediate managers who read the document and give their endorsement. This process continues until the *ringi-sho* reaches the top management level for final approval. Therefore, the process of *ringi seido* is hierarchical and consensus oriented. However, everyone involved receives an opportunity to voice his or her opinion before consensus (Meyer, 2015). In most Japanese companies, informal meetings are held to build consensus, and, prior to the formal decision, *nemawashi*, or dealing with the roots of trees, is utilized, in which opinions and support are sought. This is an important consensus achievement process which avoids any awkward direct confrontations that may disrupt internal harmony. However, it is a lengthy process to obtain consensus using *ringi seido* and *nemawashi*. "Too many meetings are held, with many unnecessary questions and suggestions raised. To make things worse, many meetings are very long, as participants tend to follow all the proper motions and are not forthright with ideas that may upset their colleagues" (Chen, 2004, p. 156). According to Chen (2004), Japanese managers spend around 40% of their time in conferences and meetings. Once an agreement is approved, however, it is easily implemented because everyone concerned has been involved, so it becomes easier to receive assistance from each relevant section (Nishida, 2007).

Leadership

In many Japanese companies that use the decision making style described above, the role of the organizational leader is to adjust differences, manage conflicts of interest or differences in opinions, and, generally, understand the flow of the group discussion rather than to have specialized knowledge. Leaders are expected to understand the emotional aspects of the people who are seeking to resolve issues (Kume, 2001). In other words, leaders in Japanese companies place more emphasis on coordinating subordinate work rather than direct leadership.

Another common characteristic of Japanese leaders is high-context communication (Hall, 1976). Due to this high-context communication style, Japanese leaders do not explicitly give instructions; instead, they give subordinates the basic framework and content of the work and then each subordinate takes charge of his or her respective task (Nishida, 2007). Japanese leaders also expect subordinates to proactively understand the intentions of the task (Ishiguro, 2012); in other words, the subordinates are expected to determine the best way to do the work.

Japanese leaders adopt a high-context communication style because of the features of O-type (Organic-type) organizations (Hayashi, 1994; Ishiguro, 2012; Tsukada, 2013). The features of an O-type organization include maintaining ambiguity regarding the range of work for individual employees and, for this reason, members of the organization work jointly through consultation. Hayashi (1994) called this consulting area a "green area" where employees "form strategic consensus under one purpose and identity" (p. 58). Hayashi (1994) also described the "green area" as a communication matrix made up of a large number of employees who work together. Members have to complete the work in the "green area" cooperatively and collaboratively. An O-type organization differs from an M-type (Mechanistic-type) organization in that the work range for individuals in an M-type organization is clear and the tasks are distributed so there is no "green area."

Therefore, it can be seen that the O-type organization is characterized by a lack of specific duties in the employment contract. Ishiguro (2012) described the features of the Japanese leader as follows:

(1) Japanese leaders seek the consensus of members in decision-making while respecting the groups and consider human relationships within the organization; (2) Instructions to followers are non-explicit and the followers are expected to understand the intentions of the leader; and (3) Japanese leaders expect followers to properly act by understanding the situation, and filling in the "green area" which is not explicit on roles and responsibilities of work (pp. 123–124).

Teamwork

Many Japanese companies place emphasis on employee teamwork, so sharing information is essential. Experienced employees assist new staff to gain skills through teamwork. In addition, an unstated rule is that the outcomes of the team belong to the team rather than to any individual employee (Nishida, 2007). Employees are required to do projects as a team, so team members must work together to achieve the team goals. In many Japanese companies, work problems are solved in the team instead of blaming the person who may be responsible. In other words, it "is desirable to help each other voluntarily and resiliently" (Hayashi, 1985, p. 58).

Specifically, if a problem occurs, first, everyone in the involved team discusses the nature of the problem. Then, the team determines "why the problem occurred" rather than assigning blame, after which solutions as to "what should be done, who should be in charge, and what kind of project should be launched" are discussed (Hayashi, 1994, p. 58). In case of a problem, the whole team takes responsibility and the individual who caused the problem and/or is in charge is not usually personally blamed (Nishida, 2007).

Formal vs. Informal Communication

In Japanese firms, bottom-up and horizontal formal communications are the key to smooth and effective business operations (see Decision Making above). However, both informal and formal communications need to be examined. On appointment, new employees are given *nyushashiki* (入社式; enter in company ceremony) followed by group activity- based induction training, during which they are required to understand the corporate mission, slogans, history and philosophy. The new employees in the same induction training sessions become *douki* (同期; cohorts), so are expected to continue to associate with each other even in private (Nishiyama, 2012). Although the new generation of Japanese employees are not particularly fond of this type of induction, they are often forced to accept these traditional practices, which help establish close relationships and group cohesiveness, thus forming the basis for effective future teamwork.

Whether loose or tight, there are often groups called *habatsu* (派閥; cliques) within the company, which are often based on where people come from (place of birth) and where they graduated. For instance, employees who graduated from a certain university give personal favors to new recruits from the same university in exchange for their loyalty, thus creating a mutually dependent relationship (Nishiyama, 2012).

Outside the company, drinking after work with colleagues is still an important communication tool in Japan, although it is not as vibrant as it used to be. Dai-Ichi Life Research Institute Inc. (2007) revealed that many employees thought drinking after work with colleagues was fun (69.8%) and necessary (61.1%), but the tendency was higher in the male management level employees than female, which explains why the membership system is dominated by male employees, who enjoy collecting information and strengthening personal ties with other employees outside the hierarchical and formal communication channels.

After 2000, due to the development of new communication technology such as groupware and Social Networking Services (SNS), internal work communication other than face-to-face has become robust and has influenced employee organizational and interpersonal communication. Groupware is mainly used to share internal information such as formal documents, whereas SNS, which includes an internal Facebook, promotes interpersonal communication between employees (Abe, 2011; Fukuda, 2013). Many large Japanese corporations used to strengthen horizontal employee ties by sponsoring internal club activities and retreats; however, the economic crisis reduced finances and many companies could no longer afford these activities. Recently, however, SNS has revitalized horizontal and informal employee communication (Wada & Yamazaki, 2007). For example, in one company, there are several communities on the message board, such as employee groups that care for children and ramen noodle lovers, who are able to exchange ideas and opinions and socialize. Another company created an SNS so as to keep in contact with former female employees who may be able to substitute for current female employees on maternity leave (Wada & Yamazaki, 2007). Therefore, new media technology has expanded workplace communication.

■ Developing Relationships and Communicating in Japan

Given the discussion of the Japanese employment system and its influence on professional relationships and communication, this section examines a series of studies to elucidate how Japanese employees develop relationships and communicate.

Nishida's research group (2002, 2007, 2008), including the authors of this chapter, conducted extensive studies on expatriate Japanese working in overseas Japanese subsidiaries in China, the U, Malaysia, and the Philippines. This research revealed that the Japanese employees had noticed the different work practices of their local colleagues. Japanese expatriate employees often felt it was difficult to work with their local counterparts because of the communication differences.

Table 7.2 gives information about the issues Japanese employees find difficult when dealing with the five host country employees in four

Table 7.2 *Difficult Work Behavior (Japanese Employees' Comments on Host Employees)*

	Toward Chinese in China	n = 76
1	Not working as a team	42 (55.3%)
2	Communicating in Chinese at work	39 (51.3%)
3	Only do their own work	38 (50%)
4	Not reporting about their work	37 (48.7%)
5	Not actively working	37 (48.7%)
	Toward Chinese in Malaysia	**n = 30**
1	Not seeking the cause of problems	14 (46.7%)
2	Easily quit job	12 (40%)
3	Only do their own work	11 (36.7%)
4	Not actively working	10 (33.3%)
4	Not asking questions when they do not understand the details of their work	10 (33.3%)
	Toward Malays in Malaysia	**n = 30**
1	Not seeking the cause of problems	14 (46.7%)
2	Low quality control and office management ability	12 (40%)
2	Not keeping time	11 (36.7%)
4	Easily quit the job	10 (33.3%)
4	Not asking questions when they do not understand the details of their work	10 (33.3%)
	Toward Americans	**n = 56**
1	Communicating in English	28 (50%)
2	Low quality control and office management ability	25 (44.6%)
3	Easily quit job	21 (37.5%)

Table 7.2 *Continued*

3	Need detailed instructions	21 (37.5%)
5	Not reporting about their work	14 (25%)
	Toward Filipinos	*n* = 21
1	Not keeping time	13 (61.9%)
1	Not actively working	13 (61.9%)
3	Not seeking the cause of problems	12 (57.1%)
4	Being late for work	11 (52.4%)
4	Not asking questions when they do not understand the details of their work	11 (52.4%)
4	Not giving clear opinions	11 (52.4%)
4	Need detailed instructions	11 (52.4%)
4	Need a lot of attention	11 (52.4%)

Adapted from Nishida (2008)

countries: the Chinese in China, the Chinese in Malaysia, the Malays in Malaysia, the Filipinos, and the Americans. Some issues commonly reported in most Asian countries were as follows: "not seeking the causes of the problems," "not working actively; doing only what is requested," and "not asking questions when they don't understand the details of their work." In particular, Japanese expatriates frequently reported that their Filipino colleagues "did not keep time" and "were late for work" and found that the Chinese in China "did not work as a team." As stated above, unclear job descriptions, which is a major part of the Japanese membership system, instills within Japanese employees a mindset to share work with others and to work as a team. Further, they are expected to stay at work even when they have finished their own work so as to give a helping hand to others. In other words, Japanese employees expected the host country employees to work according to Japanese cultural norms, so this failure to meet their expectations gave them considerable stress.

On the other hand, host country employees felt it was difficult to work with Japanese because: "they spent a long-time making decisions," "did not clearly express their opinions," "had odd ways of giving instructions," and had a "payment system based on seniority" (see Table 7.3). Some Japanese employment practices and communication practices made it difficult for the host country employees to cope with the Japanese employees. These findings were consistent with what has been discussed above in terms of decision making, leadership, and the seniority system, which are well-known features of Japanese leadership and employment practices.

In short, Nishida's findings clearly illustrate the unique features of Japanese professional relationships and communication and elucidate the

Table 7.3 *Difficult Behavior at Work (Host Employees' Comments on Japanese)*

	Chinese	n = 105
1	Long time spent in decision making	52 (49.5%)
2	Insufficient language competence in Chinese	49 (46.7%)
3	Not understanding Chinese way of working	35 (33.3%)
4	Payment based on a seniority system	32 (30.5%)
4	Reactions to requesting a salary increase	32 (30.5%)
	Chinese in Malaysia	**n = 29**
1	Not clearly expressing their opinions	17 (58.6%)
2	The way they give instructions	10 (34.5%)
2	Language problems	10 (34.5%)
4	Payment based on a seniority system	9 (31%)
5	Long time spent on decision making	8 (27.6%)
	Malays in Malaysia	**n = 30**
1	The way they give instructions	13 (43.3%)
2	Not clearly expressing their opinions	12 (40%)

Table 7.3 *Continued*

3	Long time spent on decision making	11 (36.7%)
4	Language problems	9 (30%)
5	Not listening to others' opinions	8 (26.7%)
	Americans	**n = 74**
1	The way they discuss things	27 (36.5%)
1	The way they share information	27 (36.5%)
3	How to say "No"	20 (27%)
4	Long time spent on decision making	19 (25.7%)
5	Communicating in English	17 (23%)
	Filipinos	**n = 50**
1	Scolding in front of others	14 (28%)
2	Not clearly expressing their opinions	12 (24%)
3	Disfavor due to changing jobs	11 (22%)
3	Long time spent on decision making	11 (22%)
3	Disrespecting the family	11 (22%)

Adapted from Nishida (2008)

possible Japanese relationship development and communication problems when dealing with non-Japanese in business settings.

Summary

This chapter has discussed Japanese professional relationships and communication practices through an examination of several Japanese employment system aspects such as the importance of the company membership system, lifetime employment, the seniority system, and enterprise trade unions. Although the three main pillars of Japanese company culture (lifetime employment, the seniority system, and enterprise trade unions) have been under significant pressure to change due to economic deterioration, and there have been in fact some changes in many companies, these pillars are still viable in practice and helpful in understanding Japanese relationship building and communication at work in such areas as decision making, leadership, teamwork, and informal communication.

References

Abe, M. (2011). Henkeru Japan: Furiiadoresuya ITkankyono seibinadoga shanaikomyunikeishonwo unagasu [Henkel Japan: Free address system and IT environment promote internal communication]. *Jinji Jitsumu, 48* (1104), 24–29.

Abegglen, J. C. (1958). *Nihonno keiei* (K. Urabe, Trans.). Diamond Press. (Reprinted from *The Japanese factory: Aspects of its social organization,* J. C. Abegglen, 1958, Glencoe, IL: The Free Press)

Abegglen, J. C. (2006). *21st-century Japanese management: New systems, lasting values.* NY: Palgrave Macmillan.

Abegglen, J., & Stalk, Jr. G. (1985). *Kaisha the Japanese corporation: How marketing, money, and manpower strategy, not management style, make the Japanese world pace-setters.* New York: Basic Books, Inc.

Auer, P., & Cazes, S. (Eds.). (2003). *Employment stability in an age of flexibility: Evidence from industrialized countries.* Geneva: International Labor Office.

Cabinet Office (1998, 2003, 2008). *World census of youth.* Retrieved from http://www8.cao.go.jp/youth/kenkyu.htm

Chen, M. (2004). *Asian management systems* (2nd ed.). London: Thomson Learning.

Dai-Ichi Life Research Institute Inc. (2007). *Shokubano komyunikeishonnikansuru ankeitochousa* [Survey studies on communication at work]. Retrieved from http://group.dai-ichi-life.co.jp/dlri/ldi/news/news0711.pdf

Ehara, Y., & Yamada, M. (2003). Yuragu nihonkata koyou [Wavering Japanese employment). In Y. Ehara, & M. Yamada (Eds.), *Jenda no shakaigaku* [Sociology of gender revised edition] (pp. 104–109). Housoudaigaku kyoikushinkoukai.

Fukuda, A. (2013). Shanai koyunikeishonniokeru "shanai SNS" no koukatekina katsuyouhou [Effective usage of "internal SNS" on internal communication]. *Jinji Jitsumu, 50* (1125), 26–30.

Hall, E. T. (1976). *Beyond culture.* New York: Anchor Books.

Hamaguchi, K. (2009). *Atarashi roudou shakai: Koyou shisutemu no saikouchikue* [New Labor Society: To reconstruct the employment system]. Iwanami Shinsho.

Hamaguchi, K. (2011). *Nihon no koyou to roudouhou* [Employment and labor law in Japan]. Nihon Keizai Shinbun Shuppansha.

Hamaguchi, K. (2013). *Wakamono to roudou "nyusha" no shikumi kara tokihogusu* [Young people and labor deciphering through "entering the company"]. Chuou Shinsho Rakure.

Hamaguchi, K. (2014). *Nihon no koyou to chukounen* [Japanese employment and persons of middle or advanced age]. Chikuma Shinsho.

Hayashi, K. (1985). *Ibunka inta-feisu kanri* [Intercultural interface management] Yuuhikaku.

Hayashi, K. (1994) *Ibunka inta-feisu keiei kokusaika to nihontekikeiei* [Intercultural interface management: Globalization and Japanese management]. Nihon Keizai Shinbun Shuppansha.

Higashimura, T., & Harvard University. Program on U.S.-Japan Relations. (1997). *Japanese-style/American-style: Management to meet the global challenge.* Cambridge, MA: Harvard University.

Ishiguro, T. (2012). *Tabunka soshiki no nihonjin riidaa zou: Raifusutoori intabyuu kara no apurouchi* [Japanese leadership in multicultural organization: From life history interviews]. Shumpusha.

Itagaki, H. (2011). The Japanese management system and the corporate strategies of Japanese companies. In T. Kawamura (Ed.), *Hybrid factories in the United States: The Japanese-style management and production system under the global economy* (pp. 53–74). Oxford, UK: Oxford University Press.

Iwai, H. (2010). A study of changes in the postwar Japanese life course: A research perspective of JGSS-2009 life course study and results of preliminary analysis. *JGSS Research Series, 7*, 193–204.

Iwai, H. (2013). Sengo nihongata raifukosu no henyou to kazoku syugi [Changes in the postwar Japanese life course and familism]. In E. Ochiai (Ed.), *Shinmituken to koukyouken no saihensei ajia kindai kara no toi* [Reconstruction of the Intimate and public spheres in modern Asia] (pp. 127–153). Kyotodaigaku Gakujutsu Shuppansha.

Kono, D. (2012). Dorakkaacho "Maneijimento" niokeru "nihongatakeiei"ronto sonokanrenno keieigakukakuron ["Japanese style management" and its related theories in "Management" by Dracker]. *Keieiryokusoseikenkyu, 8*, 19–29.

Kume, T. (2001). Syuudan/soshikinai no ishikettei shiron [Decision-making in groups and organizations] In S. Ishi, T. Kume, & J. Toyama (Eds.), *Ibunka komyunikeishon no riron* [Theories of intercultural communication] (pp. 177–188). Yuuhikaku.

Kuwada, K., & Tao, M. (1998). *Soshikiron* [Organizational studies]. Yuuhikaku.

Matanle, P. (2006). Beyond lifetime employment? Re-fabricating Japan's employment culture. In P. Matanle, & W. Lunsing (Eds.), *Perspectives on work, employment and society in Japan* (pp. 58–77). Hampshire, UK: Palgrave Macmillan.

McCann, L., Hassard, J., & Morris, J. (2006). Hard times for the salaryman: Corporate restructuring and middle managers' working lives. In P. Matanle, & W. Lunsing (Eds.), *Perspectives on work, employment and society in Japan* (pp. 98–116). Hampshire, UK: Palgrave Macmillan.

Ministry of Economy, Trade, and Industry (2012). *The number of small and medium sized enterprises*. Retrieved from http://www.meti.go.jp/press/2013/12/20131226006/20131226006.html

Ministry of Health, Labour and Welfare (2009). *Hataraku jyosei no jitujyou* [Female workers' current condition]. Retrieved from http://www.mhlw.go.jp/bunya/koy oukintou/josei-jitsujo/dl/09c.pdf

Meyer, E. (2015). *The culture map breaking through the invisible boundaries of global business*. US: Public Affairs.

Nippon Keidanren Jigyo Service Personnel and Wage Center (2010). *Yakuwari/koukendo chingin: Seikashugi jinji chingin seidono saisekkei* [Role/Contribution-based wage: Redesign of merit-based personnel and wage system]. Nippon Keidanren Shuppan.

Nishida, H. (Ed.). (2002). *Malaysia, Philippines shinshutsu nikkeikigyouni okeru ibunkakan komyunikeishon masatsu* [Intercultural communication conflicts at Japanese overseas subsidiaries in Malaysia and the Philippines]. Tagashuppan.

Nishida, H. (Ed.). (2007). *Beikoku, chugoku shinshutsu nikkeikigyouni okeru ibunkakan komyunikeishon masatsu* [Intercultural communication conflicts at Japanese overseas subsidiaries in the United States and China]. Kazamashobou.

Nishida, H. (2008). Kaigaishinshutsu nikkeikigyoha naniwosubekika: chousakekkakara mietekitakoto [What should overseas Japanese subsidiaries do?: Things revealed through our research]. In H. Nishida (Ed.), *Gurobaru shakainiokeru ibunkakan komyunikeishon* [Intercultural communication in global society] (pp. 289–310). Kazamashobou.

Nishiyama, K. (2012). Japanese style decision making in business organizations. In L. A. Samovar, R. E. Porter, & E. R. McDniel (Eds.), *Intercultural communication: A reader* (13th ed.). International Edition (pp. 331–412). Boston: Wadsworth Publishing Co. Inc.

Shimizu, S. (2014). *Japanese-style management: From crisis to reformation in the age of Abenomics.* London: LID Publishing Ltd.

Statistics Bureau, Ministry of Internal Affairs and Communications (2009, 2015a). *Regular employees hiring rate and turnover rate by industry.* Retrieved from http://www.stat.go.jp/data/nihon/16.htm

Statistics Bureau, Ministry of Internal Affairs and Communications (2015b). Labor force survey long time series. Retrieved from http://www.stat.go.jp/data/roudou/longtime/03roudou.htm

Toyokeizai (2015, May). Nihongata koyosisutem daikaibou [Examination of Japanese employment system]. *Weekly Toyokeizai* (6596), 42–89.

Tsukada, S. (2013). Nihon kigyo ni okeru shokuba manejimento no tokucho to josei katsuyaku shuishin [Characteristics of workplace management and the expansion of women's roles in Japanese corporations]. *Kikan seisaku keiei kenkyu [Quarterly Journal of Public Policy & Management],* 2, 23–30.

Urabe, K. (2011). *HRgaido: Jinjibuhatu IT medianokatuyou* [HR guide: Application of IT media from human resources]. *Jinji Management,* 21 (11), 13–25.

Wada, M., & Yamazaki, H. (2007). Nettode kigyoufuudokaikaku: SNS-gakaeru shanaikomyunikeishon [IT changes corporate culture: SNS changes internal communication]. *Economist, 85* (30), 76–78.

Watanabe, S. (2015). *Guroobarukanonakano nihongata keiei: Posuto shijoshugino chosen* [Japanese management system in globalization: Challenge of post free market economics]. Dobunkanshuppan.

Yamaguchi, I. (2007). The differences in communication climate and perceived organizational justice between male and female workers in Japanese workplace. *Human Communication Studies, 35,* 93–107.

Yoshino, N., & Nakahigashi, M. (2010). Japanese economic history: Overview. In N. Yoshino, M. Lacktorin, H. Chuma, Y. Aso, M. Nakahigashi, & M. Nakata (Eds.), *The postwar Japanese economy* (3–39). Yuhikaku.

Zhou, B. L. (2007). *Nikkei kigyo ga chugoku de seikou su ru tame ni: Ibunka keiei ga cyokumen suru kadai* [For Japanese companies succeed in China: Tasks of transcultural management]. Kouyoushobou.

Author Note

The second author would like to give her special thanks to Takaaki Yuzawa, for his great help in editing English expressions.

CHAPTER 8
FAMILY RELATIONSHIPS AND COMMUNICATION IN SOUTH KOREA

JUYOUNG JANG, SOYOUNG LEE,
MIAI SUNG, AND JAERIM LEE

South Korean (Korean hereafter) families have a long history of being close, supportive, and intimately involved in one another's lives, but with the rapid industrialization and modernization of Korea, families are in transition. Traditional[1] Korean families have been governed by strong familism which is a value orientation or an ideology emphasizing cohesive family relations that prioritize familial interests over individual desires and filial piety underscoring the devotion to parents and the succession of the patrilineal bloodline (Ok, 2011). This foundation of familism has functioned as a coping strategy for Koreans as they adapt to rapid social changes and has helped them be resilient under various crisis events including the period of Japanese colonial rule, the Korean War, and the Asian financial crisis in the late 1990s (Chang, 2011). It has also been the backbone of familial support and collectivistic resource management. Although the core values of familism have remained the same through the years, Korean families have altered the characteristics of familism to optimize family functions and to satisfy social demands and challenges. In this chapter, we illustrate the family dynamics and communication within the changing sociocultural contexts in Korea. First, we start by describing the changes in family ideologies and demographics in Korea. Then, we illustrate the shifting couple and parent–child relationships and communication based on family

---

[1]Throughout this chapter, the word "traditional" refers to the characteristics of Korean families that were prevalent after the mid-seventeenth century before modern Korea. Confucian family norms were much less strong in earlier times of the Korean history.

Contributed by Juyoung Jang, Soyoung Lee, Miai Sung, and Jaerim Lee. Copyright © Kendall Hunt Publishing Company.

developmental stages: young adulthood and early couple relationships, parenthood, and the empty nest period. Finally, we describe the characteristics of family relationships beyond couple and parent–child relationships (i.e., sibling relationships and extended families).

■ Changes in Family Ideology and Demographic Trends in Korea

Family Ideologies and Korean Families

Confucian family ideology might be what most people imagine when they think of Korean families. Although family relationships have somewhat changed in recent years, the influence of this ideology with regard to traditional family relationships is still prevalent in Korea (Han & Lee, 2016). This ideology defines family relationships according to a hierarchical order by generation and gender and clearly defines family members' obligations (Chang, 2011). It also stresses the patrilineal parent–child relationship. Traditional Korean family relationships were based on the Confucian family ideology, and the ideal family structure was the "stem" family (Yi, 1998) where the eldest son continued the family lineage and resided with his parents after marriage. Other sons lived in their own homes and had fewer family responsibilities and privileges than the oldest son. Married daughters were considered members of their husbands' families and had no family responsibility or inheritance rights in their family of origin.

Marriage was considered a unification of two families in traditional Korea, and thus arranged marriages were common (Kim & Tasker, 2013). Traditionally, the marital relationship was established based on *boo-wi-boo-gang* (부위부강; the husband's leadership and wife's obedience) and *boo-boo-yu-byel* (부부유별; gender differences in power, roles, courtesy, and systems) grounded in Confucianism. Neglecting family members was considered especially shameful according to Confucian ethics (Yang & Rosenblatt, 2001). Thus, a major responsibility within Korean families was ensuring the well-being of family members, especially children and the elderly. Although these traditional views are changing, they are still a strong norm in Korean families today.

Hyo (효; filial piety), a core value of Confucian family ethics, means that children should be responsible for their parents' physical and emotional well-being by respecting, honoring, and caring for their parents

(Sung, 2011). The moral reasoning of filial piety is that children ought to return the parents' endless love and devotion. Although weakened and transformed, filial piety is still practiced and endorsed in modern Korea.

Since the Korean War in the mid-twentieth century, several modified family ideologies have emerged in the process of "compressed modernization" (Chang, 2011). Most family dynamics and communication can be understood within the context of these family ideologies in Korea because they illustrate the family values that have been shaped by social changes. Three other major family ideologies currently exist in Korea in addition to the Confucian family ideology: instrumental family ideology, affectionate family ideology, and individualistic family ideology (Chang, 2011). Instrumental family ideology places a high value on providing instrumental and strategic support for family members' social achievements as the main function of the family. Affectionate family ideology, on the other hand, emphasizes providing emotional protection for family members as the main purpose of the family. Finally, individualistic family ideology respects individuality and gender equality in families' roles and responsibilities. These family ideologies have emerged sequentially in the last 50 years and have existed simultaneously in Korea rather than shifting from one to another (Chang, 2011; Sung & Lee, 2013). This coexistence of multiple family ideologies could cause tensions within families and society and complicate family dynamics in modern Korean society (Chang, 2011). For example, eliminating the head of family system and the family register law[2] in the mid-2000s has contributed to the growth of egalitarian and individualistic family ideologies among women and the younger generations, but it may have created a substantial generation gap with older generations endorsing the Confucian family ideology.

---

[2]The Korean Family Register Law established in 1960 was an identification system that documented the status of individuals regarding their relation to the head of the family, the patrilineal successor (ho-ju; 호주). Under the law, a male linear descendant was given priority as the family head, followed by a female descendant and then the wife. This system restricted women's legal rights because a woman's identity belonged to either her father's or husband's family identifying her as the father's daughter or husband's wife. In 2008, the Family Relation Registration Law replaced the Family Register Law, so individuals now register under their own record containing information on their family members (i.e., parents, spouse, children) and events (e.g., birth, marriage, divorce). It also allows children to use their mother's surname or to change their surname following their parents' divorce or adoption. Overall, these changes have strengthened individuals' rights.

Demographic Changes and Diverse Korean Families

The birth rate in Korea has decreased to one of the lowest levels in the world. The total fertility rate in 2014 was 1.21, which was next to Hong Kong and Macao (Korean Population, Health, and Welfare Association, 2014). The low birth rate is tightly linked to social forces such as the high cost of childrearing and education, the increase in women working, the tendency to delay or avoid marriage, and the Korean government's strong family planning initiatives in the 1970s and 1980s (Chin, Lee, Lee, Son, & Sung, 2012; Eun, 2011). Accordingly, the meaning of having children has slowly shifted from a normative developmental task in early adulthood and the succession of a patrilineal family to either an emotional reward or a burdensome investment (Ok, 2011).

The marriage and divorce trends also reveal changing family values. Under the Confucian family ideology, social norms regarding marriage and marital stability were strongly enforced in Korea (Anderson & Kohler, 2012). The crude marriage rate has declined over the last forty years from 9.2 in 1970 to 6.0 in 2014, and the age of the first marriage increased over 5 years, on average, from age 27.2 for men and 23.3 for women in 1970 to 32.4 for men and 29.8 for women in 2014 (Statistics Korea, 2014a). At the same time, the divorce rate nearly doubled; the crude divorce rate went from 0.4 in 1970 to 2.3 in 2013, and 28.8% of those divorced in 2014 had been married for 20 years or more (Statistics Korea, 2014a). These trends reflect the substantial attitude shifts toward marriage (Chung, 2011). Whereas marriage was once viewed as an institution and a passage to adulthood, the pursuit of intimacy and affection has become more important, and consequently, there has been a growing tendency to value marital satisfaction over marital stability (Lee, 2011; Ryu, 2013).

Single parents. As the divorce rate increases, the number of single-parent families also has increased. About 9% of households in Korea were single-parent families in 2010, and 78.2% of these single-parent families were single mother families (Kim, Chang, Choi, Kim, & Sun, 2013). Since family cohesion and parent–child communication play positive roles in adjustment to school life for the children of single parents (Jang & Hwang, 2010), positive communication and shared family time are particularly crucial in single-parent families. However, according to a study of single parents with dependent children (Kim et al., 2013), single parents were likely to experience more difficulties in work–family balance due to the heavy burden of their parental and work roles as well as economic hardships and challenges concerning their children's education. Unlike many single parents in Western countries, the majority of Korean single parents and their children never maintain contact with their ex-spouse or the noncustodial parent.

Transnational marriages and multicultural families. The number of labor migrants and transnational marriages in Korea has dramatically increased in the last twenty years, challenging the traditional view of Korea's ethnic homogeneity (Lim, 2010). Moving to a multicultural society has been mostly due to the upsurge of transnational marriages between Korean men in rural areas and foreign women, mostly because Korean women are less willing to marry rural Korean men who are poorer and less educated (Chin et al., 2012; Sung, 2015). Many foreign women, especially Southeast Asian women, have migrated to Korea for marriage, resulting in about 10% of the total marriages in 2010 (Statistics Korea, 2011). A unique characteristic of multiculturalism in Korea is that it has evolved to focus on the challenges in the family sphere rather than focusing on social issues related to migrant groups (Sung, 2015). Transnationally married couples may experience challenges in their relationships since they have different cultural backgrounds. Since most multicultural families are Korean husbands and foreign brides, the multicultural movement has emphasized the assimilation of these foreign brides into Korean culture and society, which reveals that traditional patriarchal family values are still deeply rooted in Korea (Lim, 2010).

Besides the cultural differences, demographic characteristics of transnational married couples (multicultural couples hereafter) are different from typical Korean couples. For example, the average age gap between spouses of multicultural couples is much larger (13 years) than that of average Korean couples (3.4 years; Statistics Korea, 2011). In addition, the period between marriage and childbirth is shorter than that of average Korean couples, which may contribute to problems in couple adjustment.

It has been reported that many migrated wives suffered from human rights violations during the mate selection and/or experienced domestic violence by their husbands (Y. K. Kim, 2010), leading to a high divorce rate among multicultural couples. Thus, the main factors in encouraging marital and life satisfaction for these couples are the husband's support, strong communication skills, and social support. These factors could contribute to increasing marital and life satisfaction and a better understanding of each spouse's cultural background (Han, 2006; E. Kim, 2010; Song & Lee, 2010).

Many children in multicultural families tend to experience difficulties developing Korean language competency because most of them are raised by their migrant mothers who might not be fluent in Korean. This language barrier could cause school adaptation problems and psychological distress (S.-H. Kim, 2011). Further, in multicultural families, the Korean father and paternal relatives often have negative attitudes toward their mothers using their native language, except for mothers who speak English or Japanese. Because of the sense of ethnic homogeneity, the Korean government did not encourage bilingual education for multicultural children until 2009 when the Korean government launched bilingual education programs for multicultural children through Multicultural Family Support Centers as part of integration and multicultural education efforts among diverse Korean families (Chung, Kim, & Lee, 2011). Still, the competitive Korean education environment and the social prejudice against diversity, especially ethnic homogeneity, make child rearing much harder for multicultural couples.

In sum, Korean families have experienced various social and demographic issues in the past few decades. Nevertheless, traditional characteristics of Korean families have not completely disappeared or transformed into new, modern characteristics. Rather, both traditional and modern characteristics coexist in Korean families, resulting in complex family interactions. These characteristics are explained in more detail in the following sections.

■ Couple and Parent–Child Relationships and Communication

Korean families tend to put a stronger emphasis on the parent–child relationship than the couple relationship, based on the influence of Confucianism. Although the idea of a "love marriage" is dominant in Korea, the marital relationship typically becomes more instrumental after the birth of a child (Chin, 2011; Sohn, 2011). The parent–child tie starts during pregnancy, which is often expressed as *tae-kyo* (태교; prenatal education) (Chung, Kang, & Kim, 2013; Y. H. Kim, 2011). The strong parent–child relationship starting before the birth of the child is a life-long process that remains cohesive even after the child reaches adulthood and becomes a parent. In the past, providing financial support for the elderly parents was children's important responsibility based on filial piety, but the obligation of supporting the parents has decreased, while the expectation of parental investment in children has increased. This trend is influenced by the desire for upward social mobility and the small number of children parents today typically have (Ok, 2011). Korean parents feel a stronger responsibility for their children's social achievement and future success compared to Western parents (Anderson & Kohler, 2012). This cultural expectation of parenting explains why strong parental control and intervention are perceived as parental affection (Song, 2015).

In Korean families, the couple relationship and parent–child relationship are intertwined throughout life due to the strong parent–child bond. The couple relationship is often shaped by their children's needs from the birth of a child into adulthood. For adult children, their couple relationship can be affected by how they interact with their own and their spouse's parents. Thus, it is difficult to describe a Korean couple's and parent and child's relationships separately. Rather, explaining how these relationships are interdependent from a family development perspective provides a better understanding of family relationships and communication within the cultural context of Korea.

Young Adulthood and New Couples

Despite the recent decline in the marriage rate, marriage is still considered an important rite of passage to become an adult in Korean culture and is a prerequisite for childbirth. For example, in 2014, more than half of Koreans over 15 years old believed that marriage was a must (15.2%) or preferred (42.1%). Only 2% of Koreans reported a negative attitude toward marriage (Statistics Korea, 2014b). Both Korean males (61.5%) and females (52.3%) reported that they believed in marriage (Statistics Korea, 2014b), although Korean males tended to more strongly endorse the importance of marriage and maintaining a family (Kim & Lee, 2003). Even though people still believe that marriage is necessary, it is noteworthy that an increasing number of younger people tend to believe that marriage is a choice rather than a must in modern Korean society (Chung & Chang, 2007).

Children's dependence on parents. Social situations in Korea such as an overemphasis on children's education and the highly competitive labor market contribute to children's delayed independence from their parents. As a result, the expectation of parental devotion has extended to young adults' marriage decisions and support. For example, the cost of a wedding and housing for newlyweds is overwhelming, so they tend to rely on their parents to help pay for these needs (Chung, 2011; Kim et al., 2012). In 2012, newlyweds spent KRW 44,680,000 (approximately USD $40,000), on average, for the wedding, and more than half of the cost was provided by their parents (Kim et al., 2012). Dual-earner couples with young children also often need support from their parents for childcare due to their reluctance to utilize nonfamily day care (Lee & Bauer, 2013).

Adult children's prolonged dependence on parents shaped by social situations contributes to strengthening parental influence (Chin, 2011; Lee, 2015). Still, Korean children seek parental consent in their choice of a spouse (Sohn, 2011). This dependence indicates that respecting parents' opinions and maintaining harmonious relationships within the family of origin are highly valued in Korean families. It is also not expected that married couples should be independent from their families of origin in Korea. In fact, maintaining positive relationships with their parents affects the marital adjustment of newlyweds (Kim & Kim, 1999). However, parental influence on spouse selection has somewhat weakened (Sohn, 2011) as attitudes toward marriage have shifted from a rite of passage to adulthood to a matter of personal choice and the pursuit of intimacy.

Parent–adult child relationships. Having a positive, harmonious parent–adult child relationship requires keeping healthy boundaries (Jang, 2015). Marriage forms a new family and brings out new and modified family roles, which requires adjusting family boundaries (S. Choi, 2015). Nevertheless, parents contact their adult children more often than not. In 2010, more than 60% of parents contacted their adult children living apart at least once a week while less than 50% of adult children contacted their parents. Interestingly, parents who were young, healthy, highly educated, and well prepared for retirement tended to contact their adult children more often than others (Cho et al., 2010). Parents and adult children talked about their domestic and family lives, work, and social news. Married children also contacted their parents-in-law. Wives contacted their parents-in-law at a similar level to their contact with their own parents, but husbands contacted their wife's parents less frequently (Cho et al., 2010).

Marital relationships. One of the most famous idioms that characterize Korean marital relationships is *il-sim-dong-chae* (일심동체), meaning that married couples have the same mind and the same body, which is a stronger expectation than the typical mutual understanding between spouses in the West. Traditionally, it was believed that good marital relationships should produce one voice and avoid conflicts in decision making.

Some scholars have recognized that this ideology might have directly and indirectly influenced couple communication in Korea (D. W. Lee, 2009). However, in modern Korean society, it has been redirected to understand that couples are two independent persons with two different mindsets and couples must understand their differences and establish their own realities through serious communication (Lee, 2002, 2009). Still, the mutual trust between spouses is considered one of the most important factors for a happy marriage in addition to love and economic stability.

The phrase *ee-sim-jun-sim* (이심전심) exemplifies the Korean couple communication style based on the mutual trust. *Ee-sim-jun-sim* means that people in close relationships can understand each other without verbal communication. Koreans tend to believe that intimate partners like long-married couples do not need many words to truly communicate what they think and how they feel. This tendency is a characteristic of cultures that use high-context communication, which is often found in cultures like Asia, Africa, Latin America, and the Middle East. High-context communication is likely to involve indirect, implicit, and nonverbal messages (Hall, 1976), and the information in these messages depends on contexts, including gestures, social customs, silence, nuance, and tone of voice (Nam, 2015).

The high-context communication style is especially prevalent in Korean families, which might explain why verbal communication is relatively limited between Korean spouses and in parent–child relationships. For example, Koreans hardly express affection to their spouse by saying "I love you" or giving a kiss or hug, which may look strange from a Western perspective. However, many Koreans do not feel the need to or feel uncomfortable using these direct and explicit messages given their high-context communication style. It might be helpful for the readers of this chapter to understand that lower levels of explicit communication between couples or between parents and children are not always a sign of negative functioning in Korean families as they might be in Western families.

Recent studies have found that how couples spend time together has a strong impact on Korean couples' marital satisfaction. Traditionally, spending time as a couple was not an important factor affecting marital satisfaction or happiness in Korea. Koreans believed that when husbands and wives performed their duties based on strict gender role divisions (i.e., the husband as the breadwinner and the wife as the caregiver), their marital relationship would be successful. In addition, due to the emphasis on the parent–child relationship over the couple relationship (Chung, 2011), the couple's marital satisfaction was often measured by how their children performed as successful citizens and family members. In fact, Korean couples experience more conflicts over the education of their children than over issues regarding their spouse or marital relationship (Cho et al., 2010). Further, the amount of time Korean couples spend on communication is quite short. More than half of married adults communicated with their spouse less than one hour daily in 2010 (Cho et al., 2010). However, because of the increasing emphasis on love in marriage, spending quality time with the spouse has become a major factor that influences the couple's marital happiness. For example, those who reported that they spent a longer time with their spouse had much higher marital satisfaction than those who spent their leisure or social time without their spouse (Koh, 2015).

The age of the couple is a key factor for communication in Korea. Lee (2009) found that Korean couples demonstrated different interpersonal communication trends across age groups. In particular, young couples in their 20s and 30s demonstrated effective communication skills in open and clear communication while middle age couples in their 40s and 50s were better at problem solving skills during their communication. However, Korean couples in their 40s and 50s demonstrated ineffective communication skills in listening and feedback, resulting from couples' lack of patience, biased opinions toward each other, and lack of efforts to react to the spouse's concerns. Therefore, many family life education programs emphasizing healthy couple relationships in Korea have focused on enhancing couples' communication skills, especially listening and problem solving skills customized to the age and the marital duration and specific couple relationship characteristics (Y. Choi, 2015).

Gender role expectations are another significant factor affecting the marital relationship. Husbands tend to have more traditional gender attitudes than wives, but the reported marital satisfaction of those husbands was relatively lower than of those with gender equal attitudes among older adults (Koh, 2015). Another study has confirmed that for those who felt that their couple relationships were more likely to be gender equal, their marital satisfaction was higher than those who did not believe in gender equality in their marital relationships (Kim & Park, 2005). Those who do not have gender equal relationships often report a steep decrease in their marital satisfaction over time (Koh, 2015). For example, if a retired husband does not participate in household chores and maintains patriarchal attitudes, the couple is likely to avoid couple interaction, and their accumulated conflicts remain unresolved (Lee & Kim, 2015).

Despite the increasing awareness of gender equality in parenting, mothers are still considered the main caretaker of children. In addition to the existing gender role divisions between the husband and wife, Korean men tend to spend less time with their families due to the Korean workplace culture. Many Korean employers expect a strong commitment from employees, long work hours, and social gatherings after work as an extension of work duties. Therefore, when fathers believe that avoiding these work-related activities or responsibilities would jeopardize their promotion opportunities, they are more likely to sacrifice their family time and to devote themselves to work rather than to their families. The heavy involvement in work eventually diminishes their roles as fathers and husbands at home (Jeong & Jeon, 2014). As a result, Korean men are less likely to engage in their families' lives and maintain healthy family relationships over time (J. Choi & S. Lee, 2015). However, since these family and workplace cultures are changing, the younger generations of Korean males seek more opportunities to spend time with their families, to become involved in parenting, and to develop more family leisure time (J. Choi & S. Lee, 2015; Jeong & Jeon, 2014).

Childless couples. Although the birth rate has declined, a childless marriage is still not considered a normative alternative. For example, childless couples are often stigmatized as having physical or interpersonal problems or being selfish, which often causes emotional distress or guilt. It is important to understand the different types of childless marriages in the Korean context (Choi, Sung, & Lee, 2014). Couples who postpone having a child often think that their incomes are not high enough to raise a child so they delay parenthood. These husbands usually want to have children more than their wives do, which might cause conflict between the spouses regarding the decision of when to have a child (Sung, Choi, & Lee, 2015). Involuntary childless couples are more likely to be satisfied with their own and their spouse's incomes and to own a house than other types of childless couples, which reveals that they would be able to support a child. However, these couples, especially the wives, appear to have the lowest level of subjective happiness, satisfaction, and self-esteem compared to other types of childless couples. In addition, husbands who are involuntarily childless tend to describe their couple relationships as "dating partners," which means that they consider their relationships as being very intimate but incomplete to be called a "family" due to the absence of a child (Lee, Sung, Choi, & Chun, 2014). The Korean government partially funds fertility treatments to lower-income involuntary childless couples, which is a policy response to increase the extremely low fertility rate in Korea.

Transition to Parenthood

Becoming a parent is an important developmental task for Korean couples since the parent–child relationship plays a major role in defining marital happiness (Chung, 2011). For newlywed couples, childbirth is more like a family duty rather than their choice (Chung, Chung, Kim, & Park, 2007; Kwon, 2015). The number of Korean females who participate in any type of economic activity has gradually increased in the past few decades, but about 20% of married women still quit their jobs due to marriage, pregnancy, and childcare for infants to elementary school-age children (Statistics Korea & Ministry of Gender Equality and Family, 2015). That is, despite the increase in women in the labor force, marriage and childrearing are still major barriers for Korean women to work and develop their careers (Chung, 2011). Korean mothers often give up their careers after childbirth, but only some women return to the labor force in their 40s. As evidence, the employment rate of Korean females in their 30s is the lowest compared to women in their 20s and 40s (Statistics Korea & Ministry of Gender Equality and Family, 2015). This is another example of marriage, childbirth, and career disruption among Korean females being strongly tied to each other.

Childcare support. Experiencing major life transitions, such as marriage, childbirth, parenting, and career disruption in a short time period often significantly influences Korean couples' marital relationships. Despite increasing support for childcare from the national and local governments as a way of increasing the fertility rate, it is still very expensive to raise a child in Korea. Therefore, family income and support from extended family members become important factors that influence martial satisfaction. In addition, in Korea, childrearing is still considered the mother's role and this ideology often creates feelings of guilt among employed mothers (Kwon, 2015). According to a recent survey, many Korean families raise their infants and toddlers (0–2 years old) at home and tend not to send them to day care or preschool until after 3 years old (Statistics Korea & Ministry of Gender Equality and

Family, 2015). This implies that mothers with young children are far more likely to spend longer hours taking care of their children than fathers.

Maintaining a close tie with extended family members is crucial for these young mothers to receive help while taking care of their young children. As a result, influenced by unequal gender role divisions, employed mothers, especially those with young children, often feel more stress in their family lives, spend more time taking care of family members, and are less satisfied with their marriages (Statistics Korea & Ministry of Gender Equality and Family, 2015). A positive experience in parenting and sufficient support from extended family members help young Korean couples experience a positive transition to parenthood and prevent a negative impact on marital satisfaction (Lee & Keith, 1999; Yeon & Choi, 2015). However, the transition to parenthood seems to somewhat negatively influence young couples' marital satisfaction, especially for young mothers (Chung, 2011). In order to maintain a healthy and happy marriage over time, one of the major developmental tasks among these young parents as couples is to find a work/family balance and gender equality in family roles early on.

Children's education and parenting. Traditionally, Korean families have thought that achieving fame and prestige through education is one of the most important responsibilities for children. According to this tradition, educating their children as well as possible is the most important mission of parents. By three years, most Korean children attend early childhood education programs or day care centers. In addition, families start investing a large amount of their resources in their children's extracurricular, private education or study abroad programs as early as elementary school (Chin, 2011). Due to the heavy focus on academic success, Korean children spend more time studying. For example, in 2014, on average, Korean high school students spent about 8 and a half hours, middle school students about 6 hours, and elementary school students 4 and a half hours for schooling every weekday. Additionally, high school students spent almost 2 hours, middle school students 2 hours and 40 minutes, and elementary school students 2 hours and 14 minutes on extracurricular educational activities during an average weekday (Statistics Korea, 2015). This amount of time spent on educational activities is significantly higher than American high school students who spent 5.7–6.5 hours on an average school day in 2010–2014 in all educational activities (e.g., attending classes and completing homework) (Bureau of Labor Statistics, 2015). In general, Korean high school students spent about three more hours than their American peers on an average school day in educational activities.

"Wild goose" family is an example of the heavy emphasis on children's education in Korean families. Because of globalization, English is one of the most important subjects in education, so a growing number of families decide to live apart so the children can study abroad. In these transnational families, some family members, especially fathers, remain in Korea to work and pay for their families to live and study abroad in English-speaking countries. Usually, the wives live with their children in the foreign country. This lifestyle is similar to the lives of wild geese, so these families are called "wild goose" families. "Wild goose" families typically do not have intimate, affective relationships but relationships based on the instrumental family ideology (Cho, 2004) that prioritizes the familial role of providing instrumental support because family roles in these families are performed strategically based on the traditional gender role divisions.

Korean couples often sacrifice their couple relationship for the sake of their children's education (Cho, 2015; Kim, 2007). For example, "wild goose" fathers left in Korea experience loneliness and difficulties managing one-person household lives and maintaining relationships with their family abroad (Choi, 2006; Kim & Chang, 2004). The fathers often sell their house and move into a much cheaper, smaller apartment and send between 50 and 100% of their income to their family abroad. This lifestyle tends to cause problems in family relationships and the psychological and economic well-being of fathers (Kim, 2006). At the same time, the mothers staying in the foreign countries with their children experience difficulties due to language barriers and adaptation to the new environment. It is not easy for them to be solely responsible for their children's education in addition to managing their new lives, often leading to mild depression (Yun & Shin, 2010). Their children are also likely to experience psychological distress due to culture shock, racial discrimination, language barriers, absence of a male role model, and challenges of adapting to the new environment during puberty (Ha, 2007). Communication between spouses and parent–child is crucial to maintain a sense of family for these "wild goose" families. Open communication between children and parents living with or apart from them contributes to decreasing the level of children's depression (Ha, 2007; S. Y. Lee, 2009). Still, transnational communication might not be enough to maintain healthy family interactions, resulting in unstable couple and family relationships (Choi, 2006; Um, 2002).

Parent–Adolescent Children Relationships

Due to the heavy emphasis on education, Korean parent–child communication may focus mostly on the children's educational achievement and career development. Interestingly, for Korean adolescents, family, friends, dating, and money are not considered as important communication topics as education (Chin, 2011). Because their daily lives mainly consist of school, extracurricular education programs, and additional study, relationships between parents and school-aged children or adolescents can be characterized as prolonged dependence of children on their parents (Chin, 2011) which continues until the children graduate from college, find a job, and get married. In many cases, Korean parents are expected to pay for their children's tuition. Because of this financial dependency, parents have a strong influence on their children's decision making for education (e.g., which school to attend, which major to choose) and career path. Young adult children often consult their parents regarding their career path and even marital decisions, especially if they are financially dependent on their parents. Because of this unique parent–child relationship, Korean children develop independence, self-regulation, and autonomy in their 20s rather than in adolescence. Ironically, parents may not always be satisfied with their children's independence, even when the children are in their 20s since it reduces their power to be involved in their children's lives (Chin, 2011).

Korean children tend to have much closer relationships with their mothers than their fathers. Traditionally, the mother and the father had distinct parenting roles. The father was in charge of discipline while the mother was expected to remain affectionate and loving toward the children (*um-boo-ja-mo*; 엄부자모). Throughout the period of industrialization and economic development, Korean fathers rather focused on their role as family breadwinners, which often resulted in difficulties forming close father–child relationships. The Korean workplace culture valuing long hours of work has been another barrier to fathers' interaction with their children. According to the second National Survey of Korean Families (Cho et al., 2010), 35.4% of adolescents reported a lack of communication with their fathers whereas only 11.9% experienced a lack of communication with their mothers. In the same survey, 29% of adolescents reported that they would discuss issues with their mothers, but only 0.9% of adolescents considered doing so with their fathers. These findings show a discrepancy between the quality of the mother–child relationship and the father–child relationship.

Younger Korean fathers, however, are spending more time with their children (Cho & Yoon, 2014) due to the increased awareness of the father's unique contribution to his children (J.-A. Choi & J. Lee, 2015). The media have also influenced parenting attitudes among the general public. Recent television shows highlighting fathers' participation in child care have been very popular, and the image of the "friend-like daddy" has become widespread. The Korean government is also encouraging fathers to participate in family lives such as child care and housework as a way of enhancing the overall well-being of Korean families. For example, the Ministry of Gender Equality and Family has promoted the "Family Love Day" campaign that encourages employed parents to go home immediately after their work hours and to spend time with their families.

The advancement of technology, especially the Internet and smartphones, has strongly impacted the lives of Korean families. The Internet and smartphones are efficient tools for adolescents to express their thoughts, interact with their social groups, and foster a sense of accomplishment and creativity (Bae & Cho, 2010; Bae, Cho, Cho, & Kim, 2015; Choi, Choi, & Ahn, 2011). The advanced technology also affects family communication and relationships (Lee & Lee, 2004). Appropriate use of technology within family can be a great tool to promote positive family communication and relationships. For example, with the advancement of communication technology, "wild goose" fathers in Korea and their family members abroad can communicate with each other every day through e-mail, online instant messaging, and phone calls.

On the other hand, improper use of technology may cause more harm than good. Adolescents who are overdependent on or addicted to using technology can experience mental health problems, a lack of quality communication with parents, and isolation from their family and peers (Bae & Cho, 2010; Bae et al., 2015; Choi et al., 2011; Jeon, Chung, & Lee, 2014; Yuh, 2014). While parents may recognize their children's struggle with an excessive use of the Internet and smartphones, they may feel a loss of control dealing with this issue due to the limited knowledge of new technology or inadequate parental guidelines to monitor their children's Internet and smartphone use, leading to reduced parental confidence and competence (Bae et al., 2015).

Empty Nest Period

Due to the increased life expectancy and decreased birth rate in Korea, the empty nest period has been extended compared to the past (Koh, 2015; Sung, 2011). Because the parent–child relationship is considered more important than the couple relationship, Korean couples do not typically pay enough attention to developing a quality couple relationship when they are younger. Their marital relationships are maintained through shared parental activities while their children are with them, but when they are gone, the linkage between the husband and wife is gone as well. The time of transition between caring for children and having no children to care for in the home often causes problems for middle-aged Korean couples. Couples who have maintained a child-centered family life may experience more difficulties adjusting to the empty nest transition, especially after retirement (Lee & Kim, 2015).

In the past, marital satisfaction tended to improve in later life because couples had the least conflict due to the decreased burden of child rearing (Chun, Choi, & Kang, 2006). Marital satisfaction in this stage for modern Korean couples, however, does not seem to increase compared to the satisfaction during the parenthood period, which may be different from the Western couple relationship (Koh, 2015). A plausible explanation is that the extended expectation of parental support for adult children hinders the couple's adjustment to a couple-centered lifestyle. Research has revealed that older adults with a high level of self-differentiation are likely to be more satisfied with their later life, especially those having spouse-centered lifestyles compared to those with child-centered lifestyles (Lee & Chung, 2008). Differentiation of self refers to one's capability to differentiate self from other family members and to separate feelings and thoughts (Bowen, 1978). Because of Korea's collectivistic family culture that prioritizes togetherness over individuality and a child-centered family lifestyle, parents often equate their children's achievements with their parental success and experience difficulties separating their identity from their parental roles (Song, 2015). Thus, a prolonged child-centered family lifestyle could impede parents' differentiation of self that is essential to accepting the adult children's independence, leading to maladjustment in the empty nest period (Jang, 2015).

Bilateral family relationships. Because most households are now nuclear families in Korea, it might seem that Korean adult children are independent of their parents and family of origin like Western families, but how family members maintain their relationships and what roles family members play in each other's lives make family relationships more like a modified extended family with continuing interdependence (Y. Choi, 2015; H.-K. Kim, 2011). For example, nowadays, married children keep in close contact with both the patrilineal and matrilineal relatives. This relationship implies bilateralization, moving from patrilineal kinship interactions toward close relationships with both sides of the family (Lee & Bauer, 2013).

Exchanging support within families. One of the key values of Korean families at all stages is exchanging support between family members, particularly between parents and children. Throughout the life course, parents are involved in children's decision making of personal and family matters, but parents and children co-construct their life experiences. For example, adult children often provide instrumental, financial, and emotional support for their elderly parents although this obligation has weakened recently (Lee & Kim, 2014).

Since parents and children co-construct their life experiences, even into later life, adult children are traditionally expected to pay back their parents for the parents' support in the children's younger years. However, social and parental expectations of their children's obligation to care for their elderly parents have weakened over time despite the Confucian ideal of filial piety. In 2012, only 35.6% of youth reported that the family is responsible for elder care, which is a drastic decline compared to 2002 when 67.1% claimed this responsibility (Jung, 2013). In fact, the characteristics of filial piety have been reshaped. For example, recent studies have found that pursuing social achievement to honor parents was more significant than providing financial support for elderly parents (Lee & Bauer, 2013; Ok, 2011). However, the family is still the primary source of elderly care in Korea, and the level of ambivalence about providing care for parents is relatively low due to the influence of filial piety (Lee & Kim, 2014).

Elderly parents are not the only beneficiaries in the parent–child support exchange anymore (Jung & Kim, 2012). Until the early 2000s, parents were the most common beneficiaries and they were the most satisfied with their support exchange compared to others. However, a recent study revealed a changing trend of parent–child support exchange (Jung & Kim, 2012). In this study, parents in mutual support exchange were the most satisfied with their quality of life compared to other parents who did not experience mutual support, which implies the importance of reciprocity in modern Korean parent–adult child relationships. However, the study also revealed an increase in parents who are benefactors and a decline in parents who are beneficiaries, indicating that many adult children require financial and instrumental support from their elderly parents and still rely on them. If this trend of prolonged dependence of adult children continues, it might be difficult to expect reciprocity in the support exchange between parents and adult children, resulting in a power imbalance in the parent–adult child relationship (Lee, 2015).

The motivation of caring for elderly parents has also changed. In the past, the oldest son's motivation for caring for his parents was out of obligation and the daughter's motivation was affection toward her parents, although affection is now the most frequently reported motivation for both sons and daughters (Kim & Choi, 2007). When it comes to parents-in-law, the major motivation has been fulfilling an obligation as children.

In-law relationships. Although husbands' interaction with their parents-in-law has increased compared to the past, it is often due to the children's need for support from the wife's parents rather than vice versa. The primary caregivers for the parents-in-law are often daughters-in-law, not daughters, in Korea, which is different from Western societies. This norm, again, stems from a deeply rooted Confucian tradition in Korean families that obligates daughters-in-law, especially the eldest son's wife (Sung, 2011).

Family members may hold different expectations regarding their and others' familial roles based on various family ideologies in Korea (Chang, 2011), and conflicts in in-law relationships are often caused by the differences in these role expectations (H. J. Lee, 2003). The relationship between a mother and daughter-in-law is the most salient in-law relationship in Korean families. Because in-law relationships are triadic (i.e., husband, wife, mother-in-law) not dyadic (Morr Serewicz, 2006), the role of the son/husband is crucial in the mother and daughter-in-law relationship (Jang, 2015). To be specific, a son/husband who is actively involved in communication with both his mother and wife can mediate the in-law relationship more efficiently and help maintain a satisfactory mother and daughter-in-law relationship (Sung & Lee, 2002). Conflicts between a mother and son-in-law have not yet been investigated in depth, but the conflicts seem to have recently increased as the need for child care support from the wives' mothers has increased (Jeon, Kim, & Jeon, 2011).

■ Family Relationships beyond Couple and Parent–Child Relationships

Adult Sibling and Sibling-In-Law Relationships

Given the tradition of the Korean patrilineal stem family (Yi, 1998), one's birth order and gender have played essential roles in sibling and sibling-in-law relationships. Traditionally, the eldest brother occupied the top rung of the sibling hierarchy according to the *jang-ja-woo-dae* (장자우대; giving preference to the eldest son) norm. This norm privileged the eldest brother in allocating family resources (e.g., inheritance) and he was considered the representative of the family when the father was not available. The eldest brother's privilege and power were also linked to his responsibilities for the family, including caring for his older parents and devoting himself to *jeh-sa* (제사; ancestral services on the date when an ancestor passed away). The eldest brother's wife was the actual service provider for the family according to the traditional division of gender roles. In contrast, married sisters were considered *chool-ga-we-in* (출가외인) in traditional Korea, which meant that they had no family obligations or privileges in their family of origin since they belonged to their husband's family. Thus, married sisters were excluded from any inheritance or family resources and from making major decisions in the family of origin. Having minimal interactions with their parents and siblings was the norm so they could concentrate on serving their husband's family.

Today, the traditional norms of privileging the eldest brother and excluding married sisters still remain among older generations, but egalitarianism has become influential in sibling and sibling-in-law relationships. After several major amendments, family law in Korea has granted equal rights and responsibilities to adult siblings regardless of their birth order and gender. However, both traditional and egalitarian expectations coexist among middle-aged Koreans (Sung & Lee, 2013). Eldest brothers often hope to share family duties with their younger brothers, while younger brothers often still expect their eldest brother to hold both the authority and responsibility in the family. Due to these conflicting expectations, brother–brother relationships tend to involve emotional distance, which sometimes leads to relational tensions. As the actual provider of service, brothers' wives are particularly sensitive to the unfair distribution of work for their in-laws among sisters-in-law (i.e., "Am I doing more work than the other wives (in the family)?"), which often results in negative emotions toward the other brothers' wives.

In contrast to the other sibling relationships, sister–sister relationships are intimate without concerns about financial or instrumental provisions for their own parents or siblings (Sung & Lee, 2013). This is because, on one hand, the traditional norm of discouraging married women from interacting with their family of origin is no longer powerful, and, on the other hand, traditional expectations which excluded married daughters from sharing family duties are still influential. As a result, married sisters can enjoy their relationship without having tensions caused by obligations to the family of origin. This new tendency that married sisters actively interact with their family of origin reflects the bilateralization of kinship interaction, which used to be exclusive to the husband's family of origin in traditional Korea (Lee & Bauer, 2013; Ok, 2011).

Relationships with Relatives

Traditionally, there was a broad boundary of Korean "relatives" or "kin" on the patrilineal sides (i.e., father's or husband's relatives) but a limited boundary on the matrilineal sides (i.e., mother's or wife's relatives). This tradition is not surprising given the heavy emphasis on the succession of the patrilineal bloodline in traditional Confucian families (Ok, 2011). The typical boundary of close relatives was those who shared the paternal great-great-grandfather line (Park & Hong, 2012). The key role of this patrilineal kin network was to serve ancestors by performing ancestral services on traditional holidays (e.g., lunar New Year's Day and harvest festival day) or by maintaining the family gravesite. Because ancestral services required substantial resources in traditional Korea, the kin network often allocated or pooled family resources to collaborate as a group. Other family rituals such as weddings and funerals were also major occasions when the kin network exchanged support. Based on the Confucian family ideology that highlighted mutual support among patrilineal relatives, Koreans were also expected to help the members of their kin network in times of need.

Koreans' subjective boundary of relatives has become narrower since family rituals including ancestral services have become less important and the number of ancestors that need to be served in rituals has declined. In addition, Korea's current family law makes no distinction between the paternal and maternal sides in the definition of kin. Bilateralization in kinship interaction, i.e., active interaction with both the husband's and wife's relatives, has also become apparent in Korea (Lee & Bauer, 2013; Ok, 2011). Young couples are expected to maintain close relationships with both sides of the family (Kim & Kim, 2001), and Korean couples are likely to exchange financial, emotional, and instrumental support with both sides of their extended families (Chung, 2011).

Despite the bilateralization of kinship interaction, the reasons for interacting with the husband's versus the wife's relatives seem to be different (Han & Yoon, 2004; Sung, 2006). The husband's relatives are still prioritized when it comes to whose side comes first when performing family responsibilities (e.g., elderly care, financial support, visitation on traditional holidays, participation in family rituals). In contrast, the wife's relatives are preferred as the providers of gendered support (e.g., child care, housework assistance; Lee & Bauer, 2013). However, in modern Korea, economic or instrumental support is likely to come from both families (Kim & Kim, 2001). Some scholars explain this unbalanced bilateralization in the context of familism that forces Koreans to still be the primary providers of instrumental support for their relatives (J. K. Lee, 2003) or as a result of the traditional gender role ideology that ironically has led to bilateralized interaction with the husband's and wife's relatives (Lee & Bauer, 2013).

Summary

Since the early to mid-2000s, several demographic changes have emerged in Korea that significantly affect and are affected by family dynamics and values: (a) a low fertility rate, (b) a decline in the marriage rate and an increase in the divorce rate, (c) an aging population, and (d) an increase in transnational marriages. In addition, after the Korean War, traditional Confucianism-based family ideologies have been modified to include three other types of ideologies, instrumental family ideology, affectionate family ideology, and individualistic family ideology, to meet the needs of families and a changing society (Chang, 2011). This shift in ideologies indicates that modern Korean families have experienced very complicated and drastic changes in family structures and functions. To respond to these social changes, the Korean government has developed many family-friendly policies which have strengthened societies' responsibility in promoting the well-being of diverse individuals and families (Chin et al., 2012). The Framework Act on Healthy Families, the

Act on Equal Employment and Support for Work–Family Balance, and the Multi-Cultural Family Support Act are a few examples of this new paradigm of family policy. Although these policies might not be sufficient to accomplish the social inclusion of diverse individuals and foster family-friendly social environments, it is a stepping-stone to improve the social contexts in which families are embedded through continued cooperation between the private and public sectors.

Amid the rapid social changes and critical social events challenging the well-being of family relationships, Korean families have thrived. The strong parent–child bond and instrumental couple relationship reveal how Korean families have coped with the changes in social environments and how they have maintained family resilience. Korean families are changing in the direction of embracing gender equality and individuality as well as emphasizing intimacy and affection to adapt to the current social contexts. Overall, the family is the core of Koreans' lives and the most crucial aspect of their happiness, which has been consistent over time. Koreans continue to emphasize strong cohesive and instrumental family relationships. There may be different ways of respecting others in the modern sociocultural contexts compared to some Western countries, such as how Koreans express affection and share limited resources within families, but families in Korea continue to provide strong instrumental and emotional support for each other. We hope that this chapter has provided a glimpse of how Korean families interact and communicate throughout the life course, in the past and in the present, based on various social changes.

References

Anderson, T. M., & Kohler, H-P. (2012). *Education fever and the East Asian fertility puzzle: A case study of low fertility in South Korea* (PSC Working Paper Series, PSC 12-07). Retrieved from http://repository.upenn.edu/psc_working_papers/38/

Bae, J., Cho, E., Cho, Y., & Kim K. (2015). A study on parents' observation of adolescent children's smartphone use problem and their parenting experiences. *Journal of Family Relations, 20*(1), 143–164. Retrieved from http://www.kafr.or.kr/

Bae, J. A., & Cho, Y. H. (2010). Digital media and mother-child communication. *Journal of Cybercommunication Academic Society, 27*(1), 53–91. Retrieved from http://www.cybercom.or.kr/?mod=papers

Bowen, M. (1978). *Family therapy in clinical practice.* New York & London: Jason Aronson, Inc.

Bureau of Labor Statistics. (2015). *American time use survey.* Retrieved from http://www.bls.gov/TUS/CHARTS/STUDENTS.HTM

Chang, K.-S. (2011). Compressed modernity and Korean families: Accidental pluralism in family ideology. In Korean Family Studies Association (Ed.), *Korean families: Continuity and change* (pp. 129–149). Seoul, South Korea: Seoul National University Press.

Chin, M. (2011). Korean families in mid-life: Over-emphasis on children's education. In Korean Family Studies Association (Ed.), *Korean families: Continuity and change* (pp. 355–378). Seoul, South Korea: Seoul National University Press.

Chin, M., Lee, J., Lee, S., Son, S., & Sung, M. (2012). Family policy in South Korea: Development, current status, and challenges. *Journal of Child and Family Studies, 21*, 53–64. doi: 10.1007/s10826-011-9480-1

Cho, E. (2004). Korean families on the forefront of globalization. *Economy and Society, 64*, 148–171. Retrieved from http://www.criso.or.kr/

Cho, E. (2015). Korean families reflected in wild goose family phenomenon. In Choi et al., *Speaking about Korean families: Phenomena and issues* (pp. 147–167). Seoul, South Korea: Hawoo.

Cho, H.-K., Song, H.-R., Park, J.-Y., Kwon, T.-H., Kim, K.-H., Kim, J. H., . . . Lee, J. (2010). *The second national survey of Korean families.* Retrieved from http://www.mogef.go.kr/korea/view/policy/policy02_01f.jsp?-func=view&currentPage=0&key_type=&key=&search_start_date=&-search_end_date=&class_id=0&idx=613546

Cho, M. R., & Yoon, S. K. (2014). Changing differences by educational attainment in fathers' family work – domestic labour and child care. *Korean Journal of Family Social Work, 44*, 5–30. Retrieved from http://www.kafsw.or.kr/

Choi, J., & Lee, S. (2015). Psychological salience of father status and paternal involvement with their children: Moderating effects of provider role attitudes and family-friendly organizational culture. *Journal of Family Relations, 20*(1), 91–116. Retrieved from http://www.kafr.or.kr/

Choi, J.-A., & Lee, J. (2015). Beyond oedipal fathers: Revisiting fathers in psychoanalytic theory. *Korean Journal of Psychology: General, 34*, 429–451. Retrieved from https://www.koreanpsychology.or.kr/eng/index.asp

Choi, S. (2015). Family portraits reflected in house: Where do we stay? In Choi et al., *Speaking about Korean families: Phenomena and issues* (pp. 99–123). Seoul, South Korea: Hawoo.

Choi, Y. S., Choi, H. J., & Ahn, Y. J. (2011). The effect of parents' raising attitude, self-control, and peer relationship on adolescents' Internet addiction. *Journal of Family Relations, 15*(4), 113–133. Retrieved from http://www.kafr.or.kr/

Choi, Y. S., Sung, M., & Lee, J. (2014). Portraits of childless couples in South Korea I: Psychological well-being, couple relationships, and attitudes toward children by types of childlessness. *Family and Culture, 26*(1), 40–71. Retrieved from http://www.family21.org/

Choi, Y. S. (2006). The phenomenon of "geese-families": Marital separation between geese-fathers and geese-mothers. *Family and Culture, 18*(2), 37–65. Retrieved from http://www.family21.org/

Choi, Y. S. (2015). Changes in Korean families: How to analyze them? In Choi et al., *Speaking about Korean families: Phenomena and issues* (pp. 13–41). Seoul, South Korea: Hawoo.

Chun, H., Choi, H. K., & Kang, I. (2006). The effects of marital conflicts and conflict resolution strategies on marital instability by duration of marriage. *Journal of Family Relations, 11*(1), 179–202. Retrieved from http://www.kafr.or.kr/

Chung, H. (2011). The early years of marriage. In Korean Family Studies Association (Ed.), *Korean families: Continuity and change* (pp. 331–353). Seoul, South Korea: Seoul National University Press.

Chung, H.-S., Kim, Y., & Lee, A. (2011). *Study on current situation and improvement on bilingual education of Children from multicultural families.* Seoul, South Korea: Ministry of Gender Equality and Family.

Chung, M. R., & Chang, Y. H. (2007). A study on the conception of the values of marriage, having child, and job of university students and its variables. *Research Dissertation: Educational Research Institutes, 41,* 1–17. Retrieved from http://www.sungshin.ac.kr/edure/

Chung, M. R., Kang, S. K., & Kim, M. J. (2013). The study of marital satisfaction, parenting attitude, and practice of taegyo in pregnant women. *Journal of the Korean Home Economics Association, 51,* 241–251. doi: 10.6115/khea.2013.51.2.241

Chung, O.-B., Chung, S.-H., Kim, K.-E., & Park, Y.-J. (2007). A study on the differences of family values and parental role responsibility among three generations. *Journal of Family Relations, 12*(2), 215–249. Retrieved from http://www.kafr.or.kr/

Eun, K.-S. (2011). Changes in population and family in Korea. In Korean Family Studies Association (Ed.), *Korean families: Continuity and change* (pp. 87–127). Seoul, South Korea: Seoul National University Press.

Ha, M. (2007). 'Kirogi' families weigh risks and rewards. The Korea Times. Retrieved from http://news.naver.com/main/read.nhn?mode=LSD&mid=sec&sid1=001&oid=040&aid=0000046457

Hall, E. T. (1976). *Beyond culture.* Garden City, NY: Anchor.

Han, G. H., & Yoon, S. E. (2004). Bilateralization of kinship in Korean families: Focused on intergenerational relationships. *Korea Journal of Population Studies, 27*(2), 177–203. Retrieved from http://www.pak.or.kr/sobis/pak.jsp

Han, K. (2006). Family life and cultural encounter of foreign wives in rural area. *Journal of Korean Cultural Anthropology, 39*(1), 195–243. Retrieved from http://www.koanthro.or.kr/index.asp

Han, Y., & Lee, J. (2016). South Korea, Families in. In C. Shehan (Ed.), *The encyclopedia of family studies* (pp. 1836–1841). Wiley-Blackwell.

Jang, D.-H., & Hwang, D.-S. (2010). The effects of family protective factors on children's school adjustment of male-headed family from divorced. *Journal of Public Welfare Administration, 20*(2), 63–83. Retrieved from http://www.dbpia.co.kr/Journal/ArticleDetail/NODE01611462

Jang, J. (2015). Inside *Si-World*: Mothers- and daughters-in-law in Korea. In Choi et al., *Speaking about Korean families: Phenomena and issues* (pp. 405–425). Seoul, South Korea: Hawoo.

Jeon, H. S., Chung, H. J., & Lee, J. Y. (2014). Relationships among parent–child communication, self-efficacy, and mobile device dependence perceived by adolescents. *Journal of Family Relations, 18*(4), 53–70. Retrieved from http://www.kafr.or.kr/

Jeon, S.-S., Kim, S.-K., & Jeon, G.-Y. (2011). The effect of relationship variables between mother-in-law and son-in-law on son-in-law's relationship-satisfaction and negative perception. *Journal of the Korean Home Economics Association, 49*(7), 123–133. doi: 10.6115/khea.2011.49.7.123

Jeong, Y.-J., & Jeon, G.-Y. (2014). The effects of family-friendly policies and work-family culture on parenting stress and parenting efficacy of working parents with infants. *Journal of Family Relations, 19*(1), 3–28. Retrieved from http://www.kafr.or.kr/

Jung, J. K., & Kim, G. E. (2012). The study of intergenerational support exchange between older parents and adult children. *Journal of the Korean Gerontological Society, 32,* 895–912. Retrieved from http://www .tkgs.or.kr/html/

Jung, Y. T. (2013). Study on familial relationship in connection with caring for the elderly. *Journal of Family Relations, 18*(3), 207–231. Retrieved from http://www.kafr.or.kr/

Kim, E. (2010). The effect of marital interaction on the marital instability of foreign wives in Gyeongnam. *Journal of Korean Home Management Association, 28*(3), 1–12. Retrieved from http://society.kisti.re.kr/khma/

Kim, E.-J. (2007). A study on the social economic status of the family, extra tutoring fee, parent–child relationship and children's educational achievement. *Korean Journal of Sociology, 41*(5), 134–162. Retrieved from http://www.ksa21.or.kr/

Kim, E.-J., Chang, H.-K., Choi, I.-H., Kim, S.-Y., & Sun, B.-Y. (2013). *A study on the status of single-parent families.* Seoul, South Korea: Ministry of Gender Equality and Family.

Kim, H. J., & Kim, M. C. (1999). The interrelationship between perceived health in family-of-origin, self-esteem, and marital adjustment. *Journal of Family Relations, 4*(2), 39–60. Retrieved from http://www.kafr.or.kr/

Kim, H.-K. (2011). Women's work and kin relationships since the 1960s. In Korean Family Studies Association (Ed.), *Korean families: Continuity and change* (pp. 297–328). Seoul, South Korea: Seoul National University Press.

Kim, H. S., & Lee, J. U. (2003). The study on premarital preparation of single men and women. *Journal of the Korean Home Economics Association, 41*(2), 211–224. Retrieved from http://society.kisti.re.kr/khma/

Kim, J. Y., & Tasker, F. (2013). The effects of parental divorce: A cultural-specific challenge for young adults in South Korea. *Journal of Divorce & Remarriage, 54,* 349–362. doi:10.1080/10502556.2013.800387

Kim, S.-H. (2011). A qualitative study on the problem of educating children in multicultural families. *Journal Korean Home Management Association, 29*(4), 17–33. Retrieved from http://society.kisti.re.kr/khma/

Kim. S.-J., & Kim, S. O. (2001). Kinship behavior and the satisfaction of the spouse towards it in early stage of marital couples. *Journal of Family Relations, 62*(2), 91–111. Retrieved from http://www.kafr.or.kr/

Kim, S.-K., Park, J.-S., Kim, Y.-K., Kim, Y.-W., Choi, Y.-J., Son, C.-K., & Yun, A.-R. (2012). *The national survey of marriage and childbirth.* Retrieved from http://repository.kihasa.re.kr:8080/handle/201002/9983

Kim, S.-S. (2006). The 'girogi' fathers' changes of lives and adaptation problems. *Journal of Korean Home Management Association, 24*(1), 141–158. Retrieved from http://society.kisti.re.kr/khma/

Kim, T. H., & Park, J. H. (2005). The effect of gender role attitudes on strengthening couple relationships. *Journal of Family Relations, 10*(3), 79–106. Retrieved from http://www.kafr.or.kr/

Kim, Y. H. (2011). Factors associated with the practice of traditional prenatal education (taegyo) among pregnant Korean women. *Korean Journal of Women Health Nursing, 17*, 491–498. doi: 10.4069/kjwhn.2011.17.5.491

Kim, Y. H., & Chang O. J. (2004). The so-called 'wild geese family': Issue of families that run separate household for a long time. *Journal of Family Relations, 9*(2), 1–23. Retrieved from http://www.kafr.or.kr/

Kim, Y. J., & Choi, Y. H. (2007). A study on caregiving motives of adult child: Focused on interaction effect of gender and relations to adult child-their parent. *Journal of Family Relations, 12*(3), 313–334. Retrieved from http://www.kafr.or.kr/

Kim, Y. K. (2010). Research on the actual condition and political subject of multicultural families. *Health·Social Welfare Issue & Focus, 26*, 1–8. Retrieved from https://www.kihasa.re.kr/html/jsp/main.jsp

Koh, S. J. (2015). Couple marital satisfaction: Balancing in relationship and role based on gender equality. In Choi et al., *Speaking about Korean families: Phenomena and issues* (pp. 233–255). Seoul, South Korea: Hawoo.

Korean Population, Health and Welfare Association. (2014). 2014 world population census survey: Korean version. Retrieved from http://www.ppfk.or.kr/MasterBoard/View.aspx?MenuNo=5050000&MasterID=5&SiteID=0&SiteMenuID=0&SearchField=&SearchKeyword=&TypeID=&BoardID=10843

Kwon, H.-K. (2015). Gender issues on child birth and parenting. In Choi et al., *Speaking about Korean families: Phenomena and issues* (pp. 281–299). Seoul, South Korea: Hawoo.

Lee, D. W. (2002). A conversation analysis of 'husband-wife' communication: In search of the interpersonal communication problems and solutions. *Korean Journal of Communication Studies, 10*(2), 7–45. Retrieved from http://www.kcanet.or.kr/index.php

Lee, D. W. (2009). The characteristics and transitional process of communication behavior between Korean husbands and wives across generations. *Korean Journal of Communication Studies, 17*(1), 129–151. Retrieved from http://www.kcanet.or.kr/index.php

Lee, H., & Lee, K. (2004). The change of family relations by the internet use of housewives: Focused on the intimacy among family members and the equality between couples. *Korean Journal of Human Ecology, 13,* 329–343. Retrieved from http://www.kjhe.or.kr/

Lee, H. J. (2003). The factorial structure of the conflict source between mother-in-law and daughter-in-law and related variables. *Journal of Welfare for the Aged, 19,* 31–59. Retrieved from http://www.koreawa.or.kr/

Lee, J. (2015). Revisiting young adults' instrumental dependence on their parents. In Choi et al., *Speaking about Korean families: Phenomena and issues* (pp. 379–403). Seoul, South Korea: Hawoo.

Lee, J., & Bauer, J. W. (2013). Motivations for providing and utilizing child care by grandmothers for employed mothers in South Korea. *Journal of Marriage and Family, 75,* 381–402. doi: 10.1111/jomf.12014

Lee, J., & Chung, H. (2008). Psychological adjustment of elderly couples: Based on Bowen's family systems theory. *Journal of Family Relations, 13*(1), 1–27. Retrieved from http://www.kafr.or.kr/

Lee, J., Sung, M., Choi, Y., & Chun, Y. (2014). Portraits of involuntary childless men in Korea: The meanings of child, couple relationships, and relationships with social networks. *Proceedings of the Fall Conference of the Korean Home Management Association,* 188. Retrieved from http://society.kisti.re.kr/khma/

Lee, J. K. (2003). *In the name of the family: Modern families and feminism in Korea.* Seoul, South Korea: Alternative Culture.

Lee, J. K. (2011). Imagining the South Korean family beyond patriarchy. In Korean Family Studies Association (Ed.), *Korean families: Continuity and change* (pp. 245–269). Seoul, South Korea: Seoul National University Press.

Lee, J. Y., & Kim, D. (2015). A qualitative study on the adaptation process of middle-aged and elderly couples with retired husbands. *Family and Environment Research, 53,* 179–193. doi: 10.6115/fer.2015.014

Lee, S. C., & Keith, P. M. (1999). The transition to motherhood of Korean women. *Journal of Comparative Family Studies, 30,* 453–470. Retrieved from http://www.jstor.org/stable/41603645

Lee, S.-S., & Kim, S.-H. (2014). Factors affecting the ambivalence of adult children toward their aged parents. *Korean Journal of Family Welfare, 19,* 445–469. doi: 10.13049/kfwa.2014.19.3.445

Lee, S. Y. (2009). Factors related to the depression of young Korean oversea students in the U.S. *Korean Journal of Youth Studies, 16*(5), 99–120. Retrieved from http://www.kyra.or.kr/

Lim, T. (2010). Rethinking belongingness in Korea: Transnational migration, "migrant marriages" and the politics of multiculturalism. *Pacific Affairs, 83*, 51–71. doi: 10.5509/201083151

Morr Serewicz, M. C. (2006). The difficulties of in-law relationships. In D. C. Kirkpatrick, S. Duck, & M. Foley (Eds.), *Relating difficulty: The process of constructing and managing difficult interaction* (pp.101–118). Mahwah, NJ: Erlbaum.

Nam, K.-A. (2015). High-context and low-context communication. In J. M. Bennett (Ed.), *The SAGE encyclopedia of international competence* (pp. 377–381). Thousand Oaks, CA: Sage.

Ok, S. W. (2011). Continuity and change in patrilineal culture of Korean families. In Korean Family Studies Association (Ed.), *Korean families: Continuity and change* (pp. 1–18). Seoul, South Korea: Seoul National University Press.

Park, H.-I., & Hong, H. O. (2012). *History of Korean family life.* Seoul, South Korea: Korea National Open University Press.

Ryu, D. H. (2013). Reality therapy for couple to enhance marital satisfaction of domestic violent couple. *Journal of Family Relations, 17*(4), 67–87. Retrieved from http://www.kafr.or.kr/

Sohn, S. Y. (2011). Love, sexuality, and marriage. In Korean Family Studies Association (Ed.), *Korean families: Continuity and change* (pp. 271–296). Seoul, South Korea: Seoul National University Press.

Song, J.-H., & Lee, T.-Y. (2010). A study on marital adjustment factors among multicultural couples. *Health and Social Welfare Review, 30*(2), 164–192. doi: 10.15709/hswr.2010.30.2.164

Song, M. (2015). Is parental devotion to education for children a double-edged sword? In Choi et al., *Speaking about Korean families: Phenomena and issues* (pp. 333–353). Seoul, South Korea: Hawoo.

Statistics Korea. (2011). Transnational marriage/total marriage. Retrieved from http://kostat.go.kr/portal/korea/kor_nw/2/2/3/index.board?bmode=read&bSeq=&aSeq=251920&pageNo=1&rowNum=10&navCount=10&currPg=&sTarget=title&sTxt=%EB%8B%A4%EB%AC%B8%ED%99%94

Statistics Korea. (2014a). 2014 marriage & divorce statistics. Retrieved from http://kostat.go.kr/portal/korea/kor_nw/2/2/3/index.board?bmode=read&bSeq=&aSeq=335256&pageNo=2&rowNum=10&navCount=10&currPg=&sTarget=title&sTxt

Statistics Korea. (2014b). Opinions on marriage by sex, age group and educational attainment. Retrieved from http://kosis.kr/upsHtml/online/downSrvcFile.do?PUBCODE=KP&FILE_NAME=/KP/07020323.xlsx&SEQ=3670

Statistics Korea. (2015). 2014 report on the time use survey. Retrieved from http://meta.narastat.kr/metasvc/index.do?confmNo=10152&inputYear=2014

Statistics Korea, & Ministry of Gender Equality and Family. (2015). Statistical report on women's lives. Retrieved from http://kostat.go.kr/portal/korea/kor_nw/2/1/index.board?bmode=read&aSeq=346959

Sung, M. (2006). Bilateralization phenomena in Korean families: A qualitative approach. *Journal of Korean Home Management Association, 24*(3), 59–72. Retrieved from http://society.kisti.re.kr/khma/

Sung, M. (2011). Korean family relationships in later life. In Korean Family Studies Association (Ed.), *Korean families: Continuity and change* (pp. 379–414). Seoul, South Korea: Seoul National University Press.

Sung, M. (2015). Perception of bloodline and multicultural society. In Choi et al., *Speaking about Korean families: Phenomena and issues* (pp. 127–145). Seoul, South Korea: Hawoo.

Sung, M., Choi, Y., & Lee, J. (2015). Portraits of childless couples in South Korea II: Factors predicting voluntary and involuntary childless married Koreans' psychological well-being. *Family and Culture, 26*(1), 72–101. Retrieved from http://www.family21.org/

Sung, M., & Lee, J. (2013). Adult sibling and sibling-in-law relationships in South Korea: Continuity and change of Confucian family norms. *Journal of Comparative Family Studies, 44*, 571–587. Retrieved from http://www.jstor.org/stable/23644619

Sung, M. O., & Lee, H. J. (2002). The influences of conflict between mother-in-law and daughter-in-law on the family relationship of the female elderly. *Journal of Welfare for the Aged, 18*, 185–206. Retrieved from http://www.koreawa.or.kr/

Um, M. Y. (2002). Issues of male professionals living apart from their families for a long time: The so-called. *Korean Journal of Family Therapy, 10*(2), 25–43. Retrieved from http://www.familytherapy.or.kr/

Yang, S., & Rosenblatt, P. C. (2001). Shame in Korean families. *Journal of Comparative Family Studies, 32*, 361–375. Retrieved from http://www.jstor.org/stable/41603758

Yeon, E., & Choi, H. (2015). Actor and partner effect of infant-parents' emotional value of children, parenting stress, and marital satisfaction. *Korea Journal of Association of Child Care and Education, 90*, 79–108. Retrieved from http://www.kce.or.kr/main/index.html

Yi, K.-G. (1998). *Social anthropology of Korean family*. Seoul, South Korea: Jip-Moon-Dang.

Yuh, J. (2014). The effects of loneliness, family cohesion, family conflict, and parent–adolescent communication on smartphone addiction symptoms. *Journal of Family Relations, 19*(3), 175–192. Retrieved from http://www.kafr.or.kr/

Yun, E. K., & Shin, S. H. (2010). The actor effect and the partner effect of self-esteem and mother-adolescent communication on depression in mothers and adolescents in kirogi families according to adolescent' development stage. *Journal of Korean Academy of Nursing, 40*, 620–630. doi: 10.4040/jkan.2010.40.5.620

CHAPTER 9
FRIENDSHIP, ROMANTIC RELATIONSHIPS, AND COMMUNICATION IN SOUTH KOREA

EUN-JEONG HAN

In this chapter, I will introduce some characteristics and communication styles used in friendships and romantic relationships among Koreans. I will contrast Korean characteristics in these relational contexts with the West through the lens of Hofstede's (2001) framework of cultural dimensions as introduced in Chapter 1 of this book. The first part of this chapter will be focused on friendship and the latter part will be about romantic relationships. In addition, considering the fact that Korea is known as one of the leading countries in terms of adopting new communication technologies (Hwang & Park, 2006; Kim & Yun, 2008; Park & Lim, 2014; Yi, Oh, & Kim, 2013), I will briefly touch on Koreans' social media usage patterns in friendships and romantic relationships and how they reflect a Korean culture. Lastly, there will be a brief discussion on the practical guidelines for non-Koreans who are interested in having interpersonal relationships with Koreans as well as recommendations for more effective communication with Koreans.

■ *Woo-Jeong* (우정; Friendship)

A friend can be generally defined as "someone you know well, someone you like, and someone with whom you feel a close personal bond" (Lustig & Koester, 2013, p.227). However, the definition of friendship and the things one expects from a friendship vary among people according to differences in their cultural background (French, Bae, Pidada & Lee, 2006; Martin & Nakayama, 2014). In this section, I will survey some of the cultural norms and characteristics of friendship in Korean society.

Group-Based Friendship Formation

Woo-Jeong (우정; Friendship) in Korean culture is based on memberships in social groups rather than intimate relationships between two individuals. For many Koreans, therefore, friendship is often considered an involuntary relationship while in the United States friendship is often considered voluntary (French et al., 2006). Specifically, Koreans often develop friendships with those they have grown up with (Shin, 2007) or have attended school with (Kim & Yun, 2008). In addition, Korean men often develop friendships with others in their unit during their compulsory 18-month military service.

Though increased mobility in Korean society today has lessened friendships based upon shared homelands and therefore experiences growing up, school is still the main place where Koreans forge lasting friendships. There are numerous associations of graduates from the same schools, the so-called *Dong-Chang-Hwae* (동창회; Alumni Clubs) in Korea, and most middle-aged Koreans attend *Dong-Chang-Hwae* to stay in touch with their old friends. In fact, the Korean school system itself encourages students to develop strong feelings of bonding (Kim, 2014). In almost all school settings in Korea, except colleges, Korean students do not travel to different classrooms to take subjects of their choice but take various subjects in the same classroom with the same classmates for the entire semester (Kim, 2014). In fact, according to Kim's (2014) study, more than half of Korean teenagers who transferred to schools in the United States reported that they missed school in Korea mainly because they shared everything with their classmates with whom they shared the same schedule from early morning to late afternoon. For many Korean teenagers, school in the United States, where each student moves around from classroom to classroom, is not a good place to make friends even though US students have much more free time than their counterparts in Korea (Kim, 2014).

This clearly shows that Korean friendship is rooted in a collectivistic culture. People from individualistic cultures are more likely to treat a person equally regardless of whether he/she is a member of an in-group or an out-group while people in collectivistic cultures show much more positive attitudes toward members of an in-group than those from an out-group (Guan, Park & Lee, 2009; Kim & White, 2007). In Korea's collectivistic culture, only members of the same in-group can be friends. Supporting this, one Korean exchange student told the author of this chapter "In

Korea, when we have a party, we invite only those friends everybody knows. But here in the United States it seems like a party is open to everyone whether people know each other or not. It feels weird when somebody I never met comes up to me and says 'Hi, I'm Tom's friend. Nice to meet you.' I couldn't understand why there were so many guests who did not know each other." (personal conversation)

Koreans' emphasis on an exclusionist approach toward relationships is evident in their use of language. For instance, Koreans habitually use 'we, our, us' rather than 'I, my, me,' reflecting the Korean view of self as linked to the relationship with others rather than as an independent entity (Woo, 2013). Particularly, the term *Woo-Ri* (우리; We/Us/Our) indicates "we-ness or any collective inclusive of I and any others (persons or objects)" (Han & Choi, 2011, p. 400). That is, when Koreans say *Woo-Ri*, it is assumed that they have shared many social activities such as having meals together or singing together (Han & Choi, 2011).

Age Does Matter in Friendship

While Americans often have friends who vary in age range, Koreans typically develop friendships with those who are of the same age. For Koreans, a younger or older person cannot be considered as a friend. Instead, he/she is a brother, sister, senior, or junior. In Lim and Giles's (2007) study, Korean college students believed that two individuals with even a one-year difference in age should be treated differently. Sometimes, Koreans even check the difference in months and days when two individuals are the same age (Yoon, 2004) to differentiate their relative status. The most typical ways of asking or revealing age are mentioning the name of the symbolic animal of the year of birth and of the year of entering college (Lim & Giles, 2007; Yoon, 2004).

Koreans' extraordinary consciousness of age difference is indicative of a high power distance culture. In a high power distance culture, a rigid social hierarchy exists among people and they are treated differently based on social status (Hofstede, 2001). Of the various factors that determine social position (i.e., title, rank, experience, and seniority), age is the most universal one used in almost every interpersonal relationship (Lim & Giles, 2007) and this is why Koreans are extremely sensitive to know each other's age before forming relationships.

In fact, the Korean language itself has a unique system of honorific expressions (Lim & Giles, 2007; Merchant, 1980; Yoon, 2004), and in Korean society it is critical to use appropriate honorific words in conversation with individuals who are in different social positions (Farver & Lee-Shin, 1997; Lim & Giles, 2007; Merchant, 1980; Yoon, 2004). There are six different levels or styles in terms of honorific expression in the Korean language including "plain, pan-mal, familiar, semiformal, polite, and formal" (Yoon, 2004, p.193). Among these six, two of the most commonly used styles among Koreans are *Pan-Mal* (반말; Non-polite or Casual Language) and *Jon-Dat-Mal* (존댓말; Polite Language) (Yoon, 2004). In general, Koreans use *Pan-Mal* in casual conversations with friends or with those who are younger than themselves while *Jon-Dat-Mal* is used for those who are older or in higher positions than themselves.

Also, in Korea, directly asking one's age is a socially accepted custom (Lim & Giles, 2007; Yoon, 2004) although it could be considered as rude behavior in Western countries, particularly in the United States. Koreans do it to figure out their relative positions so that they can respect others or be respected by others using the appropriate language (Lim & Giles, 2007; Yoon, 2004). Thus, even when two persons meet for the first time, they might ask each other's age by immediately saying, for example, "My name is John, nice to meet you. Do you mind if I ask what your age is?." More typically, Koreans go through a negotiation process regarding language usage in relation to age (Lim & Giles, 2007). For example, after revealing each other's age, one might say "Since I'm older than you, I think I can use *Pan-Mal* to speak to you. Would it be OK with you?" or "Since we are the same age, we are friends. You don't have to use *Jon-Dat-Mal* to me." Then, in agreement, or with each other's permission, they use the particular language called for.

It is important to understand that treating people differently based on age is the way to show respect in Korean culture (Kang, 2006). That is, Koreans believe that a younger person should show respect to an older one and an older person should have the responsibility of caring for the younger one. Thus, many Koreans tend to perceive power imbalance based on age as something positive and take for granted (Kang, 2006). However, in non-native Koreans' eyes, a difference in age is often viewed as something problematic, particularly in social interactions between a man and a woman. For example, in Lee et al.'s (2013) study, a female Korean graduate student voluntarily helped a male Korean guest speaker who visited her class to be aware of their age difference; the guest speaker was much older than her. However, her American classmates perceived this as a sign of gender-based power inequality.

Friendship Is Long-Term Commitment

For Koreans, a friendship takes a long time to form and lasts almost forever. While Americans usually need less than six months to form a friendship with someone, Koreans, and many other international students, believe it needs to take a much longer time, at least one year (Martin & Nakayama, 2014). Due to the fact that Americans easily make friends and call acquaintances friends, international students in the United States often say Americans are friendly to everyone but their friendships are too superficial (Martin & Nakayama, 2014).

Because their friendships are developed through shared experiences over an extended period of time, Koreans do not need to provide detailed information in communications with friends. Therefore, Koreans use a high-context communication style in interpersonal relationships. In high-context communication, key information of a conversation exists in the context or relationship between speaker and listener (Ino & Glicken, 2002; Ji et al., 2010; Martin & Nakayama, 2014). In Koreans' interpersonal communication, listeners need to be extremely sensitive to catch hidden meanings in what speakers say rather than literally interpreting the words themselves (Aiken, Kim, Hwang & Lu, 1995). For example, when they are asked a question, Koreans do not provide clear or specific answers but use vague terms expecting listeners to infer the true answers (Park & Kim, 1992). Similarly, when they need to convince others or defend themselves, Koreans usually use abstract or general descriptions while Americans rely on specific evidence and sound reasoning (Park &Kim, 1992). Koreans often ask a third person when they are confused as to what their conversational partners actually meant or intended. Also, in expressing and perceiving politeness in communication, Koreans tend to rely on relational cues while Americans pay attention to the message itself (Ambady, Koo, Lee & Rosenthal, 1996).

The best example of Koreans' high-context communication style is the so-called *Noon-Chi* (눈치; Sense of Understanding Contexts). *Noon-Chi* can be identified as a sense or ability of (1) figuring out what is going on, (2) inferring other's true intentions or expectations, and (3) catching a hidden meaning of what another said with little contextual cues. In an ideal situation of conversation between two Koreans, participants do not need to describe or explain what they want in detail because they are supposed to catch it through *Noon-Chi* (Kim & Yun, 2008). Thus, having *Noon-Chi* is the most critical communication skill in all types of interpersonal relationships in Korean society (Park & Kim, 2008).

Jeong (정; Affection), Euo-Ri (의리; Loyalty), and Self-Disclosure Are Essential in Friendship

While Americans expect trust and honesty from friends (Martin & Nakayama, 2014), *Jeong* is the fundamental expectation from friends among Koreans. In fact, the term *Woo-Jeong* in Korean language refers to *Jeong* among friends. In Korean society, there is almost no interpersonal relationship without *Jeong* because what makes a relationship 'personal' is *Jeong* (Brown, 1994). Similar concepts of *Jeong* in Western culture could be "affection or affinity" (Kim & Yun, 2008, p. 311) or "emotional connection" (Brown, 1994, p187). However, what makes *Jeong* different from those concepts is that it does not always contain positive emotions but can include feelings of pain or even hatred (Kim & Yun, 2008; Son, 2014).

More importantly, *Jeong* cannot be developed without people being together for an extended period of time (Son, 2014). In general, Koreans rarely say 'we have or feel *Jeong*' when they are in the early stage of an interpersonal relationship. Instead, Koreans use the term *Jeong* for friends, family members, teachers/students, managers/subordinates, or coworkers who have been together for an extended time period (Kim & Yun, 2008; Son, 2014).

As *Jeong* deepens through shared experiences and feelings whether they are positive or negative, friendship among Koreans often means being selfless or other-centered (Son, 2014) and requires *Euo-Ri* (의리; Loyalty). The concept of *Euo-Ri* is the combination of responsibility, obligation, loyalty, and trust. Thus, Koreans believe one should be willing to help a friend whenever he/she needs it, regardless of the cost, to show true friendship (Park & Kim, 1992).

In relation to the concept of *Jeong* and *Euo-Ri*, Koreans believe that friends should share almost everything; enjoy the same activities, have the same (or at least similar) opinions or attitudes toward social issues, and do almost everything together whether they like it or not. In the eyes of Koreans, friends are not independent individuals but one unit or group of interdependent ones. Americans form and maintain friendships with individuals who have various backgrounds, interests, and opinions (Martin & Nakayama, 2014) and therefore hang around with different friends to serve different needs or in different contexts. Koreans tend to be with the same friends regardless of context and share all topics with the same friends, expecting everyone to have the same or similar perspectives.

For this reason, Koreans use a "high disclosure" (Adler & Proctor II, 2014, p. 291) communication style. Although Koreans, like other Asians, share their personal information with only those they trust (Park & Kim, 2008) they tend to employ a high level of self-disclosure when they are with friends. In French et al.'s (2006) study, Korean students' level of disclosure in interactions with friends was higher than that of their American counterparts. Merchant (1980) interprets Koreans' high disclosure communication style as a "Korean's way of getting close to you" (p. 66) rather than a violation of privacy or social rules. That is, Koreans are interested in and openly search for information about another's personal issues because they believe that one should know everything about another in order to maintain a genuine and meaningful relationship (Merchant, 1980).

In sum, Koreans usually develop a friendship with those who are of the same age and who are members of the same in-group. Two of the most essential requirements for keeping a friendship are *Jeong* and *Euo-Ri*, which can be developed only through a long-term relationship. In terms of communication styles, Koreans use high disclosure and high-context communications which require *Noon-Chi*. All of these are related to a cultural background of collectivism and high power distance.

■ *Sa-Rang*(사랑; Love) and *Yeon-Ae* (연애; Romantic Relationship)

Although *Sa-Rang* (사랑; Love) is the most commonly translated Korean word to refer to love or romance, it is not equivalent to a feeling of love for Koreans (Brown, 1994). In Korean culture, *Sa-Rang* is closer to the concept of care/caring which has a connotative meaning of responsibility of a person in a higher position or with power (Kang, 2006). Thus, it may be more accurate to use the term *Yeon-Ae* (연애; Romantic Relationship) or *Sa-Gwi-Da* (사귀다; We are in a relationship) to refer to a romantic relationship between two young adults. Korean couples use *Yeon-Ae* when they are on an intimate level and consider marriage while *Sa-Gwi-Da* is used for those who have just gotten involved in a romantic relationship or for teenagers who are involved in casual dating without considering marriage. In this section,

I will discuss romantic relationships in general without consideration of depth or level.

Friend-Oriented Romantic Relationship and Unique Turning Point

Similar to their attitudes toward friendship, many Koreans believe that getting involved in a romantic relationship is a long-term commitment. Koreans do not express their interest in potential romantic partners immediately but start a romantic relationship only after spending an extended period of time observing each other. More importantly, passion is less important in Korean romantic relationships compared to that of Americans. In Seepersad et al.'s (2008) study of 227 college students, Koreans rated a much lower level of loneliness than their American counterparts when they were not in a romantic relationship. In interpreting this result, Seepersad et al. (2008) argue that since a romantic relationship is not the only source of love and intimacy for Koreans, Korean students do not rate high levels of loneliness even when they are not in a romantic relationship. Meanwhile, American students are more likely to feel lonely when they are not in a romantic relationship because American society as a whole puts a great emphasis on an individual's romantic relationship as a main source of love and intimacy (Seepersad et al., 2008).

According to DeVito (2013), turning points refer to "significant relationship events that have important consequences for the individuals and the relationship, and may turn its direction or trajectory" (p. 230). Because it is mandatory duty for all Korean men to complete military service, the time period of serving in the military, 18 months in general, is a significant turning point for young adult Korean couples. For many couples, it becomes a negative turning point which leads to the termination of a relationship for a couple of reasons. First, for Korean women, especially female college students, it is not easy to wait for their boyfriends without dating regularly or even meeting them for 18 months. Second, and more important, most female senior and junior college students graduate school and get a job before their boyfriends come back to school after completing military service. In the eyes of these women, their boyfriends who are still in military service or in college are too immature or are unprepared as a partner for marriage, compared to those men they meet in the workplace. Third, immediately after completion of military service, many Korean men tend to adopt the autocratic communication style they learned during military service and force it on their girlfriends, leading to breakups.

However, for some couples, the 18 months' military service plays a positive role in strengthening relationships and leading to marriage. Because completing a military service is a critical milestone not only for one individual man but also for the entire members of the family, Korean parents start to consider their son's girlfriend as their daughter-in-law when she shows consistent love to her boyfriend during his time of military service. That is, in Korean parents' eyes, this woman is not a girlfriend anymore but a member of their family because she has gone through a tough time waiting for their son. Supporting this, one Korean college student that the author of this chapter met said "I visited my boyfriend's military camp with his parents when he completed his first four week's basic training course. After that visit, my boyfriend's parents started to treat me like their daughter. It is obvious because they even gave me pocket money. They are now extremely nice to me." (personal conversation)

Expressing Ma-Eum (마음; Heart) Is Integral in Romantic Relationship

Korean teenagers or young adult couples often create and celebrate various special days such as the anniversary of 50, 100, and 1000 days together, and exchange small gifts with each other (Han & Choi, 2011). Missing a special day often becomes a cause for relational conflict among Korean couples, and presenting gifts plays a critical role in strengthening interpersonal relationships among Koreans (Han & Choi, 2011). This can be attributed to the Koreans' cultural tradition of giving presents as the way of expressing their *Ma-Eum* (마음; Heart). Among Koreans, *Ma-Eum* shows how much one cares or has concern for others and relationship status change is based on the degree of expressing one's *Ma-Eum* (Han & Choi, 2011). Unlike Americans who present their passion, affection or care through verbal communication, Koreans believe that expressing one's *Ma-Eum* has to be through actions (Han & Choi, 2011). Especially, in Koreans' minds, actions that require a significant amount of time, effort, or materials can represent one's genuine or sincere *Ma-Eum*. This is why Koreans, particularly those in romantic relationships, often exchange gifts.

Another common action of expressing *Ma-Eum* among Koreans is having a meal together. In fact, the most typical way of greeting among Koreans is "Did you have a meal?" The question does not really ask if you had meal or not but has various meanings depending on context. When it is used for acquaintances or neighbors, it is same as "How are you?" in the United States. When Koreans use it for friends or for people in lower social positions such as children, students, subordinates, it means "I do care about you. Let me know if you need anything. I'll be with you." In professional settings, when they want to start a business with someone, Koreans usually say "Why don't we have a meal together soon?" In a romantic relationship, the most common way of requesting a date is "I'd like to have a meal or coffee/tea with you." because it has a connotative meaning of "I'm interested in you." Thus, the action of having a meal together can be a significant turning point in a romantic relationship moving forward, perhaps, to a more intimate relationship as well as for resolving conflicts or repairing a relationship.

Affective but Reserved Communication Style

Koreans' emphasis on expressing one's *Ma-Eum* is presented through their affective communication style. In Koreans' interpersonal communications, it is more important to understand and share each other's feelings than to exchange factual information (Park & Kim, 1992). The unique term, *ee-sim-jun-sim* (이심전심; Reading Each Other's Minds), which can be translated as "from one mind to another" (Kim & Yun, 2008, p. 308) reflects Koreans' common belief that people should be able to express and understand each other's true intentions through *Ma-Eum* even if they do not talk (Kim & Yun, 2008). That is, Koreans are extremely sensitive to reading a partner's feelings, and being careful to choose an appropriate response so as not to hurt his/her feelings in conversations (Park & Kim, 1992).

However, Koreans' tendency to use an affective communication style does not mean that they frequently express their feelings nor are they encouraged to do so. Especially, touching each other or expressing one's love in public is still considered a violation of the "display rules" (DeVito, 2013, p. 113) even in contemporary Korean society although many popular Korean movies and TV shows may present public displays of passionate affection as normal. In fact, traditional Korean couples, including husbands and wives, do not openly express passion or affection for each other (Kim & Yun, 2008; Merchant, 1980; Park & Kim, 1992; Son, 2014). In Koreans' view, love is not something people need to show explicitly but it should be kept inside (Park & Kim, 1992). In Korean cultures, a real mature or strong person is one who is full of *Jeong* but keeps it inside (Son, 2014). One popular joke among Koreans is that Korean men from Keoyng-Sang province, one of the most conservative areas in Korea, speak only three sentences when they come back home from work: "Did you have a meal?" "How are kids doing?" and "Let's go to sleep." As shown in this joke, Korean men tend to hide their feelings even at home, the most private place.

Importance of Family and Chae-Myeon (체면; Social Face)

While Americans consider a romantic relationship as the choice of an individual, for many Asians including Koreans, it is a matter for the family (Dhariwal & Connolly, 2013; Martin & Nakayama, 2014). Family members of each party, particularly parents, still play significant roles in romantic partner selection among Koreans (Brown, 1994; Oh & Minichiello, 2013). Also, considering the fact that most young adult Koreans stay with their parents until they marry (Brown, 1994; Cho, Otani, Han & Horn, 2010), young adults are more likely to be influenced by or even under the control of their parents in their partner selection in romantic relationships (Oh & Minichiello, 2013). Korean-Americans in the United States also show the same tendency. According to Lee's (2003) findings from in-depth interviews with 60 Korean-Americans in the New York City, most of the participants viewed marriage as family business rather than an issue for the two individuals alone and indicated their willingness to follow or respect their parents' preference in the selection of their romantic partners.

Among various issues surrounding family, the socioeconomic status of the family seems like one of the most critical factors to affect one's partner selection and the stability of romantic relationships among contemporary Korean couples. As presented in numerous popular Korean TV soap operas and movies, Korean couples from two very different socioeconomic backgrounds are more likely to encounter rejection from their family members and fail to get married. Thus, many Koreans get involved in romantic relationships with or marry those who went to the same school or have similar professions. Some Koreans find their partners through professional marriage agencies to find appropriate partners for them (Brown, 1994; Won-Doornink, 1985). Similarly, a majority of Koreans, particularly those in the upper-middleclass, are still against inter-racial/ethnic romantic relationships or marriages (Han & Price, 2015; Kim, 2012; Yang & Rosenblatt,

2001). They believe that interracial/ethnic marriage is an option only for those who are not able to find Korean partners (Han & Price, 2015). Lee (2003) affirmed this with the finding that upper-middle class Korean-Americans prefer and tend to have romantic relationships with Koreans, Korean-Americans, or other Asians at least, while those Korean-Americans in working class families frequently get in relationships with individuals from various racial/ethnic groups.

Koreans' concern about each other's family background, socioeconomic status or race/ethnicity in romantic relationship is rooted in the unique culture of *Chae-Myeon* (체면; Social Face), which can be defined as "one's social face" or "one's self-image presented to others" (Choi & Lee, 2002, p. 335). This culture of *Chae-Myeon* reflects Koreans' extremely high level of sensitivity to how others view them. Koreans tend to compare themselves with others in many social contexts and make sure they do not deviate from typical Korean norms (Kang, 2006; Merchant, 1980; Yang & Rosenblatt, 2001). This high level of other-consciousness controls the public behavior of Koreans from what they order for lunch to who they get marry to (Kang, 2006; Merchant, 1980; Yang & Rosenblatt, 2001). At the same time, keeping *Chae-Myeon* means one behaves appropriately or meets expectations for his/her social position in various contexts (Choi & Lee, 2002; Yang & Rosenblatt, 2001). Thus, for Koreans, marrying someone who has a very different socioeconomic status has two risks: (1) it is a sign that one is different from typical Koreans and (2) one may not be able to keep *Chae-Myeon* in case his/her partner does not follow appropriate social norms due to his/her different background.

Strong Masculinity Culture, Patriarchy, and Oppression of Women

A strong culture of masculinity and the ideology of patriarchy still remain in romantic relationships among Koreans. In a society with a culture of masculinity, people are expected to have traditional roles and rules according to gender, such as that a man/husband should be a breadwinner and a woman/wife should stay home taking care of children (Hofstede, 2001). Despite visible changes in terms of women's social status and family patterns, Koreans still keep traditional ideas about gender roles (Eun & Lee, 2005; Hyun, 2001; Park & Kim, 1992; Youn, 1998). For example, the results of Youn's (1998) survey with 833 subjects who ranged in age from 15 to 23 reveal that Korean men hold conservative attitudes toward women's roles and women in general. Also, Hyun (2001) claims that patriarchy still plays a key role in oppressing Korean women. Supporting Hyun's (2001) point, in Kim's (2006) study, middle-aged Korean women who married Americans and moved to the United States reported the main reason they married Americans was to escape from the oppressively strong ideas of patriarchy in Korean society. Similarly, a majority of female Korean-American participants in Lee's (2003) study said they did not want to date Korean men who hold traditional ideas about gender roles based on Confucianism.

Furthermore, Koreans hold very conservative and traditional ideas in terms of romantic relationships (Won-Doornink, 1985; Yang & Rosenblatt, 2001; Youn, 1998). For instance, Koreans do not proudly disclose the romantic relationships they had prior to marriage because people would call individuals who had been dating with more than one person as a cheater, or similar terms regarded as dishonorable (Won-Dornink,1985). Similarly, Koreans, particularly those in the highly educated upper-middle class, maintain a negative attitude toward the idea of living together before marriage (Eun & Lee, 2005). More importantly, Koreans oppress women by keeping a double standard with regard to virginity and extramarital affairs (Yang & Rosenblatt, 2001). Specifically, in Korean society, women are expected to keep their virginity until they get married while men are encouraged to have sexual experiences before marriage partly due to peer pressure (Yang & Rosenblatt, 2001). And, men who have extramarital affairs can be easily forgiven while women are harshly criticized by not only husbands but also members of the community (Yang & Rosenblatt, 2001). Overall, in spite of their high level of education and professional positions, Korean women are still being oppressed or disadvantaged at least in their romantic relationships.

In sum, unlike Americans, who emphasize strong passion between two individuals, Koreans take a friendship-oriented approach to romantic relationships and view their romantic partners as members of their extended family. In Koreans' romantic relationships, the socioeconomic background of each partner's families is one of the most critical considerations, and it is related to Koreans' strong other-consciousness, particularly *Chae-Myeon* culture. Furthermore, in spite of rapid social changes, Koreans still hold a conservative perspective in terms of romantic relationships with a strong culture of masculinity and the ideology of patriarchy. When it comes to communication styles, Koreans tend to use affective communication because they believe that it is more important to understand another's *Ma-Eum* rather than delivering information. However, at the same time, Koreans are very reserved in expressing love in romantic relationships.

■ Use of Social Media in Friendship and Romantic Relationship

Korea is considered as one of the leading countries in terms of information technology in the world (Lewis & George, 2008; Hwang & Park, 2006; Kim & Yun, 2008; Park & Lim, 2014; Yi et al., 2013) and the number of Internet users in Korea has dramatically increased in the last decade. More than 90% of Korean households had Internet access in 2009 (Yi et al., 2013). Inevitably, interpersonal relationship patterns among younger generations of Koreans have been influenced by new communication technologies, particularly social media (Ji et al., 2010; Kwak, Choi, & Lee, 2014). In this section, I will briefly discuss some characteristics of Koreans' social media usage in interpersonal relationships and how they are relevant to Korean culture. It is worthy to note that a great number of researches on Koreans' use of social media are about *Cyworld* (싸이월드; World of Relationships) because it had been the most popular social networking site among Koreans until *Facebook* was launched in 2010 (Hjorth, 2007; Muk, Chung & Kim, 2014; Park, Lim, Sams, Nam & Park, 2011; Shin, 2010; Son, 2009).

Socialization and Bonding Close Relationships

Koreans use social media to enjoy socializing with people rather than seeking for information (Ishii & Ogasahara, 2007; Lim & Palacios-Marques, 2011; Park & Lee, 2012). In fact, socialization is an integral part of interpersonal relationships among Koreans. According to Ishii and Ogasahara's (2007) findings, Koreans socialize with friends more often (average 3.7 times per month) than Japanese (average 2.7 times per month) in offline-based relationships. Thus, it is not surprising to know that Koreans' main purpose of using social media is for the socialization. Specifically, in Ishii and Ogasahara's (2007) study, Koreans expected a higher level of social gratification and spent more time socializing with others even in online communities than their Japanese counterparts. Also, Lim and Palacios-Marques (2011) found that Koreans ranked the highest in terms of using Internet for socialization in comparison to their American and

Spanish counterparts. Similarly, Park and Lee (2012) showed that Koreans usually use a smartphone to socialize with others.

More importantly, the main purpose of using social media among Koreans is to maintain or strengthen existing close relationships rather than expanding their social networks. According to Shin (2010), *Myspace* failed to appeal to Koreans because the major functions and features of it were designed for those individuals who are interested in sharing knowledge with others or in self-promotion. Meanwhile, Koreans were attracted to *Cyworld* because it offered various services that could reinforce existing offline relationships (Shin, 2010). In fact, what made *Cyworld* popular among Koreans was its main service of searching for old classmates. Through *Cyworld*, a great number of Koreans, particularly those who are in foreign countries, were able to reconnect with their old classmates who they had lost touch with since leaving school or leaving Korea (Hjorth, 2007; Kim, Faux II, & Park, 2007). In Kim et al.'s (2007) focus group interviews with Korean immigrants in the United States, one participant made a comment about how *Cyworld* helped her to maintain relationships with old friends in Korea, reflecting Koreans' attitudes toward friendship discussed earlier. According to this Korean immigrant, keeping a friendship with someone in Korea requires continuous effort: meeting each other, having meals together, celebrating special days, and exchanging gifts, all of which are almost impossible for those living in foreign countries. However, due to *Cyworld*, she could show her efforts to keep a friendship though she was in the United States (Kim et al., 2007).

In addition to Kim et al. (2007) and Shin's (2010) works, there are numerous researches that confirm the notion that Koreans' main motive for using social media is in bonding relationships (i.e., Choi, Jung, & Lee, 2013; Chung, 2011; Hjorth, 2007; Ishii & Ogasahara, 2007; Kim, 2014; Kim, et al., 2007; Kim, Sohn & Choi, 2010). First, Kim's (2014) recent study reveals that Korean teenagers who came to the United States for study used social media to keep up with their old friends in Korea rather than communicating with new friends in the United States. Interestingly, Kim et al.'s (2010) comparative study shows that despite the fact that American and Korean students spend almost same amount of time on social networking sites, the number of friends in their contact lists were significantly different; American students had many more friends (average 412 friends) than their Korean counterparts (average 81 friends). Interpreting this result, Kim et al. (2010) argued that Koreans use social networking sites that mainly consist of their close friends for social support while Americans use it for entertainment purposes with various types of friends. This is consistent with one of the characteristics of Korean friendship that discussed earlier: Koreans keep exclusive friendships with those who are of the same age, from the same group, and who have similar interests while Americans have a wide range of friends. Thus, most of the friends listed in Americans' social networking sites may not be considered by Koreans as friends at all. Furthermore, in comparison with Japanese who share a similar Asian culture, Koreans show a stronger tendency of strengthening existing offline-based relationships in online communities than their Japanese counterparts (Ishii & Ogasahara, 2007). In other words, Koreans tend to form online communities based on their offline networks (Ishii & Ogasahara, 2007) and therefore Koreans' virtual relationships are extended versions of real-world ones.

For the same reason, even though they start relationships online for the purpose of convenience, Koreans tend to continue those online relationships through face-to-face meetings, the so-called *Bun-Gae* (번개; impromptu offline gathering). In Hwang and Park's (2006) study, those who participated in *Bun-Gae* more often showed a higher level of intimacy and satisfaction in their online relationships. Physical interactions through *Bun-Gae* helped Koreans feel emotional attachments and motivated them to maintain their online relationships for a long time (Hwang & Park, 2006). Similarly, in terms of self-disclosure in friendship and romantic relationships, Koreans hold negative attitudes toward those people who openly share personal information through online communication (Yum & Hara, 2006). This can be attributed to Koreans' belief in friendship as a long-term commitment and their preference for a reserved communication style in romantic relationships. That is, for Koreans, disclosure of self through online communication is perceived as revealing "too much information, too soon" (Yum & Hara, 2006, p. 146).

Reflecting and Maintaining Korean Cultures

In the use of social media, like their offline interpersonal relationships, Koreans show (1) a collectivistic culture (Choi et al., 2013; Kim & Yun, 2008; Lee & Workman, 2014; Lewis & George, 2008; Park et al., 2011), (2) a high-context communication style (Choi et al., 2013; Kim & Yun, 2008) with the emphasis of *Jeong*, and (3) high uncertainty avoidance (Lee & Workman, 2014). Specifically, in Lee and Workman's (2014) study of

Korean and American fashion consumers' patterns of using social media, Korean consumers rated a high level of sensitivity to gossip, what others say, as well as strong group conformity. Lee and Workman (2014) attributed this to Koreans' tendency toward high uncertainty avoidance as well as a collectivistic culture. Park et al. (2011) also found evidence of collectivistic culture including frequent use of "group-oriented terms such as 'we' and 'our country'" (p. 296) in their analysis of Korean politicians' profiles and comments on social media.

Hjorth (2007) discussed how *Cyworld* reflected Koreans' unique interpersonal communication practices as well as traditional Korean culture. For example, the concept of *Cy-Il-Chon* (싸이 일촌; Person in an intimate relationship in *Cyworld*) presents Koreans' collectivistic culture based on an exclusionist approach; treating people in in-groups and out-groups differently as well as emphasizing kinship. That is, *Cyworld* users share a different level of information with their *Cy-Il-Chon* and their non-*Cy-Il-Chon* (Hjorth, 2007). Furthermore, the *Mini-Hompi* (미니홈피; Mini Room) of the *Cyworld* represents the unique culture of *Bang* (방; Room) in Korean society (Hjorth, 2007). For Koreans, *Bang* has two contradictory symbolic meanings: (1) the place for social gatherings and (2) the exclusive space only for those in close relationships. Koreans often go to various types of *Bang* such as *No-Rae-Bang* (노래방; Karaoke/Singing Room), *Jjim-Jil-Bang* (찜질방; Spa/Sauna Room), *Pi-Si-Bang* (피시방; Internet café/Online Game Room) for social gatherings (Hjorth, 2007). However, at the same time, Koreans do not spend time at those *Bangs* with people who are not in close relationships with them. Therefore, the system of showing and sharing one's own *Mini-Hompi* with only those invited guests (*Cy-Il-Chon*), who are most likely close friends or family members, is an obvious example of the Koreans' unique culture of *Bang* in an online context. Another example of Koreans' unique interpersonal practices, Hjorth (2007) noticed in *Cyworld*, was gift-giving. In *Cyworld*, one could purchase and send various types of cyber-gifts (i.e., background music, decoration items for *Mini-Hompi*) to his/her *Cy-Il-Chon* to express friendship. This action of presenting cyber-gifts is in the same line with exchanging gifts to express *Ma-Eum* in their offline interpersonal relationships. Similarly, Kim and Yun (2008) argue that *Cyworld* users' common practice of reciprocal visits to the *Mini-Hompi* of their *Cy-Il-Chon* represented Koreans' emphasis of *Jeong*. That is, for Koreans, counter-visits to visitors' *Mini-Hompi* is a symbolic action expressing *Jeong* which is essential in interpersonal relationships (Kim & Yun, 2008).

As vast majority of *Cyworld* users switched to *Facebook* and few people are currently using *Cyworld*, the focus of recent researchers has moved to *Facebook* users. First, Choi et al. (2013) found that Korean *Facebook* users appreciated various entertainment services in *Facebook* as well as the opportunities it gives for forging global networks. However, due to their collectivistic and high-context communication styles, Koreans do not feel comfortable with 'may-know friends' notices from *Facebook* or frequent 'friend request' messages from strangers, and obtrusive signs about the size of networks in the main page (Choi et al., 2013). That is, for Koreans, having more friends does not mean receiving more social support, and it is too direct to put the number of their friends or networks in *Facebook*, which is a public space (Choi et al., 2013). Similarly, in Lee-Won et al.'s (2014) comparative study of American and Koreans *Facebook* users, Americans rated a higher level of positive self-presentation than their Korean counterparts, reflecting an individualistic culture which values standing out from the crowd.

In conclusion, for Koreans, social media plays a key role in strengthening existing friendships and intimate relationships rather than searching for information or expanding their networks. Also, in the use of social media, Koreans demonstrate a collectivistic culture, a high-context communication style, and a tendency toward uncertainty avoidance similar to the way that they conduct their offline relationships. Considering these findings, social media does not replace face-to-face communication but rather it complements or strengthens existing offline relationships among Koreans (Ahn & Shin, 2013; Hjorth, 2007).

■ Practical Implications and Guidelines

As the Korean government has allowed its citizens to travel to foreign countries freely since 1988, and relaxes regulations on the media industry, Koreans have been heavily influenced by Western cultures for the last three decades. Due to this, a growing number of young Korean adults are enjoying friendships and romantic relationships with nonnative Koreans. For those foreigners who are interested in or are likely to have interpersonal relationships with Koreans, in this section I will provide some practical advice based on the characteristics I discussed earlier.

First, check one's age before starting a relationship and treat him/her accordingly using appropriate language. It is not very rude to ask about one's age in Korean society and, in fact, it is better to ask it directly than to use inappropriate language due to unawareness of age. There are many ways you can figure out a person's age, but the easiest way would be to reveal your age first and then your Korean counterpart would automatically disclose his/her age saying "Oh, you are older/younger than me!" Or, you can ask a third person, taking the indirect way. Koreans would not think it a violation of their privacy but would perceive that you are trying to get to know them.

Second, in communicating with your Korean friends or romantic partners, be careful to study their nonverbal cues and work to understand the implicit meanings of their messages rather than simply interpreting explicit words. As Koreans rely on a high-context communication style, they do not explain everything in detail with concise language. Also, because Koreans are very concerned about keeping a harmonious relationship, they could say "yes" or "OK, fine" even if they do not agree or want to do what you have asked them to do. However, you are expected to figure out his/her true intentions through *Noon-Chi*. It takes time to develop a good sense of *Noon-Chi*. The best way to avoid being impolite or inappropriate as a nonnative Korean would be to observe others carefully and follow their lead based on whatever cues they may give you.

Third, do not make too many efforts to convince your Korean counterparts with logic in interpersonal conflict situations. Even if they believe what you say is true and that it makes good sense, they may not feel comfortable accepting it and it may even hurt their feelings. Likewise, do not ask them to provide specific evidence, particularly written legal documents, before you believe what they say. They would think you do not trust them or you do not consider them as friends. Instead, you need to show your sincere *Ma-Eum* through actions. Oftentimes, Korean men resolve interpersonal conflicts with their friends by hanging out, drinking together, perhaps, without saying anything. In case you are not able to exhibit *Ma-Eum* to your Korean friend in conflict, you would do better to consult an intermediary: a mutual friend or superior at school or in the workplace.

Fourth, in a romantic relationship with a Korean partner, you should be careful showing your love or emotions in public. Due to global circulation of Western popular culture and the spread of social media, young people in non-Western countries are becoming more open-minded in terms of the overt expression of love (Dhariwal & Connolly, 2013). However, Korean couples rarely touch each other in public or in front of their friends. Also, considering the fact that Koreans are reserved, your Korean partner, especially if it is a man, will rarely express how much he loves you. However, this does not mean he lacks passion or love for you. Instead, Koreans prefer to show how much they care for each other in their own more reserved way.

Fifth, take advantage of new communication technologies if you want to express your love and passion to your Korean partner. Use of smartphone and social media is an essential part of most Koreans' everyday lives (Son, 2009), and Korean couples maintain their romantic relationships through various applications for smartphones and social media. For example, there are numerous applications that provide unique services for couples only, such as an alarm service on 22 days, 100 days, 300 days, one year of dating, offering special event ideas for celebrating those special days with a list of appropriate gifts, exclusive message notice services, and so on. Therefore, you can express your love to your romantic partner as much as you want through new technologies in a private way although you cannot do it physically in public.

Sixth, to maintain a strong and healthy romantic relationship with someone from Korea, make efforts to take care of not only your partner but also members of his/her family, especially his/her parents. As discussed earlier, Koreans do not see a romantic relationship as a personal issue but a matter concerning the entire family. Because of this, among Koreans, it is critical to introduce a partner to family members and get permission from them for a romantic relationship. Particularly, if a Korean expects objections or rejections from family members of his/her romantic partner, he/she will often make a point of spending more time with a partner's family members than with his/her romantic partner alone. In addition to spending time, visiting a partner's family with gifts for holidays (e.g., Thanksgiving, The Lunar New Year's Day) or other special days and having a meal together could be a good strategy in maintaining a healthy romantic relationship with a Korean partner.

Lastly, the golden rule for maintaining both a friendship and a romantic relationship with a Korean is to be patient. For Koreans, close relationships are long-term commitments. It takes a long time not only to form a relationship with a Korean but also to move the relationship to a more intimate level. At the same time, however, it would be a life-long relationship once it has been established.

Before closing this chapter, I would like to recommend that readers take what they learned in this chapter with caution. In Lee et al.'s (2013) study, Koreans, Japanese and Chinese present different conflict management styles despite the fact that all of them share Asian values of Confucianism. Likewise, we cannot expect all Koreans to share same characteristics discussed in this chapter. There are individual differences based on various factors such as gender, generation, social class, religion, education level, and personality. Since Korean society is changing rapidly (Yang & Rosenblatt, 2001; Yoon, 2004), there may be differences even between college students and high/middle school teenagers in their attitudes toward friendship or romantic relationships. More importantly, in contemporary Korean society, people from the upper-middle class and working class individuals may hold different value systems. For these reasons readers should use the practical guidelines I suggested here as a general reference, not a set of rigid rules.

References

Adler, R.B. & Proctor II, R.F. (2014). *Looking Out Looking In* (14th ed.), Wadsworth

Ahn, D. & Shin, D. (2013). Is the social use of media for seeking connectedness or for avoiding social isolation? Mechanisms underlying media use and subjective well-being. *Computers in Human Behavior, 29*(6), 2453–2462.

Aiken, M., Kim, D., Hwang, C. & Lu, C. (1995). A Korean group decision support system. *Information & Management, 28*, 303–310.

Ambady, N., Koo, J., Lee, F. & Rosenthal, R. (1996). More than words: Linguistic and nonlinguistic politeness in two cultures. *Journal of Personality and Social Psychology, 70*(5), 996–1011. doi:10.1037/0022-3514.70.5.996

Brown, R. A. (1994). Romantic love and the spouse selection criteria of male and female Korean college students. *Journal of Social Psychology, 134*(2), 183–189.

Cho, Y., Otani, H., Han, K. & Van Horn, K. R. (2010).Cultural differences in asymmetric beliefs of interpersonal knowledge in vertical and horizontal relationships. *Journal of General Psychology, 137*(4), 343–361

Choi, J., Jung, J., & Lee, S. (2013). What causes users to switch from a local to a global social network site? The cultural, social, economic, and motivational factors of Facebook's globalization. *Computers in Human Behavior, 29*(6), 2665–2673. doi:10.1016/j.chb.2013.07.006

Choi, S. & Lee, S. (2002). Two-component model of Chemyon-oriented behaviors in Korea: Constructive and defensive Chemyon, *Journal of Cross-Cultural Psychology, 33*(3), 332–345.

Chung, N. (2011). Korean adolescent girls' addictive use of mobile phones to maintain interpersonal solidarity. *Social Behavior and Personality, 39*(10), 1349–1358. doi:10.2224/sbp.2011.39.10.1349

Devito, A., J (2013). *The interpersonal communication book* (14th ed.). Pearson Education. Boston, MA.

Dhariwal, A., & Connolly, J. (2013). Romantic experiences of homeland and diaspora south asian youth: Westernizing processes of media and friends. *Journal of Research on Adolescence, 23*(1), 45–56.

Eun, K. & Lee, Y. (2005). Comparative analysis of Korean family value system in international context. *Journal of Korean Population Studies, 28*(1), 107–132.

은기수&이윤석. (2005). 한국의가족가치에대한국제비교연구.한국인구학, 28(1), 107–132.

Farver, J. M. & Lee-Shin, Y. (1997). Social pretend play in Korean- and Anglo-American preschoolers. *Child Development, 68*(3), 544–556. doi:10.2307/1131677

French, D. C., Bae, A., Pidada, S. & Lee, O. (2006). Friendships of Indonesian, South Korean, and U.S. college students. *Personal Relationships, 13*(1), 69–81. doi:10.1111/j.1475-6811.2006.00105.x

Guan, X., Park, H. S. & Lee, H. E. (2009).Cross-cultural differences in apology. *International Journal of Intercultural Relations, 33*(1), 32–45. doi:10.1016/j.ijintrel.2008.10.001

Han, G. & Choi, S. (2011). Trust working in interpersonal relationships: A comparative cultural perspective with a focus on East Asian culture. *Comparative Sociology, 10*(3), 380–412. doi:10.1163/156913311X578208

Han, E. & Price, P. (2015).Uncovering the hidden power of language: Critical race theory, critical language socialization and multicultural families in Korea. *Journal of Intercultural Communication Research, 44*(2), 108–131.

Hjorth, L. (2007). Home and away: A case study of the use of cyworld mini-hompy by Korean students studying in Australia. *Asian Studies Review, 31*(4), 397–407. doi:10.1080/10357820701710690

Hofstede, G. (2001). *Cultures consequences: Comparing values, behaviors, institutions, and organizations across nations* (2nd ed.), Sage publications, Thousand Oaks.

Hwang, H. & Park, S. (2006, June). *The implication of the interconnectedness: Offline flash gathering as a catalyst for online interpersonal relationship.* Paper presented at the International Communication Association (ICA) annual meeting, Dresden, Germany

Hyun, K. (2001). Sociocultural change and traditional values : Confucian values among Koreans and Korean Americans. *International Journal of Intercultural Relations, 25,* 203–229.

Ino, S. M., & Glicken, M. D. (2002). Understanding and treating the ethnically Asian client: A collectivist approach. *Journal of Health & Social Policy, 14*(4), 37–48.

Ishii, K., & Ogasahara, M. (2007). Links between real and virtual networks: A comparative study of online communities in Japan and Korea. *Cyberpsychology & Behavior, 10*(2), 252–257. doi:10.1089/cpb.2006.9961

Ji, Y. G., Hwangbo, H., Yi, J. S., Rau, P. P., Fang, X., & Ling, C. (2010). The influence of cultural differences on the use of social network services and the formation of social capital. *International Journal of Human-Computer Interaction, 26*(11–12), 1100–1121. doi:10.1080/10447318.2010.516727

Kang, S. (2006). Identity-centered multicultural care theory: White, black, and Korean caring. *Educational Foundations, 20*(3–4), 35–49

Kim, N.Y. (2006). "Patriarchy is so third word": Korean immigrant women and "migrating" White western masculinity. *Social Problems, 53*(4), 519–536.

Kim, S. (2012). Racism in the global era: Analysis of Korean media discourse around migrants, 1990–2009. *Discourse & Society, 23*(6), 657–678. doi:10.1177/0957926512455381

Kim, T. (2014). A qualitative inquiry into the life experiences of unaccompanied Korean adolescents in the United States. *Qualitative Report, 19*(20), 1–22.

Kim, H., Faux II, W., & Park, Y. (2007). *U.S. residing South Korean's uses of self-presentational strategies and information exchange with social networking sites.* Paper presented at the National Communication Association.

Kim, Y., Sohn, D., & Choi, S. M. (2010). Cultural difference in motivations for using social network sites: A comparative study of American and Korean college students. *Computers in Human Behavior, 27*(1), 365–372. doi:10.1016/j.chb.2010.08.015

Kim, S., & White, C. (2007). *How Korean female public relations practitioners' perception of confucian values affects professional experiences.* Paper presented at the National Communication Association

Kim, K. & Yun, H. (2008). Cying for me, Cying for us: Relational dialectics in a Korean social network site. *Journal of Computer-Mediated Communication, 13*(1), 298–318. doi:10.1111/j.1083-6101.2007.00397.

Kwak, K. T., Choi, S. K., & Lee, B. G. (2014). SNS flow, SNS self-disclosure and post hoc interpersonal relations change: Focused on Korean Facebook user. *Computers in Human Behavior, 31.* 294–304. doi:10.1016/j.chb.2013.10.046

Lee, S. (2003). Marriage dilemmas: Partner choices and constraints for Korean Americans in New York city. Paper presented at the American Sociological Association, 1–20. doi:asa_proceeding_9751.

Lee, B., Kozak, M., Nancoo, C.P., Chen, H., Middendore, K., & Jerry, G. (2013). Exploring dominant discourses: Creating spaces to find voice and cultural identity. *Journal of Cultural Diversity, 20*(1). 21–29.

Lee, S., & Workman, J. E. (2014). Gossip, self-monitoring and fashion leadership: comparison of United States and South Korean consumers. *Journal of Consumer Marketing, 31*(6/7), 452. doi:10.1108/JCM-04-2014-0942

Lee-Won, R. L., Shim, M., Joo, Y., & Park, S. (2014). Who puts the best "face" forward on Facebook?: Positive self-presentation in online social networking and the role of self-consciousness, actual-to-total Friends ratio, and culture. *Computers in Human Behavior, 39,* 413–423.

Lewis, C. C. & Georg e, J. F. (2008).Cross-cultural deception in social networking sites and face-to-face communication. *Computers in Human Behavior, 24*(6), 2945–2964. doi:10.1016/j.chb.2008.05.002

Lim, T. & Giles, H. (2007).Differences in American and Korean evaluations of one-year age differences. *Journal of Multilingual and Multicultural Development, 28*(5), 349–364.

Lim, S., & Palacios-Marques, D. (2011). Culture and purpose of Web 2.0 service adoption: a study in the USA, Korea and Spain. *Service Industries Journal, 31*(1), 123–131. doi:10.1080/02642069.2010.485634

Lustig, M.W. & Koester, J (2013).*Intercultural competence: Interpersonal communication across cultures* (7th ed.). Pearson Education. Boston, MA.

Martin, J. N., & Nakayama, T. K. (2014).*Experiencing intercultural communication: An introduction* (5th ed.). New York: McGraw Hill.

Merchant, J. J. (1980). Korean interpersonal patterns: Implications for Korean/American intercultural communication. *Communication, 9*(1), 60–76.

Muk, A., Chung, C., & Kim, J. (2014). A cross-national study of the influence of individualism and collectivism on liking brand pages. *Journal of International Consumer Marketing, 26*(2), 122. doi:10.1080/08961530.2014.878204

Oh, J. E., & Minichiello, V. (2013). Psychosocial development in South Korean couples and its effects on marital relationships. *Journal of Family Psychotherapy, 24*(3), 228–245. doi:10.1080/08975353.2013.817264

Park, M. & Kim, M. (1992). Communication practices in Korea. *Communication Quarterly, 40,* 398–404

Park, Y. S. & Kim, B.K. (2008).Asian and European American cultural values and communication styles among Asian American and European American college students. *Cultural Diversity And Ethnic Minority Psychology, 14*(1), 47–56. doi:10.1037/1099-9809.14.1.47

Park, N. & Lee, H. (2012). Social implications of Smartphone use: Korean college students' Smartphone use and psychological well-being. *Cyberpsychology, Behavior, And Social Networking, 15* (9). 491–497.

Park, S. J., & Lim, Y. S. (2014). Information networks and social media use in public diplomacy: a comparative analysis of South Korea and Japan. *Asian Journal of Communication, 24*(1), 79–98. doi:10.1080/01292986.2013.851724

Park, S., Lim, Y., Sams, L., Nam, S., & Park, H. (2011). Networked politics on cyworld: The text and sentiment of Korean political profiles. *Social Science Computer Review, 29*(3), 288–299. doi:10.1177/0894439310382509

Seepersad, S., Choi, M. & Shin, N. (2008). How does culture influence the degree of romantic loneliness and closeness?. *Journal of Psychology, 142*(2), 209.

Shin, D. (2010). Analysis of online social networks: a cross-national study. *Online Information Review, 34*(3), 473–495.

Shin, Y. (2007). Peer relationships, social behaviours, academic performance and loneliness in Korean primary school children. *School Psychology International, 28*(2), 220–236

Son, A. (2014).Jeong as the paradigmatic embodiment of compassion (hesed): A critical examination of disparate and dispositional jeong. *Pastoral Psychology, 63*(5–6), 735–747. doi:10.1007/s11089-014-0611-7

Son, M. (2009). Cultures of ambivalence: An investigation of college students' uses of the camera phone and cyworld's mini-hompy. *Knowledge, Technology & Policy, 22*(3), 173. doi:10.1007/s12130-009-9083-y

Won-Doornink, M. J. (1985). Self-disclosure and reciprocity in conversation: A cross-national study. *Social Psychology Quarterly, 48*(2), 97–107

Woo, I. (2013). When cultures collide. *Therapy Today, 24*(7), 18–21 4.

Yang, S & Rosenblatt, P. C. (2001).Shame in Korean families. *Journal of Comparative Family Studies, 32*(3), 361–375.

Yi, M., Oh, S. & Kim, S. (2013). Comparison of social media use for the United States and the Korean governments. *Government Information Quarterly, 30*(3), 310–317. doi:10.1016/j.giq.2013.01.004

Yoon, K. (2004). Not just words: Korean social models and the use of honorifics. *Intercultural Pragmatics, 1*(2), 189–210.

Youn, G. (1998). Attitudes toward women in adolescent Korean sample, 18.

Yum, Y. & Hara, K. (2006). Computer-mediated relationship development: A cross-cultural comparison. *Journal of Computer-Mediated Communication, 11*, 133–152.

Author Note

My special thanks go to two Korean exchange students at John Carroll University, Hyejin Han and Ka-Hye Ahn, who provided valuable comments regarding contemporary Korean college students' attitudes toward romantic relationships.

CHAPTER 10
PROFESSIONAL RELATIONSHIPS AND ORGANIZATIONAL COMMUNICATION IN SOUTH KOREA

JAESUB LEE

■ Defining Professional Relationships

A professional relationship is an ongoing, committed workplace association between two or more people in for-profit as well as not-for-profit organizations. It is manifested in, for example, regular or repeated interactions between superiors and subordinates, unscheduled meetings among peers at the workplace, friendly coaching sessions between a mentor and a mentee, informative conversations between public relations officers and some stakeholder publics, and integrative negotiations with clients and customers (Sias, 2009).

The professional relationship is goal–oriented; it fulfills some organizational and personal needs and accomplishes stated and unstated purposes. It can be short-term or long-term association. The association can be continuous and/or discontinuous (on and off). It operates within appropriate explicit and implicit ethical standards and boundaries.

Forging and maintaining proper professional relationships or ties inside and outside of the organization significantly and positively contribute to the job/task performance and relational partners' career progresses. In particular, establishing and sustaining "good" relationships is the key to the business and career success in South Korea (hereafter Korea). In fact, a recent news report indicates that a good relationship is crucial to the Koreans' subjective sense of well-being. It is more important than their income, education, marriage, job, age, and gender (Kim, 2015).

There are several prominent features that impact the development and maintenance of professional relationships in Korea such as cultural characteristics, organization/management practices, and unique culture-specific attributes (e.g., "*Chae-myeon*," "*Yongo*," "*Noon-chi*," and "*Jeong*").

■ Korean Cultural Characteristics

Culture inevitably shapes the way that people interact with one another in social environments, including organizations, since different cultures promote unique sets of values, norms, and expectations (Forgas & Bond, 1985; Triandis & Albert, 1987). Thus, professional relationships are predictably subject to cultural influence. The most influential factor in Korean culture, social moral codes, and organizations is probably Confucianism.

Overall, the Confucian philosophy as practiced in Korean professional settings strongly encourages loyalty to organizations, respect for the hierarchy of occupational ranking, deference to elders, and harmony in one's relationships with others (Lee & Jablin, 1992). Further, Hofstede's (2001) profile of culture suggests that Korea typically enacts a long-term dynamism, high power distance, high uncertainty avoidance, collectivism, and masculinity. Fitting such profile, Korean business tends to stress future market position; fosters hierarchical bureaucracies, strong leaders, and a high regard for authority; places heavy emphasis on one's knowledge and use of appropriate communication rules and norms in interactions with others; works with employees who are tightly integrated into strong, cohesive in-groups and stay loyal in exchange of protection; and prefers men's values (e.g., being assertive and competitive) to women's (e.g., caring) when people try to solve any social issue.

On the other hand, recent empirical data (e.g., House, Hanges, Javidan, Dorfman, & Gupta, 2004) offer a somewhat different, conflicting cultural description, perhaps reflecting certain changing values and practices in Korea. In their GLOBE study, House and his colleagues (2004; Javidan & House, 2001; Javidan, Dorfman, de Luque, & House, 2006) compared 62 societies based on nine attributes of culture: assertiveness, institutional collectivism, in-group collectivism, power distance, uncertainty avoidance, gender egalitarianism, future orientation, performance orientation, and humane orientation. This study involved 17,000+ managers worldwide who answered questions pertaining to the nine cultural attributes. Each attribute was evaluated on two fronts: what a society practices ("as is") and what a society values ("should be"). Table 10.1 presents cultural attributes, what a society practices, and what a society values among select countries.

Table 10.1 *Cultural Attributes, Society Practices, Society Values in Korea and Select Countries**

Cultural Attributes	Society Practices (As is)	Society Values (Should be)
Power Distance: The degree to which members of a collective (society, organization, or group) expect power, authority, prestige, status, wealth, and material possessions to be distributed unequally	Korea: 5.61 China: 5.04 Japan: 5.11 USA: 4.88	Korea: 2.55 China: 3.10 Japan: 2.86 USA: 2.85
Uncertainty Avoidance: The extent to which a collective relies on social norms, rules, and procedures to alleviate the unpredictability of future events	Korea: 3.55 China: 4.94 Japan: 4.07 USA: 4.15	Korea: 4.67 China: 5.28 Japan: 4.33 USA: 4.00
Humane Orientation: The degree to which a collective encourages and rewards individuals for being fair, sympathetic, supportive, altruistic, generous, caring, and kind to others	Korea: 3.81 China: 4.36 Japan: 4.30 USA: 4.17	Korea: 5.60 China: 5.32 Japan: 5.41 USA: 5.53
Institutional Collectivism: The degree to which organizational and societal institutional practices encourage and reward collective allocations of resources and collective action	Korea: 5.20 China: 4.77 Japan: 5.19 USA: 4.20	Korea: 3.90 China: 3.05 Japan: 4.56 USA: 4.17
In-group Collectivism: The extent to which individuals put across pride, loyalty, and cohesiveness in their organizations, families, or close friends	Korea: 5.54 China: 5.80 Japan: 4.63 USA: 4.25	Korea: 5.41 China: 5.09 Japan: 5.26 USA: 5.77

(Continued)

Table 10.1 *Continued*

Cultural Attributes	Society Practices (As is)	Society Values (Should be)
Assertiveness: The degree to which a collective encourages and rewards individuals to be dominant, tough, confrontational, assertive, and competitive (versus modest, warm, cooperative, tender, and harmonious) in their relationships with others	Korea: 4.40 China: 3.76 Japan: 3.59 USA: 4.55	Korea: 3.75 China: 5.44 Japan: 5.56 USA: 4.32
Gender Egalitarianism: The extent to which a society minimizes gender inequality in terms of status and authority or role differences	Korea: 2.50** China: 3.05 Japan: 3.19 USA: 3.34	Korea: 4.22 China: 3.68 Japan: 4.33 USA: 5.06
Future Orientation: The extent to which a society encourages and rewards future-oriented behaviors such as long-term thinking, planning, and decision making time frame, investing in the future, and delaying gratification	Korea: 3.97 China: 3.75 Japan: 4.29 USA: 4.15	Korea: 5.69 China: 4.73 Japan: 5.25 USA: 5.31
Performance Orientation: The degree to which a collective encourages and rewards group members for performance improvement and excellence	Korea: 4.55 China: 4.45 Japan: 4.22 USA: 4.49	Korea: 5.25 China: 5.67 Japan: 5.17 USA: 6.14

* *Culture, leadership, and organizations : the GLOBE study of 62 societies by House, Robert J. ; Global Leadership and Organizational Behavior Effectiveness Research Program Reproduced with permission of SAGE PUBLICATIONS, INCORPORATED in the format. Republished in a book via Copyright Clearance Center.*

All survey items for each attribute have been measured on a 7-point scale, ranging from 1 (Strongly disagree) to 7 (Strongly agree). Higher scores represent greater attributes.

** The lowest score among 62 countries.*

Overall, in practices, Korea is among the highest ranked countries on assertiveness, performance orientation, institutional collectivism, in-group collectivism, power distance; ranked moderate on future orientation and humane orientation; ranked low on uncertainty avoidance and the lowest on gender egalitarianism. On the other hand, in what Korean society emphasizes, future orientation and humane orientation scored high relative to other countries; uncertainty avoidance, power distance, gender egalitarianism, assertiveness moderate; and institutional collectivism, in-group collectivism, and performance orientation low. Further, as shown in Table 10.1, large gaps are apparent between what Korea as a society practices and what it values, including power distance, humane orientation, institutional collectivism, gender egalitarianism, and future orientation. For example, Korean society does not value power distance, institutional collectivism very much, but practices them highly. Humane orientation, gender egalitarianism, and future orientation are valued highly, but practiced little. These gaps suggest that significant cultural changes and related behavioral confusions and transformations are taking place in Korea.

■ Korean Organizational Characteristics

The "traditional" Korean approach to management, often referred to as "K-Type" management, is founded upon Confucian principles (Lee, 1989; Yang, 2014). It is established upon Confucian work ethic that demands diligence and hard work, personal loyalty to superiors or the company. Another building block is paternalistic leadership. Paternalistic Korean managers, like a father figure in the family, assume the responsibility of looking after their subordinates, which leads to a climate of trust and loyalty. Further, they often personally take the blame for unit or team failure to protect individual employees' or team members' needs, interests, and feelings. K-Type management also tends to follow top-down decision making, hierarchical communication, bureaucratic control, flexible lifetime employment, and the use of rules, policies, and procedures to resolve or suppress conflict. In addition, it is a family or clan management and expands through conglomeration or becoming a *Chaebol* (재벌; a large business group such as Samsung, Hyundai, and LG which are usually owned and managed by family members or relatives in many diversified business areas). Close government–business relationship often has helped such expansion.

In an earlier, highly informative study of the overall characteristics of Korean organizations, Lee (1989) collected data from 87 large Korean companies and found the most common values stated in the *sahoons* (사훈; company creeds) of Korean organizations were *inhwa* (인화; harmony and unity among employees), sincerity and diligence, and *changjo* (창조; creation and development). Lee (1989) also discovered that "whereas harmony among employees is the most widely emphasized value in the Korean company sahoon, employee satisfaction is not one of the most frequently stated managerial objectives" (p. 149). With respect to organizational structure, Korean organizations have tall structures with many hierarchical levels, are highly centralized and formalized, and concentrate decision making power in the upper levels of the hierarchy. Moreover, "authority in Korean business firms is not only centralized in upper levels of management, but also concentrated in a few executive positions in many cases" (Lee, 1989, p. 155). This characteristic of Korean organizations is attributed to the prevalence of family ownership and management in Korean companies and the hiring of executives based on Hyul-yon (혈연; blood ties), Ji-yon (지연; ties based on the same birthplace or geographic area), and Hak-yon (학연; school ties). Regarding compensation, wages are primarily based on seniority and education, though performance is increasingly becoming an important determinant of salary; promotion decisions, especially at lower organizational levels, still tend to be based on seniority.

The Lee (1989) study also reported that communication typically orients along vertical hierarchies. Most communication is downward, though most directives do not contain detailed instructions. Thus, "being able to understand the superior's intentions out of the general context is one of the important qualities a subordinate should possess" (p. 159). Lee (1989) further found that Koreans are not especially open in their communication with their superiors and prefer informal settings for open communication rather than formal meetings. With respect to leadership, Korean managers tend to display a paternalistic/authoritarian style; subordinates are usually reluctant to express their opinions. Therefore, "managers are expected to understand the feelings of subordinates and make decisions accordingly" (p. 160).

Changing Human Resource Practices and Professional Relationships in Transition

As amply implied in the descriptions of Korean cultural and management characteristics, professional work relationships with the supervisor, coworker, mentor, and others are perhaps the most important predictors of employee and organizational outcomes (e.g., job performance and satisfaction, commitment to organization, turnover; Dorfman, Howell, Hibino, Lee, Tate, & Bautista, 1997). The strong emphasis on relationships between employees and supervisors/employers led to the traditional seniority-based performance appraisal systems, intensive formal and informal on-the-job training, and greater job security in Korean firms (Chung, Lee & Jung 1997).

Several scholars, however, suggest that significant changes in professional relationships are in the offing (Bae & Lawler 2000; Froese, Pak, & Chong 2008; Kim, Lee, & Lee, 2013; Rowley & Bae, 2002). Since the late 1990s, Korean firms have shifted somewhat drastically from relationship orientation to a market principle in their human resource management (HRM) practices (e.g., hiring, promoting, training, performance evaluation, and pay). The catalyst event for this shift was the financial crisis in 1997. With the US$60 billion rescue package, International Monetary Fund (IMF) imposed that Korea open the market for foreign direct investment (FDI), which in turn pushed Korean business firms to adopt global management standards or best practices such as performance- or market-based evaluation and employment. After a rapid recovery from the financial crisis, Korean firms also started to invest in overseas countries heavily, necessitating the adoption of global best practices (usually Western model). The amount of FDI by Korean business into foreign countries increased from US$3.8 billion in 1988 to US$44.5 billion in 2011 (National Archives of Korea). Further, with the advent of the amended Korean Labor Standard Act, Korean firms are able to lay off their employees almost at will (Bae, 1997). Indeed, based on the amended law, massive layoffs in the late 1990s were carried out, and Korean workers realized that their interpersonal, professional relationships at work were not as important as before. These interrelated events appear to accelerate the transition from an emphasis on relationship-based approach to market efficiency practice (Rowley & Bae, 2002). Table 10.2 summarizes changes in HRM characteristics over time in Korea.

Nonetheless, it would be yet foolish to dismiss the importance of professional work relationships in Korean firms. Culture is like a stubborn personality that only changes ever so slowly (Hofstede, 1991). A few professional work relationships, in particular, such as superior–subordinate, peer/coworker, and mentoring relationships, are highly consequential to the individual employees and the organizations in Korea.

Superior–Subordinate Relationships

Superior–subordinate relationships are hierarchical, mandatory workplace associations in which one party (e.g., manager, boss, supervisor) holds direct formal authority over the other (e.g., employee, subordinate). These are extremely far-reaching relationships. Much of the organizational works are done via superior–subordinate relationships. Supervisors frequently interact with their subordinates and thus may serve as a role model. The supervisor typically has the formal power to evaluate performance and reward and punish the subordinate. The supervisor mediates the formal flow of downward communication to the subordinate (e.g., the supervisor serves as an interpreter/filter of management messages). The supervisor usually has a personal as well as formal role relationship with the subordinate (Jablin 2001). Thus, the superior–subordinate relationship impacts lives of all parties concerned, including the organization, managers, and employees. Fittingly, superior–subordinate relationships are among the most frequently researched topics in organizational studies in the USA.

One prominent approach to the superior–subordinate relationship is the leader–member exchange (LMX) theory (e.g., Dansereau, Graen, & Haga, 1975; Graen, 2004; Graen & Uhl-Bien, 1995). The theoretical premise is that leaders (supervisors, managers) have limited personal, social, and organizational resources (e.g., time, energy, role, discretion, and positional power) and selectively negotiate and distribute their resources among their members (subordinates) with an eye for the unit's optimal job performance and productivity. Differences in the negotiated distribution of resources then lead, over time, to the formation of differential qualities of exchange. High-quality social relationships ("in-group" exchanges) boast a high degree of mutual positive affect, loyalty, relationship obligation, professional respect, trust, and

Table 10.2 *Characteristics of Human Resource Management in Korea**

HRM Areas	Old Characteristics	New Characteristics
Core Ideology	• Organization first • Collective equality • Community oriented	• Individual respected • Individual equity • Market principle adopted
Human Resource Flow	• Mass recruitment from new graduates • Job security (lifetime employment) • Generalist oriented	• Recruitment on demand • Job mobility • Development of professionals
Work Systems	• Tall structure • Line and staff—function based • Position based	• Flat structure • Team systems • Qualification based
Evaluation and Reward Systems	• Seniority (age + tenure) • Pay equality pursued • Evaluation for advancement in job/grade • No appraisal feedback • Single-rater appraisal	• Ability + performance (annual pay) • Merit pay systems • Evaluation for pay increases • Appraisal feedback • 360 degrees appraisal
Employee Influence	• Relatively less involvement • Relatively less information sharing	• More involvement • More information sharing

* Reprinted from Journal of World Business, Winter 2001, Bae Johngseok Boe and Chris Rowley, "The Impact of Globalization on HRM: The Case of South Korea" pp. 402–428. © 2001, with permission from Elsevier.

commitment. The opposite is observed in low-quality economic relationships ("out-group" exchanges) (Dulebohn, Bommer, Liden, Brouer, & Ferris, 2012; Graen, 2004).

Following the LMX theory perspective, several studies explored superior–subordinate professional relationships in Korean contexts, including feedback-seeking behaviors, turnover intentions, work attitudes, incivil treatments and retaliation, communication media choice, and silence. For example, Lee, Lee, Lee, and Park (2005) examined feedback-seeking behaviors of supervisors in Korean civil engineering companies in which superiors and subordinates work closely as a team with constant dialogues. Their findings indicated that superiors and subordinates perceived superiors' feedback-seeking behaviors differently based on the LMX quality. Superiors, for example, reported that they seek feedback from their subordinates in high-quality LMXs through direct or overt questions. However, subordinates in high-quality LMXs reported that their superiors employed direct cue monitoring strategies (e.g., paying attention to informal and unsolicited evaluative comments, casual remarks, and the manner of behavior). Subordinates may feel uncomfortable when openly expressing their honest views or evaluations of superiors' work performance in Korean organizations. Most subordinates consider their bosses as excellent leaders when they utilize direct or indirect cues monitoring skillfully to seek feedback and make appropriate inferences from such cues. Indirect cues monitoring refers to observing general behaviors such as how quickly phone calls are returned, how often advices are sought, and how long the wait for an appointment is.

Kim, Lee, and Lee (2013) investigated the extent to which LMX quality between the superior and the subordinate relates to turnover intensions among administrative office workers (e.g., marketing, human resources, and finance) in Korea. Typically, Western employees in high-quality LMXs are more committed to their organizations and jobs and have lower turnover intentions and actual turnover than their counterparts in low-quality LMXs (Dulebohn et al., 2012). For Korean subordinates, there was no significant relationship between LMX quality and turnover intentions at all. Kim and his colleagues (2013) suggest a few potential reasons. One is that Korean firms are increasingly adopting the market- or performance-based rather than relationship-based HRM practices. Further, a job is defined by what an employee's supervisor requires rather than by a formal description of the job duties that, even if it exists, is mostly ambiguous. Thus, the skill sets a subordinate develops are specific to the current organization and not transferable to other organizations or broader market and industry. In addition, under strong Korean social norm of reciprocity and loyalty, employees benefited from high-quality LMXs (e.g., better skills, knowledge, socioemotional support, pay) are socially obligated to make greater contributions to the organization that provided such benefits. The Korean interpersonal relationship principle is *inhwa* or harmony between unequals. It demands that employees give complete loyalty to their employers and supervisors (Alston 1989). All in all, the importance of interpersonal relationship itself and its linkage to job mobility or turnover decision is diminishing in Korea (Chang, 2006).

Jung and Takeuchi (2014) looked into how LMX relates to person-organization fit and work attitudes (organizational commitment and job satisfaction). Person-organization fit refers to the compatibility or congruence between an employee and an organization with respect to values, goals, or characteristics. The LMX quality was found to "moderately" correlate with person-organization fit, organizational commitment, and job satisfaction. As the subordinate has a higher quality in his/her relationship with the boss, he/she perceives a greater compatibility between oneself and the organization ($r = .36$), feel more committed to the organization ($r = .40$), and enjoy higher level of job satisfaction ($r = .42$). Traditional Korean organizations under study were very centralized and authoritarian with decision making power vested in higher levels, often at the top level . Thus, managers at lower levels in Korean organizations were not permitted to offer formal rewards even to subordinates in high-quality LMXs. Korean workers received their formal and informal rewards from the organization directly in general. Thus, the quality of LMX may not be a strong factor that affects work attitudes, perceptions, and behaviors in Korean contexts.

Confucian codes of behavior between the ruler and the subject are justice and loyalty. Such codes have been seemingly extended to the superior–subordinate relationship. That is, superiors treat their subordinates in the just manner and subordinates show loyalty to their superiors. In Korea and elsewhere, subordinates expect their supervisor to treat them with fairness and dignity in their daily interactions. When such expectations or codes of behavior are violated (e.g., rude actions like verbal insults, disrespectful behaviors, and humiliation), subordinates tend to engage in some sort of *retaliation* against their bosses. Kim and Shapiro (2008) found that Korean subordinates, when treated rudely (rather than politely) in receiving explanations from their superiors about an organizational decision on resource allocation, were more likely to engage in retaliation (e.g., slow working, taking supplies home, refusing to work on weekends, damaging equipment, and speaking ill of the organization). The likelihood of retaliation was tied to the strength of the negative emotion the subordinate felt about a supervisor's rude treatment. When a supervisor's rude behavior led to the greater negative emotional arousal (e.g., anger, anxiety, disgust, and embarrassment), the more retaliation the subordinate committed against the supervisor and the organization. Further, the rudeness–retaliation connection became stronger when the supervisor was dissimilar or a member of outgroup (rather than similar or a member of in-group) to the subordinate in terms of place of birth, dialects, customs, ways of thinking, etc.

Unexpectedly, Korean subordinates were more likely to engage in retaliatory behaviors against their supervisors than US counterparts. Korean sociocultural norm of *inwha* (harmony) requires that superiors and subordinates treat each other with respect. Once violated (e.g., rude treatment), Korean subordinates may experience an intense sense of betrayal and, thus, may enact negative behaviors toward superiors rather strongly.

Superiors and subordinates communicate with each other through various media, including face-to-face conversations, video conferencing, telephone, e-mail, and other written forms. Lee and Lee (2009) explored the extent to which cultural characteristics influenced *media choice* of Korean (and American) employees from telecommunication industries in communicating with their superiors, subordinates, colleagues, and outsiders. Findings suggested that country/culture, equivocality in tasks (i.e., ambiguity and multiple interpretations of the situation), and communication direction (i.e., upward, downward, and lateral) are important factors that affected the media choice.

Confucian moral ethics in Korea mandates respect for others (e.g., superiors, elders, and colleagues), which is often manifested through a personal, face-to-face conversation. A direct physical presence is the most appropriate way to show respect for others. Consistent with such cultural orientation, Korean employees take the direction of communication into consideration when making a media choice; in particular, when communicating upward with the boss, Korean employees preferred rich media such as face-to-face and telephone conversations regardless of task equivocality. When communicating with subordinates, colleagues, and outsiders, Korean employees used lean media like e-mail frequently largely based on task equivocality. American employees, on the other hand, varied their choice of media primarily based on task equivocality: when the task environment was ambiguous, they used rich media of face-to-face or phone conversations; if not, they preferred lean media like e-mail.

Cultural values impact communication significantly (Hirokawa & Miyahara, 1986). One interesting aspect of superior–subordinate communication in Korea is *silence*. In high or large power distance cultures like Korea, people tend to refrain from speaking up their minds or expressing their ideas, suggestions, and opinions. The act of speaking up is often taken as a challenge to the status, authority, or power of the manager (Rhee, Dedahanov, & Lee, 2014), which is likely to lead to punishment, retaliation, or negative consequences at work (e.g., unfavorable work assignments, losing a job, or not receiving a promotion). Further, subordinates are not likely to challenge superiors' inappropriate attitudes and behaviors because of the fear of being perceived as disobeying the norms of the society, and individuals who disobey social norms can become socially isolated/ostracized or marked as troublemakers.

Thus, subordinates consciously assess the risk of talking and, in the end, become reluctant to share information, opinions, and ideas with their superiors. Khatri (2009) suggested that subordinates in high power distance cultures like Korea are unwilling to get involved in decision making and want supervisors to make decisions for them. Communication is generally vertical with commands, directives, and information flowing from the top to bottom. Korean managers who frequently use authority and power when dealing with subordinates may see their employees passively withhold ideas regarding solutions to problems.

Further, collectivism in Korea is also partially responsible for employee reluctance to talk with their bosses at times. Hofstede (1991) noted that "Collectivism stands for a society in which people, from birth onward, are integrated into strong, cohesive in-groups, which, throughout people's lifetime, continue to protect them in exchange for unquestioning loyalty" (pp. 260–261). In collectivism, social harmony is the paramount value. From the early childhood, Koreans learn to be careful about what they say, especially when expressing their opinions and making suggestions that could result in conflict and destroy social harmony. They also learn to protect the reputations and images of others (Ting-Toomey & Kurogi, 1998). All in all, Korean employees are motivated not to reveal information that may hurt people or organizations. Even when they do, they are likely to express the point in indirect ways that help each other "save face." In short, Korean managers with large power distance and collectivistic views unwittingly foster silence in their interactions with employees.

Employee silence refers to "intentionally concealing information, ideas, and opinions with relevance to improvements" in the organization (Rhee et al., 2014, p. 705). It often negatively impacts organizational decision making, development and change, innovation, and employee stress, dissatisfaction, cynicism, and job performance. Van Dyne, Ang, and Botero (2003) presented three types of employee silence based on their communication motives: acquiescent, defensive, and prosocial. *Acquiescent* silence refers to intentionally and passively withholding information, opinions, and ideas on work-related issues based on the belief that speaking up is pointless and unlikely to change the situation. It is a fundamental resignation or disengagement. When Korean superiors do not react to information shared by low-level subordinates, employees may learn that information sharing is aimless and does not lead to change, thereby resorting to acquiescent silence.

Defensive silence refers to intentionally and proactively "withholding relevant ideas, information, or opinions as a form of self-protection, based on fear" (p. 1367). Employees consciously assess alternatives and decide to withhold ideas, information, and opinions as the best personal strategy at present. They may feel that information sharing is dangerous, risky, or threatening. It is comparable to the "Mum Effect" in which people keep "Mum about Undesirable Messages to the recipient" (Rosen & Tessler, 1970, p. 254) or consciously hold back bad news or delay delivering bad news to avoid personal discomfort, defensive responses of the recipient, or negative personal consequences (i.e., "kill the messenger") (Rosen & Tessler, 1970, 1972).

Prosocial silence refers to "withholding work-related ideas, information, or opinions with the goal of benefiting other people or the organization—based on altruism or cooperative motives" (p. 1368). For example, employees can withhold information because it is confidential and not meant for general discussion or distribution.

High power distance and collectivism lead most clearly to *acquiescent silence* (intentional and passive disengagement) of Korean employees to their supervisors/managers (Rhee et al., 2014). As Korean employees experienced greater power distance and collectivism, they engaged more in acquiescent silence.

Peer/Coworker Relationships

Peer/coworker relationships are usually involuntary professional associations between employees at the same hierarchical level who have no formal authority over each other. Although the term "coworker" implies any organizational member with whom the individual works (including superiors, subordinates, and peer employees) (Sias, 2009), coworker relationships in the current context are limited to professional ties among peer employees.

Coworker relationships are very important in that, beyond chitchats and gossips, they share information on career, technical knowledge, perceptions, values, and beliefs related to work and support each other emotionally (Kram & Isabella, 1985). Coworker relationships are the venues of instrumental, informational, and emotional support. They bring out their own set of gains and pains in Korean contexts, including knowledge sharing, ostracism, incivil behaviors, psychological strain, commitment, and turnover decisions.

In the current work environments (e.g., flat, team-based structure, greater interdependent tasks), coworkers are expected to *share critical knowledge and expertise* to carry out their tasks successfully. Supportive coworker relationships are a must for effective job performance. Kim and Yun (2015) reported that when Korean employees at manufacturing and construction companies share their expertise and knowledge with coworkers, their coworkers performed significantly better on their tasks. The impact of coworker knowledge sharing on job performance was especially pronounced when coworkers had low general self-efficacy (i.e., one's perception of his/her ability to perform across a variety of different situations) and when they had an unabusive supervisor. Unlike their peers with high general self-efficacy, employees with low general self-efficacy tend to lack confidence about their skills and are uncertain about their capabilities or resources on a given task. Thus, they readily accept and use their coworkers' shared knowledge. Abusive supervision (i.e., sustained display of hostile verbal and nonverbal behaviors) creates a work environment with distrust, negative affect, anxiety, emotional exhaustion, and low motivation. Abused employees become resistant and defensive and avoid seeking feedback even from their peers. Even if coworkers share their knowledge and expertise, abused employees don't accept and use them for task performance.

The workplace is also one of the most prevalent social contexts where *ostracism* takes place. Ostracism refers to "the omission of appropriate actions that would otherwise engage someone, such as when an individual or group fails to acknowledge, include, select or invite another individual or group" (Chung, 2015, pp. 367–368). Korean employees are subjected to ostracism at the workplace as well. Chung (2015) reported that Korean employees, when ostracized, perceive that they have poor working relationships with other organizational members and have incompatible perceptions about works and goals; they tend to become uncooperative, unsupportive, or even hostile to others. Thus, they experience greater conflicts with coworkers (and supervisors). Coworker conflicts such as ostracism, in particular, were found to affect an employee's emotions and moods resulting in negative job attitudes, performance, and organizational citizenship behaviors.

Workplace *incivility* between or among coworkers is another form of relational conflict. It refers to "low-intensity deviant behavior with ambiguous intent to harm the target, in violation of workplace norms for mutual respect. Uncivil behaviors are characteristically rude and discourteous, displaying a lack of regard for others" (Andersson & Pearson, 1999, p. 457). It is not much direct and severe, but quite pervasive with 71% or more of employees experiencing it in American organizations, and relatively difficult to identify immediately. The continued occurrence is the key to spot it and affects psychological well-being and job performance. Hur, Kim, and Park (2015) found that Korean employees who were subjected to coworker incivility (e.g., being ignored or excluded, being talked to with raised voice, rude behaviors, demeaning things) at a retail bank experienced emotional exhaustion (e.g., feeling frustrated, feeling working too hard, experiencing too much stress, feeling emotionally drained), which in turn decreased their job performance and satisfaction levels and intensified their turnover intention. It appears that coworker incivility depletes one's physical, emotional, and cognitive resources (e.g., emotional and mental energy, socioemotional support from others, personality) (i.e., conservation of resources theory, Hobfoll, 2001) and, thus, one experiences emotional exhaustion or burnout, which in turn negatively impacts organizational outcomes of job performance and satisfaction and turnover intention over time.

Korean employees are subject to *psychological strain* at work. Psychological strain is the negative affective state of feeling that is characterized by depleted emotional resources and lack of energy (e.g., anxiety, frustration, anger). For Korean employees, relationships at work are significant stressful psychosocial work environments. In particular, poor work relationships imply low emotional support and trust, which leads to high role conflict and unsatisfying interpersonal communication. On the other hand, supportive social relationships with coworkers and others help reduce psychological strain at work. Park and Wilson (2003) reported that among male Korean factory workers from manufacturing companies, the quality of coworker relationship (along with that of supervisor relationship and work load) is the most prominent factor to workplace psychological strain. Poor coworker relationships contributed to the high level of psychological strain. Good-quality supportive coworker relationships indeed help reduce or buffer Korean employees' psychological strain at work.

Lee and Gao (2005) found that when more satisfied with their coworkers (e.g., work-related cooperation, collegiality, ease with mutual communication), Korean retail employees tend to *affectively commit* to their organization; they identify with, get involved in, and stay loyal to the organization, which in turn leads to greater job effort and less propensity to leave the firm. Kim, Lee, and Lee (2013) reported a similar finding. Satisfaction with coworkers was significantly negatively related to *turnover intention* among administrative office workers in Korea. Interestingly, satisfaction with coworkers was more important than satisfaction with their superiors in their intention to stay or leave. It is clear that coworkers in Korean retail contexts impact each other's work attitudes and work outcomes. In Confucian cultural work environments like Korea, relationships of all sorts powerfully shape interactional dynamics and organizational outcomes. Coworkers or peers can fulfill each other's emotional needs and feelings of attachment to others in the organization and help find the workplace enjoyable.

Mentoring Relationships

Another professional relationship at work is the mentor–mentee/protégé relationship. A mentoring relationship exists "when an older, more experienced member of an organization takes a junior colleague 'under his/her wing,' aiding in the organizational socialization of the less experienced person and passing along knowledge gained through years of living within the organization" (Wilson & Elman, 1990, p. 88). Research has shown that mentoring relationships serve the function of role modeling as well as enhance protégé's career and psychological well-being (Haggard, Dougherty, Turban, & Wilbanks, 2011). Mentoring relationship can be formal or informal

(Allen, Eby, Poteet, Lentz, & Lima, 2004; Kram, 1985; Wilson & Elman, 1990). As organizational members interact with one another in informal settings, they size up each other as potential mentors and mentees that embody professional identity and competence. When they become attracted to each other, they form an informal mentoring relationship. Organizations can design and implement formal mentoring programs as well by starting formal gatherings or meetings in which people mill around to meet and assess each other as mentors and mentees.

There is little research on mentoring relationships in Korean organizations. Nonetheless, it is clear that there are many formal mentoring programs in place in large Korean corporations (Kim, Im, & Hwang, 2015; Son, 2010; Son & Kim, 2013). It is highly likely that informal social ties (e.g., school, region, and family) will serve as informal mentoring programs.

Kim and his colleagues (2015) looked into role learning (e.g., role conflict, role ambiguity) via mentoring experiences at 13 super deluxe hotels in Korea that implemented formal mentoring programs. They found that all three mentoring functions (career enhancing, psychosocial support, and role modeling) effectively reduced role conflict. Only the psychosocial function (i.e., socially amicable environments, as found in building friendships or counseling relationships with mentees) helped reduce role ambiguity concerning job-related expectations (e.g., job specifications, roles, duties, abilities, and skills). In Korean work environments, having friendly and personal interactions with mentors are more conducive to reducing role ambiguity than invoking seniority in rank, position, or experiences.

Further, just like American employees, Korean employees who are mentored hold more positive job attitudes (i.e., greater job satisfaction and organizational commitment) than those who are not. Based on online survey responses from 113 employees who participated in a formal mentoring program at K-tech in Korea, Son (2010) also discovered that mentoring functions positively and significantly relate to job attitudes (i.e., job satisfaction and organizational commitment). An employee involved in a mentoring program is better satisfied with the job and shows a stronger commitment to the organization.

Son and Kim (2013) also examined the extent to which mentees in mandatory formal mentoring programs in two Korean construction companies actually take mentors' advice and act on it. Protégés' willingness to learn and take their mentor's feedback or advice is an important factor in the mentors' selection of protégés, receiving mentoring support, and mentoring outcomes in protégés' and organizational productivity and efficiency. Findings indicated that mentees who have a quality mentoring relationship are committed to the mentoring relationship and willing to take the mentor's advice and act on it. Unlike American employees in individualistic cultures, Korean employees in collectivistic cultures place a high value on interpersonal relationships and thus easily become attached to or identify with mentors, which brings forth the mentee's commitment to the relationship and willingness to accept the mentor's advice.

Kim, Egan, Kim, and Kim (2013) looked into managerial coaching and its relationships with employee work-related outcomes. Somewhat similar to coaching in mentoring relationship, managerial coaching refers to one-to-one conversations or a set of behaviors between superiors and subordinates for a short period of time that advance subordinates' learning and task effectiveness. It emphasizes proximal (here and now), task-relevant improvement through immediate feedback exchanges. For Korean government workers employed at the energy providers, managerial coaching had a direct impact on employee satisfaction with work and role clarity and an indirect impact on satisfaction with work, career commitment (the strength of individual motivation to work in a chosen career), organization commitment, and job performance. Employees who enjoyed coaching from their managers had a greater clarity in their role and were more satisfied with work, and in turn, more committed to their career and organization and outperformed others who did not have coaching. The survey in the study also indicated that, despite the high power distance-oriented Korean managerial context, coaching behaviors are practiced by managers and leaders. Kim (2014) reconfirmed such findings with employees in a private conglomerate in Korea.

Perhaps, even more important than specific types of professional relationship, there are four unique Korean features that regulate overall relational development and maintenance. They are Chae-myeon, Yongo, Noon-chi, and Jeong.

Chae-Myeon

Koreans spend enormous amount of time and efforts to develop and maintain good relationships with others. One key effort is to look like a "desirable" relational partner or "face" to others. Face in Korean is called *chae-myeon*

(체면). Other Korean vocabularies referring to some aspects of social face are *myon-mok* (면목), *ul-gool* (얼굴), *mo-yang-sae* (모양새), *chae-mo* (체모), and *chae-shin* (체신). Unlike Western exclusive notion of personal or psychological image of self as face, Korean notion of face contains the dual character of personal and sociological images of self (Lim & Choi, 1996). Chae-myeon is, in part, something that one can claim and reinforce in Korean society just like Westerners do in their respective societies. But in Korea, chae-myeon is largely bestowed upon by the society according to one's age, status, power, intimacy, occupation, or social worth. On the whole, Korean sense of face or chae-myeon includes both the personalized image of a person that is negotiable and the normative image of a person that is defined socially in terms of ethics, competence, and demeanor (Kim & Yang, 2011; Lim & Choi, 1996).

Koreans expend a great deal of social energy to promote or protect chae-myeon in relational contexts (e.g., meeting social norms or standards of behavior). In corporate settings, persons with more relational power, position, authority, or status (superiors, managers) usually claim more chae-myeon than persons with less power or authority. Subordinates are not expected to threaten their superiors' face; thus, they are very careful not to impose upon or criticize their superiors. On the other hand, superiors are relatively free to engage in face-threatening acts toward their subordinates, at times leading to an abusive supervision (e.g., insults, bullying, humiliating talks). At other times, superiors offer subordinates no or very indirect performance feedback for a poor job performance in order not to damage subordinates' chae-myeon, and vice versa; people at all rungs of hierarchy usually ignore or understate negative aspects of the other, but amplify positive aspects of the other to support the other's chae-myeon of competence. Superiors and subordinates alike often ask for suggestions and directions, avoid explicit directives, and use pleas and indirect expressions to protect the other's chae-myeon of autonomy.

Further, superiors and subordinates as members of the organization and as individuals with certain social status or worth are expected to conduct themselves according to somewhat absolute standards (e.g., ethics, competence, demeanor) across all situations and relationships. As a manager, he/she is expected to maintain certain social values by behaving, speaking, dressing, and leading in a "manager-like" fashion. Upon the failure to live up to such expectations or the loss of chae-myeon, people would feel ashamed and "cannot lift their face to others" (Lim & Choi, 1996, p. 128). This, in turn, will hamper people's proper social functioning. On the other hand, when they successfully promoted their chae-myeon, Koreans would feel very elated and believe they are socially desirable to others.

Chae-myeon extends to all other relational contexts. It powerfully governs and regulates relational development and maintenance. For instance, Tudor (2012) witnessed that Korean financial analysts often described a company's weaknesses between lines of their reports while labeling it a "buy." Even advertisers in Korea tended to point out the positives of their own products rather than the negatives of competitors. Such behaviors of avoiding public criticism were to preserve chae-myeon and maintain harmonious relationships with each other. This ubiquitous influence of chae-myeon on relational outcome is sometimes called "face and favor" (Huang, 2001). Face and favor is to save social dignity and retain respectability and thus help maintain a mutually satisfying relationship with each other.

Yongo

Yongo (연고) refers to informal, exclusive, cooperative relational ties with high levels of trust, social cohesion, bond, and mutual assistance/ benefits and obligations. Yongo networks are formed based on regional origin (*Ji-yon*, 지연), family affiliation (*Hyul-yon*, 혈연), and high school or university attendance (*Hak-yon*, 학연). Such networks are extremely important in-groups in Korea. In-groups refer to people with whom one identifies, shares a lot in common (e.g., race, culture, gender, religion, age, language, education, socioeconomic status, and the like), is concerned for their welfare, makes sacrifices for, and is willing to cooperate without demanding equitable returns (Gudykunst, 1997). They are strong ties with similar experiences and expectations and serve as a personal identity to their members in Korea (Shim, Kim, & Martin, 2008).

Regional ties are automatically predefined by birth—being born in the same region. In Korea, the respective regions are assumed to share the same values and norms that operate like permanent personality of the individual. The shared origin of the birthplace creates an emotional attachment with extremely high levels of cooperation and loyalty. Many of Korean corporate leaders hail from the same province (e.g., Kyungsang, Southeast region of Korea) and mutually promote each other to the top rungs of the corporation.

Another powerful informal network is based on family or bloodline. Confucian teachings and ideals of families extend to the sphere of corporate leadership. Based on "family egoism," it is believed to be natural to give family members and relatives favors in order to achieve its goals even at the frown of external or nonfamily members of the organization (e.g., nepotism). Family members receive overwhelming support in all business matters (e.g., hiring, job assignment, promotion, and other opportunities) and, for that, unconditionally dedicate their efforts and time to ensure family success in business.

University or high school alumni ties are formed as individuals study at the same university or high school at the same time (dong-ki relationship) or across time (sun-bae/senior/elder - hu-bae/junior/younger relationship). The elder is expected to take care of the junior, who in turn shows uncompromising loyalty. A large alumni network of a prestigious Korean university is especially important to one's managerial career and business success. It may be the best guarantee for a thriving career.

The influence of yongo networks is omnipresent in corporate scenes in Korea. They do not show up on the official organizational charts, but most corporate decisions are made and problems are resolved through yongo networks, socially mutually dependent relations (Horak, 2015). These informal relationships often turn into formal superior–subordinate relationships as people are hired and promoted to higher positions via yongo networks.

Similar Korean terms to yongo are *inmaek* (인맥) that indicates a social network in general. *Yonjul* (연줄) refers to social ties that exist for a purpose, often to obtain one's personal gains and benefits (Rowley & Warner, 2014). Yongo ties permeate all aspects of relational matters across all and every conceivable social contexts, including professional relationships in Korea.

Noon-Chi

Noon-chi (nunchi, noonchi or *noonch'i,* 눈치) is a crucial variable to all relational matters in Korea. "Literally, a Korean could not survive in Korea without this perceptive skill" (Robinson, 1996, p. 129). It is one culture-specific concept that reflects the essence of Korean psychology in both cultural characteristics and interpersonal relations (Jeong, 2015). The Korean word noon-chi literally means "eye measured" or "measuring with eyes." It means eye sense or playing things by eye.

Noon-chi in nominative usage refers to "tact, savoir faire, sense, social sense, perceptiveness, an eye for social situations" (Robinson, 1996, p. 129) or "a sense that is able to understand the needs or mood of others, or the states of a social situation instantly, based not on what is being said, but on appreciating an underlying communication" (Jeong, 2015, p. 8).

People with greater noon-chi will be better able to read one's mind, probe one's motives, study one's face, grasp a situation, and see how the wind blows. Having an acute sense of noon-chi is indispensable to professional relationships, especially relationships with senior members in the Korean workplace. Having a "fast" noon-chi is a paramount virtue in subordinates. For example, without having proper noon-chi, becoming an outstanding secretary to a Korean CEO is simply impossible. The secretary has to be full of noon-chi in all matters by anticipating and figuring out needs, desires, intention, and mood of the CEO without having an exchange of explicit verbal messages. That includes opening the car door at the right time, examining and briefing on the daily schedule, checking out the place of meeting, and ensuring everything is in order, telling an amusing story to change the negative mood, arranging special meals for certain occasions, working with all means of transportation for a timely arrival (despite all the traffic jams), being able to speak foreign languages, handling long hours on duty cheerfully, standing by 24/7 for any emergencies, and even being able to address the needs of CEO family (Yoo, 2015). Superiors like subordinates who keep their attentive noon-chi and assess what superiors want and how superiors feel all the time. However, too much or excessive noon-chi that keeps the subordinate on the constant alert may make him/her extremely nervous, tense, insecure, anxious, and fearful.

Subordinates with good noon-chi tend to utilize visual perception to discover the hidden agenda behind all forms of expressions in social interactions with their superiors. Korean subordinates use noon-chi to interpret their superiors' facial expressions and words often by observing and understanding "minute nonverbal cues, on reading between the lines, and on hearing between the sounds" to penetrate the mask that hides their desires (Robinson, 1996, p. 129).

The Sawon (2014), a blog on Corporate Korea, suggests that Koreans work so late because of noon-chi. Koreans work the second most hours among member countries in the Organisation for Economic Co-operation and Development (OECD, 2015). Koreans believe that leaving on time (e.g., at 5 or 6 p.m.) gives off the impression of not working hard or not working as hard as their colleagues and boss. The general rule in a Korean company is to leave after your direct team leader or superior has left. Perceptions reign supreme in a Korean office, and creating the impression of working hard by staying late is something all Koreans with any amount of noon-chi will do. Even if your contract says working hours from 9 a.m. to 6 p.m., working until 8 or 9 p.m. will be the common "noon-chi" finish time.

Like an outstanding secretary to a Korean CEO, the height of the art of noon-chi would be to give someone something before he or she asks for it. Noon-chi often encourages deception for a higher goal of harmony. Koreans tend not to express anything that has the potential to make people or the social atmosphere feel unpleasant or awkward. Thus, indirect or watered-down talks are commonplace, and employees avoid hurting anyone's feelings with the truth, which preserves harmony as well as face (Jeong, 2015; Lim & Choi, 1996; Robinson, 1996). Noon-chi operates in all and every interactions of social associations in Korea.

Jeong

Jeong (정) is culture-specific affect that reflects the essence of Korean psychology in both cultural characteristics and interpersonal relations (Jeong, 2015). It is "a psychological sense of bonding or relational tie with a person, extending to a place, an object or anything that one has constructed a lasting sentimental relationship with over time" (Jeong, 2015, p. 7). It is not the same as sentimental feelings of loyalty and reciprocity. Jeong is about the quality of relationship. It represents a primitive way of relating, of being more fused and less separated that leads to the sense of oneness, sameness, mutual support, and sacrifice. It is this Jeong that makes Korean employees say "we" rather than "I," "our leader, our company" rather than "my leader, my company."

Jeong is manifested in all types of relationships in Korea. Once people enter a sort of "we-ness" tie, a jeong relationship activates instantly. Koreans often bring attention to the aspect of jeong, as they develop long-term relationships through bonding. Once established, jeong brings out strong mutual attachment and rarely diminishes in its size or presence.

In social interactions, jeong is realized through fidelity and devotion, often without conscious reasoning or evaluation of alternative behaviors or responses. A Western blogger (I'M NO PICASSO, 2009) describes his best view of people in a relationship with jeong as follows: "you will do for another person, take care of another person, take on another person's problems, and in return, they do the same for you. You share each other's burdens, without justification, without keeping score." Because of jeong, people sometimes will do things for each other even when they don't really want to. Such jeong-based behaviors of mutual fidelity and devotion can cause tensions, conflict, dissatisfaction, and rage because they can impose one's own expectations and demand for the other party to respond in kind possibly against one's needs and desires. Personal boundaries or needs are easily compromised by jeong-related behaviors. At other times, jeong becomes the primary criterion that decides insiders from outsiders, resulting in nepotism and favoritism (Jeong, 2015).

Professionals from various industries and contexts also come to work together and develop a relationship with jeong over time. Public relations practitioners and journalists in Korea often work closely together. Public relations professionals in Korea are the major sources of news items for mass media reporters. One interesting aspect of this source-reporter professional relationship is inherent tension and antagonism. Each party works with different roles, goals, values, and needs. Public relations professionals as news sources attempt to influence the news-making process, and journalists strive to stay objective, attempting to avoid undue influence by sources (Shin, Lee, & Park, 2012). As they interact with one another over time, they develop jeong relationship that may influence their ethical conduct of business.

Berkowitz and Lee (2004) conducted interviews with 10 journalists and 10 public relations practitioners in Korea and inquired about how jeong develops, how it manifests in their professional activities, and what effects and outcomes result. Their findings suggested that jeong emerges through common experiences and repeated interactions over an extended period of time and facilitate a flow of personal and business information. One journalist interviewee said that "I think Cheong [Jeong] was formed in the course of calling three times a week and meeting at least twice a month" (p. 434). Jeong was most clearly manifested in private and personal unreservedness that was unrelated to official business, yet respecting the professional standards and obligations of each party. Further, both parties protected each other and sacrificed themselves, instead of taking advantage of each other. They helped each other when either party was in need. They criticized and praised each other's organization. Instead of being or becoming a burden for both parties, journalists and public relations practitioners felt that jeong enabled a two-way, balanced practice of professional relationships, resulting in mutual goodwill in the communication activities that support professional responsibilities. One public relations interviewee noted that "In some cases, PR staff are criticized for maintaining a close relationship with reporters. In retrospect, I carefully tried not to be a burden to them or do harm to the reporters with whom I have established Cheong. There is a tendency for both sides to protect each other and sacrifice themselves, instead of taking advantage of each other" (p. 435). Another practitioner illustrates a balanced approach to a professional relationship: "The reporter for whom I feel Cheong has a great deal of information and knowledge of our organization. He objectively criticizes and praises our organization as applicable. He is really a good observer for our organization" (p. 435). Koreans are most likely to go see someone in jeong-bonded relationship for counseling or advice. Such relationships enable Koreans to readily talk, share, understand, and exchange thoughts. Koreans live by and die by jeong.

Summary

To be functional and productive at work, it is essential for Koreans to have good professional relationships. They are expected to forge and maintain great ongoing, committed, goal-oriented professional associations with superiors, subordinates, peers/coworkers, mentors, mentees, clients/customers, and many other working partners.

Cultural orientations powerfully influence the ways in which Koreans establish and sustain professional relationships, including Confucianism, collectivism, power distance, uncertainty avoidance, and masculinity. Distinctive managerial practices also strongly shape up Korean professional ties at work, including paternalistic leadership, loyalty, hierarchical structure, centralized decision making, family control, and close ties between business and government. In addition, uniquely Korean motivators of chae-myeon, yongo, noon-chi, and jeong complicate professional relationship terrains.

Furthermore, economic jolts in the late 1990s forcefully induced a reexamination of cultural values and managerial practices in professional contexts. In particular, market-oriented or performance-based human resources management practices are growing in popularity, imposing Koreans to explore alternative, yet profitable, relationship models in professional contexts. This trend is likely to continue and inevitably invite confusions and tensions in relational matters. From their birth and on, Koreans learn to navigate fluidly a myriad of tangled and barb-wired relational landscape. It will be interesting to see, over a decade or so, how Koreans manage relational challenges in professional contexts.

References

Allen, T. D., Eby, L. T., Poteet, M. L., Lentz, E., & Lima, L. (2004). Career benefits associated with mentoring for protégés: A meta-analysis. *Journal of Applied Psychology, 89,* 127–136.

Alston, J. P. (1989). Wa, Guanxi, and Inhwa: Managerial principles in Japan, China, and Korea. *Business Horizons, 32,* 26–31.

Andersson, L. M., & Pearson, C. M. (1999). Tit for tat? The spiraling effect of incivility in the workplace. *Academy of Management Review, 24*(3), 452–471.

Bae, J. (1997). Beyond seniority-based systems: A paradigm shift in Korean HRM? *Asia Pacific Business Review, 3*(4), 82–110.

Bae, J., & Lawler, J. J. (2000). Organizational and HRM strategies in Korea: Impact on firm performance in an emerging economy. *Academy of Management Journal, 43,* 502–517.

Bae, J., & Rowley, C. (2001). The impact of globalization on HRM: The case of South Korea. *Journal of World Business, 36*(4), 402–428.

Berkowitz, D., & Lee, J. (2004). Media relations in Korea: Cheong between journalist and public relations practitioner. *Public Relations Review, 30,* 431–437.

Chang, E. M. (2006). Individual pay for performance and commitment HR practices in South Korea. *Journal of World Business, 41,* 368–381.

Chung, K. H., Lee, H. C., & Jung, K. H. (1997). Korean management: Global strategy and cultural transformation. New York: Walter de Gruyter.

Chung, Y. W. (2015). The mediating effects of organizational conflict on the relationships between workplace ostracism with in-role behavior and organizational citizenship behavior. *International Journal of Conflict Management, 26*(4), 366–385.

Dansereau, F., Graen, G. B., & Haga, W. J. (1975). A vertical dyad linkage approach to leadership within formal organizations: A longitudinal investigation of the role making process. *Organizational Behavior and Human Performance, 13,* 46–78.

Dorfman, P. W., Howell, J. P., Hibino, S., Lee, J. K., Tate, U., & Bautista, J. A. (1997). Leadership in Western and Asian countries: Commonalities and differences in effective leadership. *Leadership Quarterly, 8,* 233–274.

Dulebohn, J. H., Bommer, W. H., Liden, R. C., Brouer, R. L., & Ferris, G. R. (2012). A meta-analysis of antecedent and consequences of leader–member exchange: Integrating the past with an eye toward the future. *Journal of Management, 38,* 1715–1759.

Forgas, J. P., & Bond, M. H. (1985). Cultural influences on the perceptions of interaction episodes. *Personality and Social Psychology Bulletin, 11,* 75–88.

Froese, F. J., Pak, Y. S., & Chong, L. C. (2008). Managing the human side of cross-border acquisitions in South Korea. *Journal of World Business, 43,* 97–108.

Graen, G. B. (Ed.). (2004). *New frontiers of leadership, LMX leadership: The series* (Vol. 2). Greenwich, CT: Information Age Publishing.

Graen, G. B., & Uhl-Bien, M. (1995). Development of leader-member exchange (LMX) theory of leadership over 25 years: Applying a multi-level multi-domain perspective. *Leadership Quarterly, 6,* 219–247.

Gudykunst, W. B. (1997). Cultural variability in communication: An introduction. *Communication Research, 24,* 327–348.

Haggard, D. L., Dougherty, T. W., Turban, D. B., & Wilbanks, J. E. (2011). Who is a mentor? A review of evolving definitions and implications for research. *Journal of Management, 37*(1), 280–304.

Hirokawa, R. Y., & Miyahara, A. (1986). A comparison of influence strategies utilized by managers in American and Japanese organizations. *Communications Quarterly, 34,* 250–265.

Hobfoll, S. E. (2001). The influence of culture, community, and the nested-self in the stress process: Advancing conservation of resources theory. *Applied Psychology, 50*(3), 337–421.

Hofstede, G. (1991). *Culture and organization: Software of the mind.* London: McGraw-Hill.

Hofstede, G. (2001). *Culture's consequences: Comparing values, behaviors, institutions and organizations across nations* (2nd ed.). Thousand Oaks, CA: Sage.

Horak, S. (2015). Approaching Korean business and management ideals through the lens of *Yongo:* A scholar-practitioner perspective. *Journal of Asia-Pacific Business, 16,* 210–222.

House, R. J., Hanges, P. J., Javidan, M., Dorfman, P. W., & Gupta, V. (Eds.). (2004*). Culture, leadership and organizations: The GLOBE study of 62 societies.* Thousand Oaks, CA: Sage.

Huang, Y. (2001). OPRA: A cross-cultural, multi-item scale for measuring organization-public relationship. *Journal of Public Relations Research, 13*, 61–90.

Hur, W., Kim, B., Park, S. (2015). The relationship between coworker incivility, emotional exhaustion, and organizational outcomes: The mediating role of emotional exhaustion. *Human Factors and Ergonomics in Manufacturing & Service Industries, 25*(6), 701–712.

I'M NO PICASSO. (2009). *Soju, noonchi, and jeong.* Retrieved November 30, 2015, from http://imnopicasso.blogspot.com/2009/06/soju-noonchi-and-jeong.html.

Jablin, F. M. (2001). Organizational entry, assimilation, and disengagement/exit. In F. M. Jablin & L. L. Putnam (Eds.), *The new handbook of organizational communication: Advances in theory, research, and methods* (pp. 819–864). Thousand Oaks, CA: Sage.

Javidan, M., & House, R. J. (2001). Cultural acumen for the global manager: Lessons from project GLOBE. *Organizational Dynamics, 29*(4), 289–305.

Javidan, M., Dorfman, P. W., de Luque, M. S., & House, R. J. (2006). In the eye of the beholder: Cross-cultural lessons in leadership from Project Globe. *Academy of Management Perspectives, 20*, 67–90.

Jeong, H. (2015). *Archaeology of psychotherapy in Korea: A study of Korean therapeutic work and professional growth.* New York: Routledge.

Jung, Y., & Takeuchi, N. (2014). Relationships among leader-member exchange, person-organization fit and work attitudes in Japanese and Korean organizations: Testing a cross-cultural moderating effect. *International Journal of Human Resource Management, 25*(1), 23–46.

Khatri, N. (2009). Consequences of power distance orientation in organizations. *Vision: The Journal of Business Perspective, 13*, 1–9.

Kim, K. L. (2015, November 24). *Will people with high income be happy? Life satisfaction depends on stable income and human relationship.* Hankyoreh (Newspaper). Retrieved November 30, 2015, from http://www.hani.co.kr/arti/economy/economy_general/718924.html. [Korean]

Kim, S. (2014). Assessing the influence of managerial coaching on employee outcomes. *Human Resource Development Quarterly, 25*(1), 59–85.

Kim, S. L., & Yun, S. (2015). The effect of coworker knowledge sharing on performance and its boundary conditions: An interactional perspective. *Journal of Applied Psychology, 100,* 575–582.

Kim, S. S., Im, J., & Hwang, J. (2015). The effects of mentoring on role stress, job attitude, and turnover intention in the hotel industry. *International Journal of Hospitality Management, 48,* 68–82.

Kim, S., Egan, T., Kim, W., & Kim, J. (2013). The impact of managerial coaching behavior on employee work-related reactions. *Journal of Business Psychology, 28*(3), 315–330.

Kim, T. G., Lee, J. K. & Lee, J. J. (2013). Do interpersonal relationships still matter for turnover intention? A comparison of South Korea and China. *International Journal of Human Resource Management, 24,* 966–984.

Kim, T., & Shapiro, D. L. (2008). Retaliation against supervisory mistreatment: Negative emotion, group membership, and cross-cultural difference. *International Journal of Conflict Management, 19*(4), 339–358.

Kim, Y., & Yang, J. (2011). The influence of Chemyon on facework and conflict styles: Searching for the Korean face and its impact. *Public Relations Review, 37,* 60–67.

Kram, K. E. (1985). *Mentoring at work: Developmental relationships in organizational life.* Glenview, IL: Scott, Foresman.

Kram, K. E., & Isabella, L. A. (1985). Mentoring alternatives: The role of peer relationships in career development. *Academy of Management Journal, 28,* 110–132.

Lee, H. C. (1989). Managerial characteristics of Korean firms. In K. H. Chung & H. C. Lee (Eds.), *Korean managerial dynamics* (pp. 147–162). New York: Praeger.

Lee, K. S., & Gao, T. (2005). Studying organizational commitment with the OCQ in the Korean retail context: Its dimensionality and relationships with satisfaction and work outcomes. *International Review of Retail, Distribution and Consumer Research, 15*(4), 375–399.

Lee, J., & Jablin, F. M. (1992). A cross-cultural investigation of exit, voice, loyalty, and neglect as responses to dissatisfying job conditions. *Journal of Business Communication, 29,* 203–228.

Lee, T. S., Lee, D. W., Lee, H., & Park, H. S. (2005). Superior–subordinate relationships in Korean civil engineering companies. *Journal of Management in Engineering, 21*(4), 159–163.

Lee, Z., & Lee, Y. (2009). Emailing the boss: Cultural implications of media choice. *IEEE Transactions on Professional Communication, 52*(1), 61–74

Lim, T., & Choi, S. (1996). Interpersonal relationships in Korea. In W. Gudykunst, S. Ting Toomey, & T. Nishida (Eds.), *Communication in personal relationships across cultures* (pp. 122–136). Thousand Oaks, CA: Sage.

National Archives of Korea. (n.d.). Retrieved November 30, 2015, from www.archives.go.kr/.

OECD. (2015). *Hours worked* (indicator). doi: 10.1787/47be1c78-en.

Park, K., & Wilson, M. G. (2003). Psychosocial work environments and psychological strain among Korean factory workers. *Stress and Health, 19*, 173–179.

Rhee, J., Dedahanov, A., & Lee, D. (2014). Relationships among power distance, collectivism, punishment, and acquiescent, defensive, or prosocial silence. *Social Behavior and Personality, 42*(5), 705–720.

Robinson, J. H. (1996). Professional communication in Korea: Playing things by eye. *IEEE Transactions on Professional Communication, 39*, 129–134.

Rosen, S., & Tesser, A. (1970). On reluctance to communicate undesirable information: The Mum effect. *Sociometry, 33*, 253–263.

Rosen, S., & Tesser, A. (1972). Fear of negative evaluation and the reluctance to transmit bad news. *Journal of Communication, 22*, 124–141.

Rowley, C., & Bae, J. (2002). Globalization and transformation of human resource management in South Korea. *International Journal of Human Resource Management, 13*, 522–549.

Rowley, C., & Warner, M. (2014). The changing contours of Korean management and business. *Asia Pacific Business Review, 20*(1), 1–8.

Shim, T. Y., Kim, M, & Martin, J. N. (2008). *Changing Korea: Understanding culture and communication*. New York: Peter Lang.

Shin, J., Lee, J., & Park, J. (2012). Perceptual dynamics of pluralistic ignorance and social distance: Public relations practitioners and journalists in South Korea. *Asian Journal of Communication, 22*, 19–43.

Sias, P. M. (2009). *Organizing relationships: Traditional and emerging perspectives on workplace relationships*. Los Angeles: Sage.

Son, S. J. (2010). *The relationship among trust, mentoring functions received and work attitudes in a Korean corporation*. Dissertation Abstracts International Section A, 71, 161.

Son, S., & Kim, D. (2013). What makes protégés take mentors' advice in formal mentoring relationships? *Journal of Career Development, 40*(4), 311–328.

The Sawon. (2014). How Korean 눈치 (Noonchi) or "self-awareness" affects Korean corporate culture. Retrieved November 30, 2015, from http://thesawon.blogspot.com/search?q=noonchi.

Triandis, H. C, & Albert, R. D. (1987). Cross-cultural perspectives. In F. M. Jablin, L. L. Putnam, K. H. Roberts, & L. W. Porter (Eds.), *Handbook of organizational communication: An interdisciplinary perspective* (pp. 264–295). Beverly Hills, CA: Sage.

Tudor, D. (2012). *Korea: The impossible country*. Tokyo: Tuttle Publishing.

Van Dyne, L., Ang, S., & Botero, I. C. (2003). Conceptualizing employee silence and employee voice as multidimensional constructs. *Journal of Management Studies, 40*, 1359–1392.

Wilson, J. A., & Elman, N. S. (1990). Organizational benefits of mentoring. *Academy of Management Executive, 4*, 88–94.

Yang, I. (2014). The informal organization of Korean companies: Implications for Korean MNCs. *Thunderbird International Business Review, 56*(6), 577–588.

Yoo, J. H. (2015, Nov. 6). *Catching thoughts and eyes: Shadow of boss with anxiety-filled life*. Naver News. Retrieved November 30, 2015, from http://news.naver.com/main/read.nhn?oid=011&sid1=101&aid [Korean]

CHAPTER 11
CONCLUSION

GEORGE B. RAY

This book provides in-depth discussions of essential components of relational communication in specific contexts in China, Japan, and Korea. Chapter 1 offers a fine overview of some basic concepts in communication and culture, with an integrative summary of cultural features that are common or at least somewhat common across China, Japan, and Korea. It is a major premise of this book that culture exerts a fundamental influence on communication. Of course, it is clear that there is a transactional relationship between people and their cultures. By examining various cultural patterns of communication we can see how relationships both shape, and are shaped by culture. In this concluding chapter we will take a look at some common themes that emerge from the nine main chapters. We will also consider communication and relationships from the perspective of cultural communication.

■ Themes in East Asian Relationships and Communication

When we look at relationships and common communication settings, we begin to identify similarities between China, Japan, and Korea. Let us note some common themes across the three main contexts, beginning with family communication.

Family Relationships

There are important traditional value systems shared by all three cultures, due, in part, to the influences of Confucianism and Buddhism (as noted in Chapter 1). The chapters on family relationships all refer to some sense of filial piety, harmony, and respect for age, especially in China and Korea. It is striking, however, that modern trends in all three societies reveal significant changes. Economic and demographic forces as well as governmental policies in China have resulted in notable departures from traditional patterns. Industrialization across the entire region and the one child policy in China have led to smaller families, parents working longer hours outside the home, and more females entering the workforce. Furthermore, as noted in Chapter 5, in Japan there has been a steady trend toward more single parent households and adults getting married later in life or sometimes choosing not to get married. Chapter 8 also notes that adults in Korea are getting married later. At the same time, multigenerational households are becoming less common in these three societies.

It is not clear how trends in family life are affecting communication practices in East Asian families. Characteristics of family communication in China display adherence to the traditional norms of filial piety, harmony, and respect for older generations. Harmony still prevails, yet it is not clear how contemporary Chinese families manage conflict. However, in Japan and Korea modern families foster more open and direct communication including conflict. It is also noted that in China families are becoming more conversation oriented and less conformity oriented. Another trend is that in Korea and Japan, although fathers have become more involved in child rearing, mothers tend to bear greater responsibility for child care. The influence of mothers in child rearing in Japan exists to the extent that, as noted in Chapter 5, some have claimed that Japan is a maternal society. This trend in Japan is not easily interpreted in light of Hofstede's research from the 1990s (Hofstede, 1991) showing strong masculinity tendencies in Japan. Contemporary norms for marriage indicate that in Japan and Korea traditional approaches (practical, parents are involved in choices) and modern customs (romantic, more personal/individual choices) are both occurring, whereas the trends on marriage are less clear in China.

In a general sense, it appears that all three societies are shifting from a traditional, hierarchical, male-dominated family system to a more contemporary model in which there is more gender equality. In East Asia more traditional family structures based on cultural heritage (Ditlmann, Purdie-Vaughns, & Eibach, 2011) are arguably the most important factors in maintaining and strengthening cultural norms for families. If, in fact, families in these three societies are moving away from the more traditional customs, a compelling question arises as to what will replace the influence of cultural heritage. Thus, we find a dynamic tension between the old and the new, as younger families feel freer to deviate from cultural traditions. Chapters 2, 5, and 8 do not necessarily give the impression that current patterns represent revolutionary change. Nevertheless, gradual, cumulative changes have led to remarkable variation in family structures over the past 50–60 years.

Personal Relationships

In the realm of personal relationships we again see several qualities shared by all three societies. Chapters 3, 6, and 9 all refer to strong group influences on relationships. Partly due to collectivism, individuals in all three cultures exhibit a sense of belonging to or being connected to groups outside the family and this exerts a significant influence on one's identity. The family, certainly, remains important as kinship ties provide a natural and lasting basis for personal relationships. Yet, in these three cultures, outside groups provide a vital context for relationships. In China, for example, *guanxi* is a fundamental aspect of how individuals relate to groups to which they belong. As noted in Chapter 4, guanxi is characterized by a strong sense of mutual interest and reciprocity, and entails the presence of human sentiment (*renqing*). Guanxi is necessary for the formation and maintenance of social networks to which one belongs. Similarly, in Japan, *nakama*, although not precisely the same thing as guanxi, establishes the relational space for one's social network and requires active maintenance. In Chapter 9, the authors note that in Korea *woo-jeong* is a kind of friendship that originates in and is maintained through membership in groups outside the family, especially those formed with classmates in school. Chapter 9 discusses a crucial role that education plays in the formation of long-term friendships (see also Chapters 3 and 6).

Thus, we find that personal relationships outside the family setting play a significant network-oriented role. In all three societies such networks tend to endure over long periods of time. Belonging to and maintaining these networks requires a major commitment and those in the network are highly aware of the social obligations that go along with membership in the extended group. In Japan and Korea, for example, presenting gifts to others is a serious consideration that implicitly acknowledges the status of one's relationship with another. There are definite and potentially lasting consequences for not presenting an appropriate gift or overlooking an occasion when a gift is called for.

Obligations such as gifting inherently involve face. Chapter 1 discusses face as a theoretical insight that can help us comprehend and organize certain propositions about human behavior. Theories such as face negotiation can also provide vocabularies that assist us in developing mutual understanding of various constructs. In the case of face and facework, those of us from individualistic cultures such as the United States may not immediately grasp the fundamental importance of face, in contrast to culture bearers from collectivistic cultures. Chapter 1 asserts that face may be considered as more other-oriented in East Asian cultures. Indeed, each chapter on friendship and personal relationships affirms this assertion. In all three societies, as our authors comment, one is attuned to what others think of one. From this perspective we may reach two observations. First, as mentioned in Chapter 9, friendship is grounded more in one's membership in social groups, as opposed to intimate or personal ties between individuals. It is also noted in Chapter 9 there is the sense that group membership is often involuntary in nature. Second, one is ever aware of her or his group identity and expectations for appropriate behavior in reference to the group. Group membership is taken quite seriously and one must demonstrate his or her on-going commitment to the group.

One implication of demonstrating commitment to the group is that instead of direct verbal disclosure of one's feelings for the group, there is greater emphasis on nonverbally signifying that one honors his or her membership in and loyalty to the group. As Chapter 6 points out and as noted by Hofstede (2001), collectivistic cultures encourage norms that put the interest of the group ahead of personal interest. Thus, we would expect that before acting in a social situation, one's first thoughts and natural inclinations are oriented toward what would be viewed favorably by the group.

Finally, in regard to dating and courtship, we find similarities as well as dissimilarities. There are similarities in relation to movement away from arranged marriages and less overt expressions of passion and romance. It appears that arranged marriages are increasingly uncommon. However, a modern vestige of arranged marriages may be evident to the extent that one's parents have particular interests in the selection of one's partner, including the practice of arranged dating in China. Discussing how those in intimate, romantic relationships express affection is easier to understand, for US Americans perhaps, by contrasting the tendencies in East Asia with American patterns. In all three cultures and in comparison to American patterns, intimate partners express affection in a more subdued manner;

there is greater emphasis on inner feelings of affection which are implicitly understood. As far as commitment to the relationship is concerned, among East Asian couples, serious commitment can be communicated more indirectly and can be inferred from subtle nonverbal cues. Finally, it is interesting to note some trends in modern dating practices in East Asia. Blind dates are common in China as well as the use of dating scripts. In Japan, online dating services seem to have become less popular and having friends introduce potential dating partners is more accepted. In Korea online relational communication is very prominent between friends, and romantic partners make extensive use of online communication, especially through the use of smartphone applications geared toward couples.

As noted, the structure of the family in East Asia is in transition and it is to be expected, therefore, that personal relationship formation and maintenance are changing as well. Inasmuch as the family provides the foundation for so many relational influences, socialization in the family setting initiates perspectives on relationships early in life. Formation and maintenance of personal relationships are clearly in the midst of change. The traditional and the modern, the old and the new, and preferences of the younger and the older are all present in the dynamic relational atmosphere in East Asia.

Professional Relationships

Discussions of relationships in organizations offer insights into patterns of change which are, in some ways, related to change in families and friendships. Chapter 7 does not discuss traditions stemming from Confucianism; however, the chapters on China and Korea both refer to influences of Confucianism, especially in regard to harmony. Yet, modernity has led to remarkable changes in the nature of organizations. It must be recognized that in comparison to well-established customs with deep cultural roots that have shaped family life and friendship, the industrialization across the region in the last 60 years has had a significant impact. This impact was felt in the family and in friendship patterns, but it seems more direct and rapid in the organizational setting since these societies have experienced remarkable industrialization. Therefore, the operation of industries that compete in global markets has led to change in response to forces external to the region.

What is similar across East Asian professional relationships is a trend toward contemporary corporate structures that have been moving away from traditional patterns. Chapter 4 discusses traditional influences from Confucianism, Classical Legalism, Daoism, Maoism, and later *Chi* theory. The chapter on China shows how each tradition has left a mark on relationships in organizations. Harmony remains important, along with benevolent leadership, guanxi, and seniority. More authoritarian management styles have given way to recent shifts toward the promotion of greater organizational efficiencies. There is also a noteworthy trend in more effective upward-flowing communication and encouraging employees to identify problems (remonstration). In China the benefits of guanxi which foster group allegiance may be in tension with the need for separate groups to more effectively collaborate.

Similarly, in Japan and Korea long-standing customs that supported a hierarchical, male-dominated organization structure are undergoing change. High uncertainty avoidance in both cultures and the influence of the three pillars of management philosophy in Japan (social contract, seniority, trade unions) have resulted in modern adaptations based more on assessing individual performance and timely goal setting and goal completion. Yet, in Japan and Korea, traditional customs are only slowly fading away. Developing organizational goals is still influenced by personal ties between employees, and in Japan, seniority and the social contract are still influential. There apparently is greater gender equality in China in the workplace, whereas gender equality has been slower to develop in Japan and Korea.

In all three societies personal relationships in organizations are complex blends of the old and the new. In China guanxi extends into the workplace and can hold advantages as well as disadvantages, as already mentioned. In Korea there is an emphasis on *che-myon* which employees endeavor to maintain; however, boundaries between personal and more formal co-worker relationships can become blurred with the resulting problematic outcomes. Chapter 10 also notes that mentoring in organizations might help reduce conflict in Korean organizations, yet there is not much research on mentoring and its effects. Chapter 10 refers to problematic upward communication in that employees may feel their critical judgments are not appreciated by upper management. Therefore subordinates may be reluctant to express their objections or negative criticisms. In Japan, there is an elaborate process through which decisions are reached. Much time is spent in developing and reviewing proposals and decisions, with emphasis on achieving consensus and avoiding conflict. Decisions can be quickly implemented as a result of achieving consensus, but there is the sense that so much time is spent on reaching consensus that the process can become very slow and laborious.

The main theme in the chapters on professional relationships is that organizations have felt the need to adapt to current economic realities. To implement new management strategies and policies in cultures where collectivism and uncertainty avoidance have prevailed is difficult at best. Change has been occurring, but traditional customs are still observed in varying ways. A central task for management is to encourage patterns of communication that can take advantage of certain traditional values (e.g., loyalty to the organization, harmony, social cohesion) while finding ways to adapt to demands of the global marketplace.

■ Cultural Communication

As Philipsen (2002) notes, the term cultural communication may have first appeared in the field of anthropology (Schwartz, 1980; Hanson, 1982). In the 1970s researchers in the ethnography of speaking and the ethnography of communication (e.g., Bauman & Scherzer, 1974; Gumperz & Hymes, 1972; Hymes, 1972; Hymes, 1974) made significant progress in studying the interaction of language and social life. Later, in the field of communication, Philipsen and his associates (e.g., Carbaugh, 1988; Fitch, 1998; Katriel, 1986; Philipsen, 1975; Ray, 1987) began a series of investigations focusing on the manner in which cultural patterns of communication are manifested in speech communities. It is from this ethnographic line of research that Philipsen developed the concept known as cultural communication. Philipsen (2002, p. 62) offers this definition of cultural communication: "I have proposed that cultural communication refers to that communicative conduct that is infused with cultural particulars of the means and meanings of communicative conduct." A central feature of cultural communication is the notion that cultures embody knowledge of the means of communicative interaction and the distinctive meanings of culturally patterned forms of communication. Even though culture provides the broad framework for communication practices, it is in specific instances of interaction and performance within speech communities where cultural patterns are evident.

The concept of cultural communication can be illustrated by considering, for example, Chapter 6 in which Seward and Long discuss friendship in Japanese culture. The authors refer to Yoneyama's (1973) model of Japanese social relationships which shows the self existing within a set of three concentric circles: *miuchi, nakama,* and *tanin.* Enacting appropriate forms of communication in each relational context requires knowledge of the relationship one has with another, past experiences with the other, status differences, the importance of gifts in certain situations, and various other cultural prescriptions. Examining and specifying the knowledge of relevant cultural prescriptions can reveal the structure of cultural communication in the formation and maintenance of friendships in Japanese culture. Cultural prescriptions apply to all forms of communication including requests, directives, showing respect, interacting intimately, enacting forms of politeness, acknowledging status, offering compliments, engaging in conflict, forms of direct and indirect communication, and innumerable other communication practices. Because of the many communication variables, situational constraints, and culture-specific characteristics, it is a major task to analyze cultural communication for any one cultural or subcultural group.

Despite the considerable effort required to analyze any specific case or several closely related cases of cultural communication, this effort is nevertheless necessary in order to develop a deeper understanding of the intricate patterns of communication within any cultural group. In this respect we can see how it is less useful to describe Chinese culture and communication, for example, than it is to describe some prominent patterns of communication in Chinese family settings. The detailed focus of cultural communication requires in-depth analysis which Philipsen shows can be conducted through ethnographic methods.

The chapters in this volume provide a valuable framework for organizing our knowledge of various forms of communicative conduct within three contexts of relational communication. One could pursue the next step leading to research which could be based on ethnographic methods. The production of numerous ethnographic case studies could then be the basis for comparative analysis across groups. Such comparative analyses are, of course, far beyond the goals of this book. However, it is hoped that readers can understand how knowledge of cultural communication can play a role in larger scale scholarly projects.

Beyond the use of ethnography from a methodological perspective we want to emphasize a fundamental insight deriving from the chapters in this book. All the chapters present and analyze native knowledge of forms of communication that enable the formation and maintenance of personal relationships in East Asia. We stress that the frameworks, terms, and concepts in each setting help us understand how members of the culture organize and make sense of their cultural communication. Our primary aim is not to consider cultural communication in East Asia from the standpoint of US American communication patterns or, more generally, Western communication patterns. Rather, we want to elucidate how members of East Asian cultures communicate on their own terms. We can discover, to take just one example, how in China (Chapter 4) all features of and parties to communication in organizations make use of *yin* and *yang*, which can interact to produce *chi*. The energy and force that characterize chi can have strategic value in an organization, bringing new life and vitality to efforts or projects in need of renewal. As Chapter 4 argues, chi can have a major impact on management style and those who are unfamiliar with chi can learn about this distinctive aspect of personal relationships in Chinese organizations. Such insights lead us to rethink and examine our own knowledge, values and beliefs, and in doing so we learn more about our own culture and ourselves.

■ Conclusion

If we consider the descriptions of communication and relationships across the three settings for each of the three cultures we place ourselves at an excellent vantage point for analyzing and interpreting cultural communication in East Asia. This knowledge is not only worthwhile in its own right, but can help fulfill the academic and practical needs for scholars and students. Also, the contents of this book can serve as a platform for the consideration of intercultural communication processes and lead us to develop new awareness of and appreciation for cultural differences and similarities.

Finally, let us mention a potential East Asian–US American dimension to this book. Long ago in the field of American history, the question was asked, "how shall we understand American history without understanding European history?" (Cohen, 2002, p. 2). Cohen then poses a parallel question, asking us to examine the influence of Asian history on American history, and, by extension, the influence of Asian cultures on American culture. From a US American perspective, it is common to consider the presence of the United States in conflict, peace, and commerce in East Asia. However, we must readily acknowledge that life in the United States and the identity of US Americans have been influenced by East Asian cultures.

Over the last 25 years globalization has emerged as a potent force that has altered and transformed the ethnic composition of many countries, including the United States. Those of us who teach, study, and conduct research in the area of intercultural communication not only are keenly aware of the effects of globalization but also feel the continuing need to examine global dynamics in immigration, trade, and cultural exchange. Ultimately we seek to understand more fully and facilitate the ongoing development of intercultural communication competence. If this book helps move us along that path, then we feel that we will have made a solid contribution to the study and practice of effective intercultural communication.

References

Bauman, R. & Scherzer, J. (Eds.). (1974). *Explorations in the ethnography of speaking*. Cambridge: Cambridge University Press.

Carbaugh, D. (1988). *Talking American: Cultural discourses on Donahue*. Norwood, N.J.. Ablex.

Cohen, W. I. (2002). *The Asian American century*. Cambridge, MA: Harvard University Press.

Ditlmann, R.K., Purdie-Vaughns, V., & Eibach, R.P. (2011). Heritage-and ideology-based national identities and their implications for immigrant citizen relations in the United States and Germany. *International Journal of Intercultural Relations, 35*(4), 395–405.

Fitch, K. (1998). *Speaking relationally: Culture, communication, and interpersonal Communication*. New York: Guilford.

Gumperz, J. J. & Hymes, D. H. (Eds.). (1972). *Directions in sociolinguistics: The ethnography of communication*. New York: Holt, Rinehart & Winston.

Hanson, A. (Ed.). (1982). *Studies in symbolism and cultural communication* (Publications in Anthropology No. 14). Lawrence, KS: University of Kansas Press.

Hofstede, G. (1991). *Cultures and organizations: Software of the mind*. New York: McGraw-Hill.

Hofstede, G, (2001). *Culture's consequences: Comparing Values, behaviors, institutions, and organizations across nations* (2nd ed.). Thousand Oaks, CA: Sage.

Hymes, D. H. (1972). Models of the interaction of language and social social life. In J.J. Gumperz and D.H. Hymes (1972) (Eds.). *Directions in sociolinguistics: The ethnography of Communication* (pp. 35–71). New York: Holt, Rinehart & Winston.

Hymes, D. H. (1974). *Foundations in sociolinguistics.* Philadelphia: University of Pennsylvania Press.

Katriel, T. (1986). *Talking straight: Dugri speech in Israeli Sabra culture.* Cambridge, UK: Cambridge University Press.

Philipsen, G. (1975). Speaking "like a man" in Teamsterville: Culture patterns of role enactment in an urban neighborhood. *Quarterly Journal of Speech, 61,* 13–22.

Philipsen, G. (2002). Cultural communication. In W. B. Gudykunst & B. Mody (Eds.), *Handbook of international and intercultural communication* (2d ed., pp. 51–68). Thousand Oaks, CA: Sage.

Ray, G. B. (1987). An ethnography of nonverbal communication in an Appalachian speech community. *Research on Language and Social Interaction, 21,* 171–188.

Schwartz, T. (Ed.). (1980). *Socialization as cultural communication: Development of a theme in the work of Margaret Mead.* Berkeley: University of California Press.

INDEX

practical marriage and social
pressure, 54–55
renqing, 44
Cultural construction
blind date, 56–57
friendship relationships,
46–47
notion of dating, 55–57
sex before marriage, 57
Cultural heritage
Buddhism, 8–10
Confucianism, 4–7
Cultural meaning system, 21
Cultural perspective, 21–22
Culture, theoretical tools
Hall's high *vs.* low context cultures, 13
Hofstede's dimensions, 11–12
Ting-Toomey's face negotiation
theory, 13–15
Cyclic course concept
circle, 71
dynamism, 71
rotation, 71
stability, 71–72
yin and *yang,* 71

D

Daoism, 68–69
Defensive silence, 236
Dependent arising., 9–10
Difficult work behavior
with host country employees,
155–157
with Japanese country employees, 158–159

E

East Asian relationships
China (*see* China)
Japan (*see* Japan)
Korea (*see* South Korea)
Elderly in Japanese families,
105–106
Employee silence, 235–236
Environmental crisis, 15

F

Face negotiation theory, 13–15
Facework, 13–14
Family demography, Japan
aging society, 93
low fertility rate, 94
regional difference, 95
smaller family size, 94–95
stem family *vs.* nuclear family,
94
Family ideology, South Korea
and communication, 167
Confucianism, 166
demographic changes, 168–170
patrilineal parent-child relationship, 166
social achievements, 167
Formal *vs.* informal
communication
douki (cohorts), 154
groupware, 155
habatsu (cliques), 154
induction training sessions, 154
internal work communication,
155

CPSIA information can be obtained
at www.ICGtesting.com
Printed in the USA
LVOW12s0553130716

495920LV00002B/2/P